THE CAVENDISH Q & A SERIES

COMPANY LAW

Cavendish
Publishing
Limited

TITLES IN THE Q&A SERIES

BUSINESS LAW
CIVIL LIBERTIES
COMMERCIAL LAW
COMPANY LAW
CONFLICT OF LAWS
CONSTITUTIONAL & ADMINISTRATIVE LAW
CONTRACT LAW
CRIMINAL LAW
EMPLOYMENT LAW
ENGLISH LEGAL SYSTEM
EQUITY & TRUSTS
EUROPEAN COMMUNITY LAW
EVIDENCE
INTERNATIONAL TRADE LAW
JURISPRUDENCE
LAND LAW
PUBLIC INTERNATIONAL LAW
REVENUE LAW
SUCCESSION, WILLS & PROBATE
TORTS LAW
'A' LEVEL LAW

COMPANY LAW

Jennifer James LLB, BCL
Senior Lecturer in Law
University of Reading

Cavendish
Publishing
Limited

First published in Great Britain 1993 by Cavendish Publishing Limited,
The Glass House, Wharton Street, London WC1X 9PX.
Telephone: 0171-278 8000 Facsimile: 0171-278 8080

© James, J 1996
First Edition 1993

British Library Cataloguing in Publication Data. A catalogue record
for this book is available from the British Library.

ISBN 1-85941-269-6

Printed and bound in Great Britain

Contents

Introduction to the Second Edition   vii

Introduction to the First Edition   ix

Table of Cases   xi

Table of Statutes   xix

1   Formation of Companies and Consequences
    of Incorporation   1

2   The Company and Insiders   35

3   The Company and Outsiders   69

4   The Directors   99

5   The Shareholders and their Rights   155

6   Share Capital   193

7   Loan Capital   251

8   Administering the Company   281

Index   305

Introduction to the Second Edition

Those students who have studied company law are well aware that the subject is less open to judicious question spotting than many others. Hence, those preparing for examinations, at least those who are sensible, ensure that they have an overview of the whole subject even if they choose to concentrate revision in a limited number of areas. Revision so conducted permits a student to answer a question which is principally on topic X while pointing out that he/she realises that minor points Y and Z also arise — even if there is little the candidate can say on those points. An overview of company law also enables a candidate to tackle general questions which cut across a major part of the syllabus, for example, questions on disclosure or the distinctions between public and private (particularly 'quasi-partnership') companies. When selecting specific areas for detailed revision, it is obviously sound practice to ensure that where topics are linked both are studied; there is little point in knowing all about the rules relating to the fiduciary duties of directors without being equally at home with the procedures for the enforcement of those duties.

Since no two syllabus are identical and individual lecturers will have laid stress on particular topics which they will have approached in differing ways, there can be no definitive list of typical examination questions. However, in the second edition of this book I have tried to produce questions which would be at home on an examination paper of any university or equivalent body and, I hope, the legal practice course. Since, as I have said, company law is an integrated subject many questions cut across topics so that, in addition to questions which are principally directed at one or two topics, my final chapter consists of a 'mixed bag' which embrace a multitude of themes.

The draft answers appended to questions are not meant to be a model answer such as could be used to write an assessment, rather they are the type of answer which a good student could hope to achieve in the course of an unseen, written examination. Answers are around 2,000 words which a well prepared student should be able to write in about 40-45 minutes. Those who find they cannot write this quickly should try to speed up their output perhaps by using recognised abbreviations of standard terms.

In suggesting answers to questions I have assumed that a student is permitted to take statutes into his/her examination. Consequently, I have not cited anything other than section numbers as authority for propositions unless the wording of a statute is of particular significance. Students denied access to the legislation could legitimately expect to receive some credit for remembering the content of relevant sections. All statutory references are to the Companies Act 1985, as amended, unless otherwise indicated and a student writing examination answers should always indicate at the outset if this also applies to his/her answers.

In common with the procedure adopted by most examiners, I have presumed that all companies have articles identical in form to those contained in the appropriate Table A promulgated under the Companies Act 1985, unless and to the extent that the contrary is indicated.

In common with the procedure adopted by most examiners, I have presumed that all companies have articles identical in form to those contained in the appropriate Table A promulgated under the Companies Act 1985, unless and to the extent that the contrary is indicated.

Jennifer James
November 1995

Students of company law are well aware that it is an extremely integrated subject and is less susceptible to judicious question spotting than many others. Consequently, sensible students ensure that they have an overview of the whole subject even if they choose to concentrate revision in a limited number of areas. Revision so conducted permits a student to answer a question which is principally on topic X while pointing out that (s)he realises that minor points Y and Z also arise - even if there is little the candidate can say on the points. An overview of company law also enable a candidate to tackle general questions which cut across a major part of the syllabus, for example, questions on disclosure or the distinctions between public and private (particularly 'quasi-partnership') companies. When selecting specific areas for detailed revision it is obviously sound practice to ensure that topics which are linked are both studied; there is little point in knowing all about the rules relating to the fiduciary duties of directors without being equally at home with the procedures for the enforcement of those duties.

Since no two syllabus are identical and individual lecturers will have laid stress on particular topics which they will have approached in differing ways, there can be no definitive list of typical examination questions. However, in this book I have tried to produce questions which would be at home on an examination paper of any university or equivalent body and, I hope, the new legal practice course. Since, as I have said, company law is an integrated subject many questions cut across topics so that in addition to questions which are principally directed at one or two topics my final chapter consists of a 'mixed bag' which embrace a multitude of themes.

The draft answers appended to questions are not meant to be a model answer such as could be used to write a written assessment, rather they are the type of answer which a good student could hope to achieve in the course of an unseen, written examination.

In suggesting answers to questions I have assumed that a student is permitted to take statutes into his/her examination. Consequently, I have not cited anything other than section numbers as authority for propositions unless the wording of a statute is of particular significance. Students denied access to the legislation could legitimately expect to receive some credit for remembering the content of relevant sections. All statutory references are to the Companies Act 1985, as amended, unless otherwise indicated and a student writing examination answers should always indicate at the outset if this also applies to his/her answers. Talk of statutes reminds me that the answer to an increasing number of company law questions is s. 459 CA 1985 and it is a rare answer which will not make some reference thereto.

In common with the procedure adopted by most examiners, I have presumed that all companies have articles identical in form to those contained in the appropriate Table A promulgated under the Companies Act 1985, unless and to the extent that the contrary is indicated.

Jennifer James
September 1993

Table of Cases

A

A Company, Re [1983] 1 WLR 927;
[1983] 2 All ER 854 ....48, 52, 172, 190
A Company (No 005287 of 1985), Re [1986] 1 WLR 28;
[1986] 2 All ER 253 3
A Company (No 00477 of 1986), Re [1986] BCLC 376 177
A Company (No 007623 of 1984), Re [1986] BCLC 362 ....171, 172, 190
A Company (No 006834 of 1988), Re [1989] BCLC 365,
ex p Kremer..178
A Company (No 005134 of 1986), Re [1989] BCLC 383,
ex p Harries...172, 190
A Company (No 00789 of 1987), Re [1990] BCLC 384,
ex p Shooter 161, 173
A Company (No 00330 of 1991), Re [1991] BCLC 597,
ex p Holden..173, 178
Aberdeen Rly Co v Blaikie Bros (HL 1854) 1 Macq 46............................62, 107, 122,
140, 150, 260
Adams v Cape Industries plc [1990] Ch 433;
[1990] 2 WLR 657..11
Alexander Ward & Co Ltd v Samyang Navigation
Co Ltd [1975] 1 WLR 673; [1975] 2 All ER 424 67
Allen v Gold Reefs of West Africa Ltd
[1900] 1 Ch 656...37, 42, 45, 50, 65, 164, 245
Allen v Hyatt (1914) TLR 444 ....102, 106, 116,
129, 138
Armagas Ltd v Mundogas SA [1986] AC 717;
[1986] 2 WLR 1063...97
Ashbury Railway Carriage Co v Riche (1875) LR 7 HL 653 ....70, 71, 77, 84
Automatic Bottlemakers Ltd, Re [1926] Ch 412.......................................279
Automatic Self-Cleansing Filter Ltd v Cunninghame
[1906] 2 Ch 34...59
Aveling Barford v Perion [1989] 1 WLR 360;
[1988] 3 All ER 1019 ....244, 271, 273

B

Bahia & San Francisco Rly Co Ltd, Re (1868) LR 3 QB 584 229
Bailey Hay & Co Ltd, Re [1971] 1 WLR 1357;
[1971] 3 All ER 693 296
Bamford v Bamford [1970] Ch 212;
[1969] 2 WLR 1107...57, 107, 115, 126, 198
Barclays Bank Ltd v TOSG Trust Fund [1984] AC 626;
[1984] 2 WLR 650..92, 97
Barleycorn Enterprises Ltd, Re [1970] Ch 465;
[1970] 2 WLR 898..269
Barrett v Duckett [1995] BCLC 243 ....95, 105, 159, 217, 218
Barron v Potter [1914] 1 Ch 895...60, 187

Barry Artist Ltd, Re Re [1985] 1 WLR 1305 44
Beattie v E & F Beattie Ltd [1938] Ch 70;
  [1938] 3 All ER 214 39
Benjamin Cope & Co, Re [1914] 1 Ch 800.......................................269, 279
Bentley-Stevens v Jones [1974] 1 WLR 638;
  [1974] 2 All ER 653 158
Berry and Stewart v Tottenham Hotspur FC Ltd [1935] Ch 718........................227
Birch v Cropper (1889) 14 App Cas 525...215
Boardman v Phipps [1967] 2 AC 46; [1966] 3 WLR 1009...............................139, 150
Boulting v ACTAT [1963] 2 QB 606; [1963] 2 WLR 529 ....45, 68.
Brady v Brady [1989] AC 755; [1988] 2 WLR 1308 ....193, 239, 242
Brazilian Rubber Estates & Plantations Ltd, Re [1911] 1 Ch 425..................111, 148
Breckland Group Holdings v London & Suffolk
  Properties [1989] BCLC 100 61
Brightlife Ltd, Re [1987] Ch 200 278
British Thomson-Houston Co Ltd v Federated
  European Bank Ltd [1932] 2 KB 176..89
Brown v British Abrasive Wheel [1919] 1 Ch 290.............................50, 166
Burland v Earle [1902] AC 83...159
Bushell v Faith [1970] AC 1099;
  [1970] 2 WLR 272..16, 38, 56, 60, 187

C
Cane v Jones [1980] 1 WLR 1451; [1981] 1 All ER 533.......................41, 43
Carney v Herbert [1985] AC 301; [1984] 3 WLR 1303 ....239, 241
Charterhouse Investment Trust Ltd v Tempest Diesels Ltd
  [1986] BCLC 1 239
Cimex Tissues Ltd, Re [1995] BCLC 409.......................................256, 257
City Equitable Fire Insurance Co Ltd, Re
  [1925] Ch 407..28, 110, 117,
                                                               147, 188, 272
City Investment Centres Ltd, Re [1992] BCLC 956 144
Clemens v Clemens Bros Ltd
  [1976] 2 All ER 268 ....38, 51, 127, 128, 167, 195
Coleman v Myers [1977] 2 NZLR 225. ....102, 103
Cook v Deeks [1916] 1 AC 554 ....108, 123, 139, 165
Cotman v Brougham [1918] AC 514..72
Cumana Ltd, Re [1986] BCLC 430 173
Cumbrian Newspapers Group Ltd v Cumberland and
  Westmoreland Herald Ltd [1987] Ch 1; [1986] 3 WLR 26 127
Cuthbert Cooper Ltd, Re [1937]...181

D
Dafen Tinplate Ltd v Llanelly Steel Co [1920] 2 Ch 124 ....37, 51, 65
Daimler Co Ltd v Continental Tyre and Rubber Co Ltd
  [1916] 2 AC 307..10
Daniels v Daniels [1978] Ch 406; [1978] 2 WLR 73 ....56, 62, 104, 120

Dawson International v Coats Paton plc 1988 SLT 854 ....68, 129
Denham & Co, Re (1883) 25 Ch D 752..81
Destone Fabrics Ltd, Re [1941] Ch 319..268
DHN Food Distributors Ltd v Tower Hamlets LBC
    [1976] 1 WLR 852; [1976] 3 All ER 462 ....11, 25
Dimbula Valley (Ceylon) Tea Co v Laurie [1961] Ch 353;
    [1961] 2 WLR 253..224
Dixon v Kennaway & Co [1900] 1 Ch 833 227
Dorchester Finance v Stebbing [1989] BCLC 498 ....28, 111, 148
Duomatic Ltd, Re [1969] 2 Ch 365; [1969[2 WLR 114..293

E

Ebrahimi v Westbourne Galleries Ltd [1973] AC 360;
    [1972] 2 WLR 1289...12, 68, 161, 171,
                                                                                           172, 179, 181, 216
Eley v Positive Life Ass Co (1876) 1 Ex D 88...39, 52, 66
Elgindata Ltd, Re [1991] BCLC 959 ....146, 160, 161, 261
Emma Silver Mining Co v Grant (1879) 11 Ch D 918 19
English and Scottish Mercantile Investment Co
    Ltd v Brunton [1892] 2 QB 700...280
Erlanger v New Sombrero Phosphate Co
    (1878) 3 App Cas 1218 19
Estmanco (Kilner House) Ltd v GLC [1982] 1 WLR 2;
    [1982] 1 All ER 437 167
Euro RSCG SA v Conran (1992) Times, Nov 2 129
Evans v Rival Granite Quarries Ltd [1910] 2 KB 979 278

F

Flitcroft's Case (1882) 21 Ch D 519 200
Foss v Harbottle (1843) 2 Hare 189...35, 39, 55, 61, 74, 94,
                                                                          99 -101, 104, 117, 119, 120,
                                                                          126, 129, 149, 156, 158, 159,
                                                                          163, 188, 198, 217
Freeman & Lockyer v Buckhurst Park Properties Ltd
    [1964] 2 QB 480; [1964] 2 WLR 618 86

G

Gaiman v National Assoc For Mental Health
    [1971] Ch 317, [1970] 3 WLR 42...41
General Auction Estate & Monetary Co v Smith
    [1891] 3 Ch 432...255, 266
George Newman Ltd, Re [1895] Ch 674...296
German Date Coffee Co, Re (1882) 20 Ch D 169...75
Gething v Kilner [1972] 1 WLR 337; [1972] 1 All ER 1164..............................102, 129
Gilford Motor Co Ltd v Horne [1933] Ch 935..10, 184
Gluckstein v Barnes [1900] AC 240..20

Government Stock Investment Co v Manila Rly Co
[1897] AC 81 277
Great Wheal Polgooth Co, Re (1883) 53 LJ Ch 42 19
Greenhalgh v Arderne Cinemas Ltd
[1946] 1 All ER 512 ....166, 167
Greenhalgh v Arderne Cinemas Ltd
[1951] Ch 286, [1950] 2 All ER 1120 ....37, 38, 51, 127, 166, 195
Greenhalgh v Mallard [1943] 2 All ER 234 45
Guinness plc v Saunders [1990] 2 AC 663; [1990] 2 WLR 324 ....67, 151

H
Halifax Building Society v Meridian Housing
Association Ltd [1994] BCLC 540 75
Halt Garage Ltd, Re [1982] 3 All ER 1016 296
Heald v O'Connor [1971] 1 WLR 497; [1971] 2 All ER 1005 241
Hedley Byrne v Heller [1964] AC 465; [1963] 3 WLR 101 129
Hely-Hutchinson v Brayhead [1968] 1 QB 549;
[1967] 3 WLR 1408 ....62, 151
Heron International Ltd v Lord Grade [1983] BCLC 244 129
Hickman v Kent or Romney Marsh Sheepbreeders'
Assoc [1915] 1 Ch 881 ....17, 21, 36, 39, 52, 65, 158
Hilder v Dexter [1902] AC 474 199
Hivac Ltd v Park Royal Scientific Instruments Ltd
[1946] Ch 169...141
Hogg v Cramphorn Ltd [1967] Ch 254; [1966] 3 WLR 995............................126, 198
Holders Investment Trust, Re [1971] 1 WLR 583,
[1971] 2 All ER 289 ....38, 51, 167, 168
Horsley and Weight Ltd, Re
[1982] Ch 442; [1982] 3 WLR 431...72, 79, 244
Houldsworth v City of Glasgow Bank (1880) 5 App Cas 317 32
House of Fraser v ACGE Investments Ltd
[1987] AC 387; [1987] 2 WLR 1083 222
Howard Smith Ltd v Ampol Petroleum Ltd
[1974] AC 821; [1974] 2 WLR 689 ....107, 115, 121, 126, 198
HR Harmer Ltd, Re [159] 1 WLR 62; [1958] 3 All ER 689....................................191
Hutton v West Cork Railway Co (1883)) 23 Ch D 654...79

I
IDC Ltd v Cooley [1972] 1 WLR 443; [1972] 2 All ER 162 ....123, 137,
139, 140
Illingworth v Houldsworth [1904] AC 355...277
Imperial Mercantile Credit Assn v Coleman
(1873) LR 6 HL 189 62
Introductions Ltd, Re [1970] Ch 199; [1969] 2 WLR 791 72
Island Export Finance Ltd v Umunna [1986] BCLC 460 140

J
JE Cade Ltd, Re [1992] BCLC 213 177
Jones v Lipman [1962] 1 WLR 832; [1962] 1 All ER 442............................10, 25, 184

K
Kelner v Baxter (1866) LR 2 CP 174...20, 21
Kenyon (Swansea) Ltd, Re [1987] BCLC 514.............................68, 172, 190
Kuwait Asia Bank EC v National Mutual Life
   Nominees Ltd [1991] 1 AC 187; [1990] 3 WLR 297.......................................28, 103

L
Lee v Lee's Air Farmming Ltd [1961] AC 12;
   [1960] 3 WLR 758..12
Lindgren v L & P Estates Ltd [1967] Ch 572; [1968] 1 All ER 917 28
Littlewoods Mail Order Stores Ltd v IRC
   [1969] 1 WLR 1241; [1969] 3 All ER 855 ....8, 11
Loch v John Blackwood Ltd [1924] AC 783......................................170, 190
Lo-Line Electric Motors Ltd, Re [1988] Ch 477;
   [1988] 3 WLR 26...144, 275
London & Mashonaland Exploration Co Ltd v New
   Mashonaland Exploration Co Ltd [1891] WN 165...129

M
MC Bacon Ltd, Re [1990] BCLC 324 268
Macaura v Northern Assurance [1925] AC 619.............................5, 10, 24
MacDougall v Gardiner (1875) 1 Ch D 13 158
Mace Builders v Lunn [1987] Ch 191; [1986] 3 WLR 921.........................273
Mackenzie Ltd, Re [1916] 2 Ch 450..221, 223
Macro (Ipswich) Ltd, Re [1994] 2 BCLC 354 ....112, 261
Manurewa Transport Ltd, Re [1971] NZLR 909 278
Marquis of Bute's Case [1892] 2 Ch 100..81
Melhado v Porto Alegre Rly Co (1874) LR 9 CP 503.............................21, 39
Movitex v Bulfield Ltd [1988] BCLC 104 150

N
Neptune (Vehicle Washing Equipment) Ltd v Fitzgerald
   [1995] 3 All ER 811 ....14, 80, 151
New British Iron Co, Re [1898] 1 Ch 324 67
New Bullas Ltd, Re [1993] BCLC 1389; [1993] BCC 251 277
Niltan Carson Ltd v Hawthorne [1988] BCLC 298....................116, 122, 153
Norman v Theodore Goddard [1991] BCLC 1028......................................111
Northern Engineering Industries,Re [1994] 222
NW Transportation Ltd v Beatty (1887) 12 App Cas 589.............................151, 164
Nurcombe v Nurcombe [1985] 1 WLR 370;
   [1985] 1 All ER 65 ....104, 159, 240

O

OC Transport Services Ltd, Re [1984] BCLC 251...128, 195
Old Silkstone Collieries Ltd, Re [1954] Ch 169;
   [1954] 2 WLR 77...222
Oshkosh B'Gosh Inc v Dan Marbel Inc Ltd [1989] BCLC 507..............................78
Ooregum Gold Mining Co of India v Roper [1892] AC 125 202
Ossory Estates plc, Re [1988] BCLC 213 203

P

Panorama Developments Ltd v Fidelis Furnishing
   Fabrics Ltd [1971] 2 QB 711; [1971] 3 WLR 440 ....90, 229, 288
Pavlides v Jensen [1956] Ch 565; [1956] 3 WLR 224...56
Pennell v Venida (1974) (unrep) 57
Percival v Wright [1902] Ch 421 ....55, 61, 100-102,
                                                                104, 106, 116, 119, 137,
                                                                149, 157, 188, 195, 217
Permanent House (Holdings) Ltd, Re [1989] 5 BCC 151 278
Phonogram Ltd v Lane [1982] QB 938; [1981] 3 WLR 736....................................22
Produce Marketing Consortium Ltd (No 2), Re
   [1989] 1 WLR 745; [1989] 3 All ER 1 ....27, 146, 261
Prudential Asurance v Newman Industries
   [1982] Ch 204; [1982] 2 WLR 31...104, 120, 159
Purpoint Ltd, Re [1991] BCLC 491..146, 260

Q

Quin & Axtens v Salmon [1909] 1 Ch 311......................................17, 21, 40, 59, 188

R

RA Noble Ltd, Re [1983] BCLC 273..171, 190
Ratners Group plc, Re [1988] BCLC 685 220
Rayfield v Hands [1960] Ch 1; [1958] 2 WLR 851..175, 196
Read v Astoria Garage Ltd [1952] Ch 637;
   [1952] 2 All ER 292 ....52, 66
Regal (Hastings) Ltd v Gulliver [1967] 2 AC 134n;
   [1942] 1 All ER 378 ....106, 110, 123, 137,
                                                                       140, 141, 149
Richardson v Pitt-Stanley [1995]...9
Rolled Steel Products Ltd v British Steel Corporation
   [1986] Ch 246; [1985] 2 WLR 908..71, 84
Royal British Bank v Turquand (1856) 6 E & B 327....................................85, 90, 91
Ruben v Great Fingall Consolidated [1906] AC 439. ....91, 229
Russell v Northern Bank Development Corpn Ltd
   [1992] 3 All ER 294; [1992] 1 WLR 588 ....45, 77

S

Salomon v Salomon & Co [1897] AC 22 ....3, 4, 8, 10, 12,
19, 25, 183, 238
Saltdean Estate Co Ltd, Re [1968] 1 WLR 1844;
[1968] 3 All ER 829 ....221, 222
Sam Weller Ltd, Re [1990] Ch 682;
[1989] 3 WLR 923..172, 173, 176, 190, 216, 254
Saul Harrison & Sons plc, Re [1995] BCLC 52, 54, 161, 189, 191
Scottish CWS v Meyer [1959] AC 324; [1958] 3 WLR 404................................11, 161
Scottish Ins Corpn v Wilsons & Clyde Coal Co
[1949] AC 462; [1949] 1 All ER 1068..216, 220
Sevenoaks Stationery (Retail) Ltd, Re [1991] Ch 164;
[1990] 3 WLR 1165 ....143-145, 275
Sheffield Corpn v Barclay [1905] AC 392 ....228, 230
Short v Treasury Commissioners [1948] 1 KB 116;
[1947] 2 All ER 298 254
Sidebottom v Kershaw Leese [1920] 1 Ch 154 ....37, 50, 166
Siebe Gorman v Barclays Bank [1979] 2 Lloyd's Rep 142 ....257, 277
Smith v Croft (No 2) [1988] Ch 114; [1987] 3 WLR 405....................62, 105, 160, 165
Smith & Fawcett Ltd, Re [1942] Ch 304;
[1942] 1 All ER 542 ....107, 227
Smith, Stone & Knight v Birmingham Corpn
[1939] 4 All ER 116 9
Southard & Co Ltd, Re [1979] 1 WLR 1198;
[1979] 3 All ER 556 ....12, 25, 183
Southern Foundries v Shirlaw [1940] AC 701;
[1940] 2 All ER 445 ....45, 49, 66
Swabey v Port Darwin Gold Mining Co Ltd
(1889) 1 Meg 385...66
Swaledale Cleaners Ltd, Re [1968] 1 WLR 1710;
[1968] 3 All ER 619 227
Swift 736 Ltd, Re [1993] BCLC 1 302

T

Thomas Marshall (Exporters) Ltd v Guinle
[1979] Ch 227; [1978] 3 All ER 193 141
Trevor v Whitworth (1887) 12 App Cas 409...201, 231

U

Underwood Ltd v Bank of Liverpool [1924] 1 KB 775..86, 90

V

Victor Battery Co Ltd v Curry's Ltd [1946] Ch 242;
[1946] 1 All ER 519...240, 241
Virdi v Abbey Leisure Ltd [1990] BCLC 342...178

W
Wallersteiner v Moir [1974] 1 WLR 991;
[1974] 3 All ER 217 ....62, 104, 120
Webb v Earle (1875) LR 20 Eq 556 215
Welton v Saffery [1897] AC 299 ....42, 46, 50, 175
Whaley Bridge Printing Co v Green (1879) 5 QBD 109 19
Wharfedale Brewery Co Ltd, Re [1952] Ch 913 216
William Jones & Sons Ltd, Re [1969] 1 WLR 146;
[1969] 1 All ER 913 222
Winkworth v Edward Baron Developments Ltd
[1968] 1 WLR 1512; [1987] 1 All ER 114 104
Wood v Odessa Waterworks Co (1889) 42 Ch C 636 37
Woolfson v Strathclyde Regional Council 1978 SC 90..................12, 183
Wragg Ltd, Re [1897] 1 Ch 796..169, 199, 203, 238

Y
Yenidje Tobacco, Re [1916] 2 Ch 426 ....178, 180
Yeovil Glove Ltd, Re [1965] Ch 148; [1964] 3 WLR 406 ....263, 264, 267

Table of Statutes

Companies Act 1948
s 210...11, 181

Companies Act 1985
s 1...3, 13, 36, 41
s 2 ....3, 5, 13-15, 36, 41, 70, 77, 83, 201, 289
s 3A...14, 72, 73, 75
s 4...15, 42, 48, 54, 73, 78, 84
s 5...15, 42, 49, 73, 78, 232
s 8 ....3, 14, 61
s 9 ....21, 36-40, 43, 45, 49, 56, 60, 64, 66,
                         78, 101, 121, 155, 157, 163, 194, 210, 245, 294
s 14 ....16, 17, 21, 36, 37, 39, 40, 65-67,
                                                  158, 175, 176, 195, 196
s 17...39
s 24 10
s 28..78
s 35 ....15, 26, 73-75, 77,
                                                  83, 84, 89, 163, 266
s 35A...81, 86, 87, 91, 92,
                                                  96-98, 153, 266
s 35B 92, 97
s 36C..22
s 42...43, 44, 49
s 54..232
s 80...57, 99, 115, 121, 125,
                                                  196, 197, 210, 211
s 80A...115, 125, 197, 210
s 89...57, 115, 197, 211, 254
s 91...115, 125
s 92...115, 197
s 94...196, 197, 210, 211
s 99...16, 169, 199, 202, 203, 213, 238
s 100..199, 202, 238, 254
s 101..202
s 102..203
s 103..9, 169, 203
s 106..202
s 111A..32
s 112...115, 199, 202, 203
s 113..115, 203
s 114...115
s 117...220
s 118...202
s 121...16, 46, 125, 166, 188, 194, 196, 210, 219, 254
s 125...128, 164, 223, 224
s 127...223, 224
s 135..7, 16, 44, 204, 205, 220, 232, 233, 246, 254

Companies Act 1985 (cont)
s 136...206
s 137...206
s 142...294
s 143 ....7, 204, 230, 233, 245, 259
s 151..204, 239, 241, 242, 248
s 152...248
s 153..239, 242, 243
s 154..241, 248
s 155..239, 241, 243, 248
s 156..205, 248
s 160...246
s 162..170, 236, 246
s 164...236, 246
s 168...236, 246
s 169...236, 246
s 170...236, 246
s 171...236, 246
s 173..205, 236, 246, 247
s 175...236, 247
s 176...205, 247
s 177...205, 247
s 182..226, 227, 238
s 183...227
s 186...227, 228
s 202...290
s 204...291
s 206...291
s 209...290
s 211...290
s 217...290
s 218...290
s 221...282
s 226...283, 284
s 232...152
s 233...284
s 234...285
s 235...286
s 238...283
s 241...283
s.242...282, 283
s 242A...283
s 245..262, 263, 284
s 249A...7
s 249B...285
s 248C...285
s 250...286
s 252...283

Companies Act 1985 (cont)
s 253..283
s 263...236, 246
s 282..17, 100, 106, 135
s 283...226, 288
s 285..86
s 286...226, 288
s 291..94
s 293..106
s 303..28, 54, 56, 59, 60,83, 88, 94, 101, 120,
                         121, 155, 157, 170, 177, 181, 187, 207, 295
s 309...54, 114, 126
s 312..244
s 317...63, 99, 108, 122, 151, 273
s 319..56, 79, 108, 152, 186
s 320...7, 63, 99, 108, 152, 272
s 322..63, 116, 122, 273
s 322A..74, 122, 153, 165
s 330...7, 108, 131-134, 152-154, 173, 248, 249
s 331...131, 133, 134, 153
s 332..134
s 334...134, 249
s 335...134, 171
s 337...134, 153
s 338 132-134
s 341...132, 173, 249
s 346...132, 153, 272
s 349..6, 10, 23, 180
s 351..289
s 352...226, 288
s 353...226, 288
s 359...227, 228
s 361..228
s 363..291
s 365..292
s 366..294
s 366A..189, 294
s 368...54, 189, 294
s 379A..6, 197, 210, 286, 287
s 380..294
s 381A..6, 17, 246, 287, 295, 296
s 381B..296
s 381C..6, 296
s 382A..287
s 384..285
s 385..285
s 385A..285
s 386..286

s 393..286
s 391...286, 295
s 391A..286
s 393..286
s 395...256, 262
s 399..294
s 425..241
s 459...3, 7, 12, 15, 18, 20, 35, 38, 40, 47, 51,
                              52, 54, 55, 57, 58, 64, 68,99, 105, 112, 113, 117,
                              119, 124, 128, 155, 156, 158, 160-162, 167, 168,
                              170-173, 176-178, 181, 182, 185, 187-191, 195, 196,
                              214, 215, 217-219, 224, 245, 254, 261, 297
s 461...128, 173, 176, 177, 191, 216, 224, 232
s 711A..75, 90
s 713..292
s 727...131, 135
s 741...26, 94, 152, 164, 255, 271
s 744..251

Companies Act 1989
s 25..286
s 27..286
Schedule 11 286

Company Directors Disqualification Act 1985
s 1...142, 274
s 2..142
s 5..142
s 6 ....142-144, 274, 275, 302
s 8..142, 143
s 10...142
Schedule 1 ....143, 274
Financial Services Act 1986
s 146...30
s 148...31
s 150...31
s 151...31
s 152...31

Insolvency Act 1986
s 76...205, 237, 247
s 79...170
s 122...234, 301
s 122(1)(g) 17, 20, 64, 68, 95, 99, 114, 119, 155, 170,
                              175, 178-180, 182-185, 188, 189, 214, 216, 217
s 123...234, 302
s 125...170, 184, 190
s 175...269, 274

Insolvency Act 1986 (cont)
s 213...6, 26, 302
s 214 ....6, 26, 110, 112, 131, 145-147,
157, 260, 261, 265, 302
s 238 271-273
s 239...114, 235, 268, 273
s 240...268, 271
s 245 ....235, 256, 258, 266-268, 273
s 249...271
s 435...271
Schedule 6, para 11 267

Misrepresentation Act 1967
s 2..32

Statutory instruments

Table A (S1 1985 No 805)
art 24 226
art 32 ....46, 195, 196, 210
art 34 220
art 35 ....125, 236, 246
art 37 29294
art 53 44
art 64 ....100, 136
art 70 ....16, 20, 28, 54, 55, 60-62,77, 83, 85, 88, 89,
....94, 100, 101,104, 106, 120, 121, 155, 157, 187, 276
art 85 ....63, 108, 122, 151, 260

Chapter 1

Formation of Companies and Consequences of Incorporation

Introduction

Questions are rarely set solely upon the rules relating to the formation of companies. However, in tackling questions upon the consequences of incorporation, some appreciation of the rules of formation (and the differing types of company) is appropriate. Factors which might influence the decision to incorporate, the effects of incorporation and 'lifting the veil' are common areas for questions. Questions involving 'lifting the veil' generally require some form of critical analysis rather than a mere recitation of decisions. Another, broader, type of question regularly encountered involves advice about incorporation and running of companies and possible types of investment in a company either in general or for specified persons (generally a brilliant but unbusiness-like inventor, his aware brother-in-law and a doddery relative of means). Material relating to formation should also be incorporated in questions relating to the different legal regime applicable to public and private (particularly quasi-partnership) companies and general questions about disclosure.

The law relating to promoters and pre-incorporation contracts can be regarded as part of the formation of a company. Questions on promoters may be linked with the liability of directors and a question could combine a pre-incorporation contract with a post-incorporation contract. However, the increasing use of 'off-the-shelf' companies for small private companies renders promoters and pre-incorporation contracts of diminishing importance. Some courses may require students to be familiar with methods of raising capital and the prospectus requirements — such material is likely to form a small part of a problem or be examined by means of a simple essay which merely demands a competent recitation of fact but obviously every question setter has their own hobbyhorse(s).

Students should be familiar with:

- How a company can be formed and the differing types of company
- Advantages and disadvantages of incorporation

- Effects of incorporation
- Circumstances in which the separate legal personality of the company will be disregarded both at common law and also by statute (particularly fraudulent and wrongful trading)
- Promoters, particularly their duties and rights
- Liability for pre-incorporation contracts

Students should be aware that related issues which could be linked to questions based on this area include:

- the distribution of power within a company
- enforcement of the articles of association
- liability and/or protection of directors/investors including disqualification of directors
- restructuring of share capital

Question 1

Do the advantages of incorporation really compensate for the bureaucracy involved in running a company?

Answer plan

A question such as this, a variant on the very well-worked theme of the advantages and disadvantages of incorporation, can only be tackled by someone who knows the material and should only be tackled by someone who is desperate! It is very difficult to score high marks on such a question since there is little scope for anything but a neat summary of the advantages of incorporation and a further summary of the bureaucratic requirements alluded to – a rare question where a list might be beneficial. It should be noted, however, that the wise student does not comment on the dullness of the question.

Answer

Incorporation of an existing or projected enterprise (not necessarily a business) can be achieved either by forming a company from scratch in compliance with the procedures laid down in the Companies Act 1985 or by buying a pre-existing company 'off-the-shelf'. In either case the company will require a memorandum of association (s 1), which must contain certain information (s 2), and articles of association. The content of the articles, which are the company's internal rules, can be determined by the founders of the company but if none are registered the appropriate form of Table A will automatically apply (s 8) if the company is limited by shares. The advantage of purchasing an off-the-shelf company is that the company already exists and there is no delay between deciding to form a company and the company coming into existence through the registration process; there is merely a transfer of shareholding. This obviates the problem of pre-incorporation contracts and the possibility of having stationery printed bearing a name which, by the time the company is registered, has been taken by another company. However, an off-the-shelf company would not have been formed with the specific requirements of the promoters in mind and alterations of the memorandum or articles might be required. Indeed problems can arise when the new shareholders of the company fail to make the necessary amendments. For example, in *Re A Company* (1986) a 'shareholder' who wished to use s 459 to bring an action against his fellow 'shareholders', was denied *locus* when it was discovered that the shares in the company, which had been purchased off-the-shelf, had never been transferred to the purchasers. For most people interested in forming (or buying) a company the appropriate form of company will be a private company limited by shares (s 1).

The United Kingdom has traditionally had more companies than other European countries of comparable size (approximately 1,000,000 at present). What are the attractions of incorporation? The principal advantage of incorporation, from which a variety of benefits flow, is that a company is a distinct legal entity with rights and duties independent of those possessed by its shareholders, directors and employees, it is a legal person. In consequence, for example, business conducted in the name of a registered company is separate from the personal affairs of the human beings who act for the company and separate also from the affairs of any other business those human beings may conduct on behalf of another registered company. Corporate personality was created by statute in the first half of the 19th century but the full significance of this provision was not appreciated until the famous case of *Salomon v Salomon & Co* in 1897.

In *Salomon*, S converted his existing, successful, business into a limited company of which he was the managing director. S valued his business at £39,000 (an honest but optimistic valuation) and received from the company in discharge of this sum, cash, a debenture (an acknowledgement of debt) and 20,001 £1 shares out of the issued share capital of £20,007. S's wife and five children each held one of the remaining issued shares (seven being the minimum number of shareholders at that date), probably as his nominee. The company went into insolvent liquidation within a year with no assets to pay off the unsecured creditors. The issue for the courts was whether S was liable for the company's unpaid debts. The House of Lords, reversing the Court of Appeal, held that the company had been properly formed and was a legal person in its own right separate from S notwithstanding his dominant position within the company. The company was not S's agent and consequently, S's liability was to be determined solely by reference to the Companies Act. The Act required a shareholder to contribute to the debts of a company only where he held shares in respect of which the full nominal value had not been paid. S had paid for his shares in full by transferring the business to the company so he had no liability to the creditors of the company. Thus, *Salomon's* case established that legal personality would be recognised even when one shareholder effectively controlled the company and had fixed the value of the assets used to pay for his shares.

The effects of separate legal personality are many and include:

(a) A company can sue and be sued in its own name.

(b) A company has perpetual succession. A company cannot die simply because all its shareholders are dead although it can be wound up or struck off the Register by the Registrar of Companies if it appears to be moribund. Because a company exists unless and until it is wound up or de-registered, property once transferred to the company remains the property of the company to do with as it pleases. There are no death duties to pay on the property because the company does not die and no costs are incurred in transferring the legal title to the property on a change of shareholder or director.

(c) The shareholders, directors and employees are not liable for criminal or tortious acts committed by the company although they may incur personal liability concurrent with that of the company. For example, a company might, through the combined acts or omissions of several employees, establish and operate an unsafe system of work which caused the death of an employee. The company would be liable but an individual director or employee would not be liable unless he or she was personally negligent or the company was acting as an agent or employee of that individual.

(d) The shareholders, directors and employees are not liable on (nor can they enforce) contracts entered into by the company. As with criminal and tortious liability, an individual may incur personal liability concurrent with that of the company if s/he also enters into the contract. Furthermore, when the company acts as the agent of a shareholder or director (or employee but this a rare event) the individual is liable under the normal rules of agency.

(e) A company may be formed with limited liability (s 2(3)). Limited liability allows the shareholders of a company to limit their responsibility for a company's debts — after all the company is a separate person so why should the shareholders incur liability for the debts of another. Liability may be limited to a pre-determined sum payable on winding up (company limited by guarantee, s 2(4)) or to the nominal value of the shares held unless this sum has been paid by the current or a former shareholder (company limited by shares, s 2(5)). Since most shares are issued fully paid shareholders have, effectively, no liability for the company's debts.

(f) Where a company has transferable shares, ownership of the company can be split or transferred without affecting the company itself.

(g) Formation of a company may bring financial benefits. For example, a company can raise money to create floating charges and, perhaps, to minimize the tax liability of shareholders.

There are drawbacks to separate legal personality in that the property of the company, not being that of the members, cannot be insured by a member and the company cannot claim on an insurance effected by a person on property which he then owned but subsequently transferred to the company (see *Macaura v Northern Assurance* (1925)). Moreover, the assets of the company are the property of the company and a shareholder, even a controlling shareholder, cannot simply help himself to the company's cash. In addition there are a limited number of situations where Parliament or the courts have decreed that corporate personality should be ignored. For example where the directors have engaged in fraudulent or wrongful trading they incur liability to creditors (ss 213, 214 Insolvency Act 1986). Section 349(4) imposes liability upon an officer of the company who has signed company cheques etc on which the name of the company does not appear in full.

But what bureaucratic drawbacks are there to incorporation? In return for the advantages of incorporation Parliament requires the observation of mandatory rules on the operation of a company. These rules are lengthy and complex and there can be no doubt that in most companies many administrative rules, for example on the conduct of meetings, are largely ignored. Perhaps in recognition of the widespread lack of use of some of the rules, the government has recently sought to reduce the administrative burden on companies, especially smaller companies, by the insertion of new sections into the 1985 Act. Sections 381A to 381C permit a private company to dispense with meetings and pass resolutions by unanimous written agreement. Section 379A permits a private company to elect to disregard certain requirements of the Companies Act if all the shareholders agree either in person or by proxy.

Such reforms are small measures; there is still an immense amount of law imposing obligations upon companies, shareholders and directors, which would not apply to a sole trader or to a partnership. These obligations fall into five broad groups.

(a) Much of company administration is subject to statute (ss 348-362) and there are rules as to the qualification of directors and the company secretary (ss 282-310). The conduct of meetings of shareholders or directors is subject to statutory control (ss 366-384) although many of these rules are ignored in small companies.

(b) The power of the directors, who in smaller companies will almost certainly be majority shareholders, are limited in that certain things cannot be done while others can be done only with the agreement of the shareholders. Many of these constraints on directorial power relate to the ability of the directors to benefit themselves (ss 311-348). For example, s 330 provides that the directors cannot lend money to a director (there are innumerable exceptions) and s 320 restricts the ability of a director to engage in 'substantial property transactions' with his/her company. The power of the directors to raise capital by the allotment of shares is restricted (ss 80-116).

(c) The ability of the directors or shareholders to do as they wish with the shares of the company is restricted (ss 80-181) so that, for instance, the share capital of the company cannot be reduced without the approval of the court (s 135) and a company cannot buy its own shares (s 143 — there are exceptions). The wishes of minority shareholders may have to be taken into account (ss 125-128, 459) despite the wishes of the majority.

(d) The major statutory requirement which imposes a continuing burden relates to company accounts. The financial results of the company must be presented to the shareholders in a balance sheet and profit and loss account (ss 221-262A). The length and technicality of the accounting rules mean that company accounts must, in effect, be prepared by a qualified accountant and a company must have its accounts checked (audited) by a qualified accountant (ss 384-394A). A summary of the audited accounts must be sent to the Registrar of Companies where it is open to public inspection (full accounts for larger companies). The obligation of a company to produce audited accounts in compliance with the Act imposes an annual financial burden on a company which is much resented by many companies. Recently, 'small companies' (defined in s 249A) have been either wholly (for those with a turnover of less than £90,000) or partially exempted from the statutory audit unless members holding at least 10% by value of a class of shares require the company to obtain an audit.

However, there can be little doubt that British businesspeople think that the bureaucratic drawbacks are more than outweighed by the benefits of incorporation. Why else would one of the most common occupations in Britain be company director.

Question 2

'The doctrine laid down in *Salomon v Salomon & Co Ltd* has to be watched very carefully ... The courts can and often do draw aside the veil ... The legislature has shown the way with group accounts and the rest. And the courts should follow suit' (*Littlewoods Mail Order Stores Ltd v IRC* (1969) *per* Lord Denning MR).

Discuss.

Answer plan

While questions on lifting the veil are fairly common, such questions (including this one) are not well answered by saying there are a large number of cases where the courts will lift the veil and then listing them. A question such as this calls for effective deployment of the cases and a discussion of Lord Denning's view that the courts should be more interventionist in disregarding corporate personality.

Answer

The fundamental attribute of corporate personality is that the company is a legal entity distinct from its members — a company is a legal person. Corporate personality was created by statute in the first half of the 19th century but the full significance of this provision was not appreciated until the famous case of *Salomon v Salomon & Co* in 1897 to which Lord Denning refers.

In *Salomon*, S converted his existing, successful, business into a limited company of which he was the managing director. S valued his business at £39,000 (an honest but wholly inaccurate valuation) and received from the company in discharge of this sum, cash, a debenture and 20,001 £1 shares out of the issued share capital of £20,007. S's wife and five children each held one of the remaining issued shares (seven being the minimum number of shareholders at that date), probably as his nominee. The company went into insolvent liquidation within a year with no assets to pay off the unsecured creditors. The issue for the courts was whether S was liable for the company's unpaid debts. The House of Lords, reversing the Court of Appeal, held that the company had been properly formed and was a legal person in its own right notwithstanding the dominant position of S within the company. The company was not S's agent and, consequently, S's liability was to be determined solely by reference to the Companies Act. S had paid for his shares in full (by transferring the business to the company) and so his liability to creditors was exhausted; the full nominal value had been paid. Thus, *Salomon's* case established that, in the absence of fraud, legal personality would be recognised even when one shareholder effectively controlled the company and had fixed the value of the assets used to pay for his shares (note now the valuation requirements for non-cash consideration for shares in public companies s 103). While on the facts of this case the company was not the agent of S, merely being a controlling shareholder will not over-ride the statutory effect of incorporation. There is no reason why a company cannot be the agent of its controlling shareholder and, in such cases, the shareholder-principal is liable for debts contracted by the company as his agent under the normal rules of contract. See, for example, *Smith, Stone & Knight v Birmingham Corpn* (1939) where the degree of day-to-day control exercised by the holding company meant that the subsidiary was regarded as its agent.

The effects of separate legal personality, about which Lord Denning seems somewhat ambivalent, are many — as we have seen the members are not liable for the debts of the company other than to the extent that statute provides, ie to pay the nominal value on winding up except to the extent that it has already been paid. Since most shares are issued fully paid shareholders have, effectively, no liability for the company's debts. Separate legal personality allows a company to sue and be sued in its own name, to hold property in perpetual succession distinct from the property of members, to issue freely transferable shares, to create floating charges and, perhaps, to minimise the tax liability of shareholders; nor are the directors or shareholders liable for the criminal or tortious acts of the company. For example, in *Richardson v Pitt-Stanley* (1995), the Court of Appeal declined to hold a director liable to an injured employee of the company who suffered economic loss through the failure by the company to take out the compulsory insurance against accidents at work. To do so would be said the court 'a case of piercing the corporate veil with a vengeance'. There are drawbacks to separate legal personality in that the property of the company, not being that of the members, cannot be insured by a member and the company cannot claim on an insurance effected by a person on property which he then owned but subsequently transferred to the company (see *Macaura v Northern Assurance* (1925)).

Parliament, as Lord Denning indicated, has in a very limited number of cases restricted the effect of incorporation. Is there any theme behind these exceptions which might indicate areas in which the courts should lift the veil of incorporation? And, perhaps more importantly, do these exceptions indicate that the courts ought to be more willing to lift the veil? There are a number of minor provisions. For example, s 24 makes a person who is a shareholder, after a six-month period in which the company has had less than two shareholders, jointly and severally liable for the company's debts. Section 349(4) imposes liability upon an officer of the company who has signed company cheques etc on which the name of the company does not appear in full. However, the most important provisions are those relating to fraudulent or wrongful trading and the special rules for groups. Sections 213 to 215 of the Insolvency Act 1986 impose liability for the debts of a company where a person has engaged in fraudulent or wrongful trading. The rules on group accounts are immensely complicated but, broadly, they are designed to ensure that the accounts of associated companies are looked at as a whole to provide a 'true and fair view'. What can we discern as the concern of Parliament in providing exceptions to *Salomon's* case? It is clear that an element of wrongdoing or impropriety should disqualify a person from the manifold benefits of corporate personality (particularly that of limited liability) and the courts have not been reluctant to follow this lead. Such cases seem currently to be called cases where the corporate form is 'a mere facade' but the description changes with the years. The veil has been lifted to prevent a person escaping specific performance of a contract by selling the contracted land to a company which he controlled (*Jones v Lipman* (1962)), or to prevent a person evading the effect of a valid restraint clause (*Gilford Motor Co Ltd v Horne* (1933)). A further example of the public policy approach to lifting the veil is *Daimler Co Ltd v Continental Tyre and Rubber Co Ltd* (1916) in which the court, during the First World War, had regard to the nationality (German) of the shareholders of a British-registered company. The principal difficulty with this approach is knowing when the court will regard the corporate form as a mere facade. Motive may be important (see *Adams v Cape Industries plc* (1990)) but even this is of limited help. Is forming a company to minimise your tax liability a case where your motive should cause the courts to lift the veil?

Leaving aside the 'facade' cases, is there, as Lord Denning suggested, good reason and Parliamentary encouragement to disregard legal personality in other cases? In *Littlewoods Mail Order Stores Ltd v IRC* (1969), Lord Denning suggested that it would not be inappropriate for the courts to lift the veil between individual companies which form part of an economic group. This approach is well recognised in Germany and, German law being the pre-eminent influence on EC Draft Directives, is provided for in the Ninth Draft Directive on company law — albeit in unworkable fashion. Limited support for Lord Denning's approach can be found in a number of cases which were reviewed in *Adam v Cape Industries plc* (1990) a case on enforcement of a foreign judgment against an English company. For example, in *Scottish CWS v Meyer* (1959), the appellant company controlled a subsidiary in which M was a substantial shareholder. The subsidiary, at the behest of the CWS, sought to destroy itself thereby reducing the value of M's shareholding. The House of Lords had no difficulty in finding that M had been subject to oppression as a member (contrary to s 210 CA 1948) by CWS despite the fact that he was not a shareholder in CWS. The court looked to the business realities of the situation and not the strict legal position. M was effectively a member of the CWS group. This case could be explained as demonstrating a purposive approach to the statute (as could some others) rather than a recognition of the integrity of the economic grouping. The same cannot be said of *DHN Food Distributors Ltd v Tower Hamlets LBC* (1976). In this case DHN had two wholly owned subsidiaries, one owned the land which DHN used under licence for its business and one owned the transport used in the business. The land was subject to a compulsory purchase order and the Lands Tribunal fixed the compensation payable at a minimal level having ruled that DHN had merely lost a licence and deprivation of the land did not affect the business of the subsidiary since it had none. The Court of Appeal ignored the separate legal status of the three companies and treated them as one economic grouping so that compensation was payable for the disruption of the business of the group. The court took the view that it should look at the realities of the relationship rather the legal structure under which the business had chosen to trade. This approach was doubted in the House of Lords in *Woolfson v Strathclyde Regional Council* (1978), in which a single business (a shop) had gradually taken over a number of adjacent retail units and incorporated them into the original shop by knocking doorways through walls. The original shops, having been acquired at different times, were leased to different companies all of which were, effectively controlled by W. However, the structures and shareholdings of the various companies were not identical. Consequently, the House of Lords was able, on the facts, to distinguish DHN where there had been a complete coincidence of shareholding. Nevertheless, the House went further and doubted the correctness of DHN other than as an interpretation of the particular statute authorising compensation.

Thus, whatever the merits of the economic reality approach, it seems unlikely to find favour in British courts in the near future. That strict adherence to the legal structures can cause unfairness to shareholders has been recognised and ameliorated by the courts in the case of the winding up of quasi-partnership companies (*Ebrahimi v Westbourne Galleries Ltd* (1970)) and in the interpretation of unfair prejudice in the context of s 459. Such strict adherence may cause loss to creditors (as when a company abandons its insolvent subsidiary) and as yet this position has not been ameliorated by the courts (see the somewhat caustic comment on this by Templeman LJ in *Re Southard & Co Ltd* (1979)). However, such reforms are probably best left to Parliament — the potential imposition of liability for wrongful trading upon a shadow director may prove a more effective means of controlling the use of high-risk subsidiaries than the possibility of subsequent lifting the veil. If Parliament does not intervene we may find that the implementation of an amended Ninth Directive requires the recognition of economic reality regardless of the primacy of the principle of separate legal personality.

Notes

Depending upon the time available, a student could illustrate the strength of the *Salomon* case by referring to other examples, eg *Lee v Lee's Air Farming Ltd* (1961), and giving the facts of some of the lifting the veil cases. Greater discussion of wrongful trading could also be useful.

Question 3

Laura, a talented designer, and her husband, Bernard, are running a small business engaged in the printing and selling of silk scarves and ties. They are seeking to expand the business and have persuaded Laura's parents to provide funds for expansion. Laura's parents do not wish to participate in the day-to-day running of the business nor do they need an income from their investment but they would like to be consulted on major matters of policy and to be able to recover their capital in the future. Laura and Bernard wish to retain control of the business but want to give Laura's brother, Mark, who works for them, greater involvement in the business. Laura and Bernard have decided to form a company in which they will own the majority of shares and be directors. They seek your advice about how to structure the company and to accommodate the wishes of Laura's parents, Mark and themselves.

Answer plan

Again a fairly typical question which might apply to many small family businesses. The answer should address the specific concerns of those involved rather than be a general description of company formation. Since the decision to incorporate has been taken, there is no need to consider the advantages and disadvantages of incorporation.

Answer

Laura and Bernard wish to incorporate their existing business. The appropriate form of company will be a private company limited by shares (s 1). L and B may choose to establish a new company; the company will require a memorandum of association, which must contain certain information (s 2), and articles of association, before it can be registered by the Registrar of Companies. The content of the articles, which can be called the company's internal rules, can be fixed by the founders of the company but if none are registered the appropriate form of Table A will apply (s 8). Alternatively, they may choose to buy a pre-existing company 'off-the-shelf'. The advantages of an off-the-shelf company are that the company becomes theirs immediately without going through the registration process; all that is required is a transfer of shareholding, but such a company would not have been formed with their specific requirements in mind and alterations of the memorandum or articles might be required. Perhaps the most important thing for them to grasp is that their company is a separate legal person and that, by establishing it, they can no longer treat the business as entirely their own affair. To take an extreme example, they must as directors formally approve any contracts they enter into with the company (see *Re Neptune (Vehicle Washing Equipment) Ltd* (1995) in which the only director was required, formally, to inform himself of his interest in a contract entered into by the company).

Turning to the mechanics of formation. The memorandum must give the name of the company which must appear on the company's seal, business letters, cheques etc and be affixed outside all places of business — brevity reduces printing costs. The final word of the company's name must be 'Limited' (which can be abbreviated to Ltd). There are restrictions upon the names which can be used (ss 25-34). The principal restriction is that their company cannot have the same name as an existing company. Consequently, if their name is Smith, Smith Ltd is unlikely to be acceptable. Indeed a name which has been registered may, within 12 months of registration, be directed to be changed by the Secretary of State if it is too like the name of an existing company. Other names are banned if the name would be a criminal offence or be 'offensive'. Yet further names can be used only if the Secretary of State gives permission, eg names suggesting a connection with local or central government. It is possible to change the name of the company at a later date if need be.

The memorandum requires the company to state whether its registered office is in England and Wales or in Scotland. Finally, s 2(1)(c) requires the company to state the objects of the company. This provision whereby the company sets out what it intends to do is of diminishing importance. L and B would probably adopt s 3A and register the objects of the company as being to carry on any trade or business whatsoever. L's parents might wish to restrict the company's business to the existing trade rather than see their money being expended on new schemes; limiting the memorandum would provide some protection for their investment (if they became shareholders) in that they could seek to restrain activities not sanctioned by the objects clause (s 35). However, the effect of s 35 is that a shareholder can only restrain contemplated acts and not those already legally binding on the company. If the directors (likely to be L and B) overstep the objects clause in their dealings on behalf of the company, L's parents could sue them for breach of directors' duty but in a company like this prevention rather then cure is more apposite. The objects of the company can anyway be changed (ss 4 and 5) but a shareholder with a 15% shareholding in any class of share has *locus* to object to the change although the change may still be sanctioned by the court.

Section 2(5) of the memorandum requires a statement of the amount of the company's share capital, how the share capital is divided up and the 'value' of each share. This value, the nominal value, is an arbitrary figure not necessarily bearing any relation to the asset value of the company or its earning potential. The minimum nominal value of a share is one penny and, at present, a company must have at the outset at least two shareholders. Thus, the company could have two one-penny shares and L could buy one and B the other. These two shares have to paid for in cash. Two shares creates a rather inflexible share structure and most private companies have a share capital of £100 or £1,000 divided into £1 or 10 pence shares. L and B could give Mark a stake in the business by allotting shares to him. If L and B wished to retain control of the company they need to ensure that their shareholding is at least 51% (sufficient to pass an ordinary resolution) or preferably 75% (sufficient to pass a special resolution) although Mark might not regard less than 25% as a very worthwhile shareholding in the company. L's parents could also be given shares in the company but unless they had a majority, which would not suit L and B, they would have no effective control over their investment. As shareholders, L's parents would have to be notified of meetings and would have *locus* under s 459 to raise the issue of unfair prejudice etc.

Assuming L and B are the principal shareholders, they may choose to pay for the shares by transferring the business to the company or by agreeing to work for the company — this is perfectly acceptable (s 99). Assuming the value of the business is to exceed the modest nominal value currently encountered, L and B may be owed money for the business by the company. This debt could be secured by debenture giving, in theory, L and B priority over other creditors on winding up. Indeed, by incorporating, L and B appear to have removed their personal assets from the perils of the company's insolvency. In practice, the benefits of limited liability do not exist for founders of small private companies — the banks who form the major creditor for most businesses require personal guarantees (often secured on the directors' homes) from directors etc before extending the company credit. The share structure of a company can be changed, see for example, ss 121 (alterations) and 135 (reduction). Since L and B are the promoters of the company, the articles should reveal any profits which they have made on incorporation.

Turning to the articles of association, the main issue is the extent to which Table A should be adopted. Most private companies amend Table A and in such cases it is safest to draft a self-contained set of articles for the company lest there be any doubt about what rules have been adopted. Common amendments are to insert a restriction upon the transferability of the company's shares — in this case L and B will not want M or any other shareholder transferring shares to outsiders, to vary the rules on quorums at meetings and the maximum number (and age) of directors. It is in the articles that L and B might choose to insert a provision permitting L's parents to block changes of policy. This could be achieved in one of two ways. L's parents could be given weighted voting rights (approved by the House of Lords in *Bushell v Faith* (1970)) in respect of certain transactions. For example, Table A, art 70, which most companies adopt, vests the running of the company in the directors subject to 'directions given by special resolution'. If L's parents are given weighted voting rights they can ensure that they can always issue 'directions'. Such a clause should be protected against alteration. Alternatively, L's parents could be given a right to veto in the articles (protected against alteration) which, by virtue of s 14, gives them a contractual right of veto if they are shareholders. The difficulty with the latter approach is that the ability of shareholders to enforce the contract which is contained in the articles is uncertain. The traditional view is that a shareholder can enforce the articles only insofar as the relevant article creates a 'membership' right, ie a right attaching to each and every share which relates to the holding of shares. This view derives from the first instance decision of Astbury J in *Hickman v Kent or Romney Marsh Sheepbreeders' Assoc* (1915) and would appear to preclude the enforcement of a right vested only in L's parents. However, powerful arguments have been raised against this interpretation of the s 14 contract. Lord Wedderburn in particular relies heavily upon the House of Lords' decision in *Quin & Axtens v Salmon* (1909), where a shareholder was held entitled to enforce an article which required his consent to the sale of company land, to advance the view that a shareholder has a personal right to require the company to act in accordance with its articles. Variations on Lord Wedderburn's argument would restrict the shareholder to having a right to ensure that the appropriate corporate body carries on the affairs of the company. The uncertainty surrounding the s 14 contract makes this route an uncertain one for L's parents. Either of these proposals would limit L and B's ability to run the company as they wished. Perhaps a free-standing shareholder agreement would provide a contractual means of restraining L and B's actions.

Since L and B are forming a private company they should be informed of the provisions for written resolutions (s 381A) allowing decisions to be made by written agreement without the need to call a meeting and elective resolutions permitting a company to exempt itself from some of the formal requirements of the Acts.

If L and B are to be the first directors of the company (only one is required by law, s 282) no further directors are required although there is no reason why M could not be invited to be a director. The proceedings of the directors will be governed by the articles. All directors are subject to the usual rules pertaining to directors' duties. These duties which derive from equity, the common law and statute are immensely complex and the directors should be advised of the need to seek proper legal advice before entering into transactions. The company would almost certainly be classified as a quasi-partnership company (even if M becomes a shareholder-director) and any serious breakdown in the relationship of the three principals could lead to a petition for just and equitable winding up under s 122(1)(g) of the Insolvency Act 1986 — a parallel provision would operate if the business had been run as a partnership. Further, attempts to exclude M's participation in the company, or attempts to block L's parents exercising any right to consultation and/or veto, could be unfair prejudice and consequently in breach of s 459.

The final question to be addressed is how to protect the financial stake being provided by L's parents. Ordinary shares in a private company are not readily marketable and offer no protection against insolvency; they are not an appropriate choice. Preference shares are subject to the same handicaps although redeemable shares would guarantee a return of capital if the company was still a going concern. The best solution would appear to be a secured loan, preferably redeemable at a fixed date, in their favour. Obviously, the company must have an asset of sufficient value to stand as security for the loan and a specified asset subject to a fixed charge is more likely to guarantee repayment than a floating charge. A charge on the assets of the company must be registered.

Question 4

Archie, Brian and Colin, who are all self-employed plasterers, agree to combine their businesses and to operate as a company, Cornice Ltd. A document is prepared which says: 'It is hereby agreed that all expenses incurred by Colin in the formation of Cornice Ltd shall be repaid from company funds within 12 months of the date of incorporation of the company' and is signed: 'For and on behalf Cornice Ltd, as agents only, Archie and Brian.'

Advised by an accountant, Colin duly formed Cornice Ltd and its shares were divided equally among the three participants who all became directors. The articles of the company provide that: 'Any person who has incurred expenses in connection with the formation of the company shall be entitled to reimbursement of those expenses by the company.' After formation, Brian signed a cheque, bearing the name Cornice, in favour of the accountant for his advice in connection with the formation; this cheque has not been paid. It has also emerged that Archie made a profit from the incorporation which he did not reveal to Colin. Colin protested about the failure to pay the accountant and Archie's undisclosed profit and Archie and Brian then resolved not to reimburse him for his expenses and agreed to take no action to recover the profit from Archie.

Advise Colin and the accountant.

Answer plan

Three principal issues arise in this question:

- whether Colin can initiate proceedings to recover the profit made by Archie
- whether Colin has any claim for the expenses which he incurred in forming the company either against the company or against Archie and Brian
- whether the accountant has any claim against the company or Brian for his services

Answer

While the law is a little hazy as to who is a promoter, it is a question of fact in all cases; there is no doubt that Archie, Brian and Colin are the promoters of Cornice Ltd. They are the people who decided to form the company, who set it going and who organised the registration all of which are factors in determining if a person is a promoter (see *Emma Silver Mining Co v Lewis* (1879) and *Whaley Bridge Printing Co v Green* (1880)). In contrast, despite any help he may have provided, the accountant is not a promoter if he merely acted in a professional capacity (*Re Great Wheal Polgooth Co* (1883)).

A promoter owes certain obligations to the company which he is forming — essentially a duty of good faith in all dealings with the incipient corporation. This is because promoters are in a position of total dominance over the company and there is much scope for them to profit from the promotion. The courts have had to determine whether a promoter cannot derive a profit from the promotion or whether to allow the retention of profit in certain cases. The courts have adopted the second view. In *Erlanger v New Sombrero Phosphate Co* (1878), the House of Lords held that a promoter could keep any profit he made out of the promotion provided that full disclosure was made to an independent board of directors. While still valid, this test is almost impossible to satisfy. Promoters of private companies, as in this case, are likely to become the first directors and have a continuing involvement with the company; there is no independent board. Consequently, the courts have treated disclosure to the members as full disclosure (*Salomon v Salomon* (1897)) provided that the initial members do not intend to bow out once disclosure has been achieved. A has not made full disclosure of his profit to all shareholders and, even if this is an indirect profit, he has broken the duty which he owes to the company. That indirect profit-making is a breach of duty is well illustrated by *Gluckstein v Barnes* (1900) in which the promoter sold property (Olympia) to a company they were promoting, which profit was duly disclosed. The promoters did not reveal that prior to their acquisition of Olympia they had acquired certain debts (for less than face value since it was generally thought they would never be paid) secured on the property. Prior to transferring the property to the company they arranged for these debts to be paid and the profit they made when the debts were discharged was not disclosed. The promoters were required to repay this profit to the company.

While there may be no doubt that A has broken his duty to the company, can C do anything about it? The duty is owed to the company and the company appears to have resolved to do nothing about A's action. Since a company is an abstraction, a person acting on behalf of the company must initiate litigation. By virtue of Table A, art 70, this power is vested in the board who, in this case, have decided not to sue. C as a shareholder cannot force the company to sue A nor has he the power to sack the board but he may be able to bring a derivative action on behalf of the company alleging fraud by the controlling shareholders. However, given the inauspicious start to the joint venture, he might be better advised to seek a just and equitable winding up under s 122(1)(g) of the Insolvency Act 1986 or bring an action for unfair prejudice (s 459) on his own account and seek to be bought out of the company.

C's next cause for complaint is the failure to obtain reimbursement for the expenses which he incurred in the course of promotion. A promoter is not entitled to reimbursement from the company unless he can establish a valid contract to pay. Is there such a contract? The document signed by A and B purports to bind the company to reimburse C but the case of *Kelner v Baxter* (1866) has long established that a company cannot be bound by a contract entered into prior to its incorporation — the company did not exist at the relevant time so it cannot contract. In *Kelner* the promoters ordered wines and spirits on behalf of a hotel company they were forming. The goods were not paid for by the company nor could they be recovered since they had been consumed; the company was not liable on the contract although the promoters were. Nor can the articles be said to ratify the pre-incorporation contract: *Kelner v Baxter* also held that a principal which did not exist at the time its agent purported to act on its behalf cannot ratify the acts of the 'agent'. If the company was to enter into a new contract with C post-incorporation he could sue on the new contract but he would have to show that he had provided consideration which was not past.

C may seek to rely on the provision in the articles authorising the reimbursement of promotion expenses. This article plainly authorises the directors to pay these expenses if they choose but it almost certainly does not entitle C to demand payment. Section 14 provides that the articles of the company bind the company and its members. The wording of the section seems tolerably clear — that the articles create a contract between the company and its members. Since a contract exists, even if a rather odd one in that it can be altered by one party (s 9), it would seem that C could sue on the articles and obtain his due. Unfortunately, the courts have interpreted the s 14 contract rather oddly. The traditional view is that a shareholder can enforce the articles only insofar as the relevant article creates a 'membership' right, ie a right attaching to each and every share and which relates to the holding of shares. This view derives from the first instance decision of Astbury J in *Hickman v Kent or Romney Marsh Sheepbreeders' Assoc* (1915) and would appear to preclude the enforcement of a right which, while vested in all shareholders (and others), does not relate to the ownership of shares. What constitutes a membership right is far from clear but it seems clear that a reimbursement of promotion expenses does not fall into this category (*Melhado v Porto Allegre Rly Co* (1874)). However, powerful arguments have been raised against Astbury's interpretation of the s 14 contract. Lord Wedderburn in particular relies heavily upon the House of Lords' decision in *Quin & Axtens v Salmon* (1909), where a shareholder was held entitled to enforce an article which required his consent to the sale of company land, to advance the view that a shareholder has a personal right to require the company to act in accordance with its articles. Variations on Lord Wedderburn's argument would restrict the shareholder to having a right to ensure that the appropriate corporate body carries on the affairs of the company. The conventional view seems likely to be applied to a case such as this and C would not be reimbursed.

C would, however, be able to bring an action against A and B personally for the reimbursement of his expenses. Section 36C provides that a contract 'which purports to be made by or on behalf of a company at a time when the company has not been formed has the effect ... as one made with the person purporting to act for the company as agent for it, and he is personally liable on the contract accordingly'. The courts have interpreted this section (and its forbears) purposively and there seems little doubt that A and B will be liable. *Phonogram Ltd v Lane* (1982) illustrates the operation of the section. L had entered into a contract with the plaintiff on behalf of a company he was forming to manage a rock group (Cheap, Mean and Nasty - unknown to me I admit!) and had received approximately £12,000 on behalf of the intended company to aid his endeavours. The company was never formed and, even though it was accepted that the money had not necessarily benefitted L personally, he was liable to reimburse the plaintiff.

The final issue concerns the accountant who has not been paid. Obviously, the accountant must establish some legal right if he wishes to bring an action to recover the sum due. First, he could seek to sue the company on the pre-incorporation contract but this will not succeed because:

- it is not clear that he was contracting with the company rather than with C personally;
- even if he was contracting with the company, the company, as we have seen, is not liable on a pre-incorporation contract.

Second, he could sue the company as the drawer of the cheque and if the company fails to pay he might be able to seek a winding up order, although it is unlikely that the sums would justify this. He could not sue the company on the provision in the articles which seems to authorise the payment of incorporation expenses because he is not a shareholder and is not a party to the s 14 contract. Indeed, even if he was a shareholder, he would face the same difficulties as C in enforcing what appears to be a non-membership right. If a court was prepared to disregard the conventional view on the s 14 contract and hold that all the articles constituted contractual rights (or that a member had a right to have the articles complied with) he would still have to depend upon C suing on his behalf (unless he was a shareholder). If C sued on behalf of the accountant, the rules of privity would seem to provide that any damages payable to C would reflect C's loss and not that of the accountant (if C has to reimburse the accountant his losses might be recoverable). Third, he could sue Brian as the signatory of a company cheque which does not bear the full name of the company. Section 349(4) states that any person who signs a cheque on behalf of a company on which the name of the company does not appear in full — B signed on behalf of Cornice and not Cornice Ltd — is personally liable on the cheque. While the omission of 'Ltd' seems minor and there is no question of the accountant being misled as to the status of the body with which he was dealing, the law is strict. The omission of '&' in the name of a company has triggered the section and, while the courts feel that claims under this provision may be wholly unmeritorious, they have left it to Parliament to amend the law. If the accountant sues B under this provision, B in entitled to an indemnity from the company provided that it is solvent.

Both C and the accountant should be able to recover their money provided that A and B are solvent. One cannot see much future for Cornice Ltd, however.

Question 5

Rendell Ltd has a number of wholly owned subsidiaries including Barbara Ltd and Vine Ltd. The directors of Rendell Ltd are also directors of these two subsidiaries.

Land belonging to Barbara Ltd is being compulsorily purchased by the government for a road-widening scheme; the amount of compensation has not yet been agreed.

Vine Ltd, while originally engaged in house building, has incurred huge losses in speculative property dealings which were entered into by the managing director of the company without the knowledge of the other directors who took no active part in management. The creditors of Vine are pressing Rendell to pay its subsidiary's debts.

Advise Rendell Ltd and its directors.

Answer plan

A number of issues arise. They can be split into those affecting the holding company and those affecting its directors.

Rendell Ltd are seeking:

- to obtain the best possible compensation for the land acquisition
- to escape liability for the debts of Vine Ltd
- to avoid the speculative building contracts
- to pursue all or some of the directors of Vine in respect of the losses already incurred

The directors of Rendell are trying:

- to escape any liability for their actions and inactions as directors of Vine

Answer

Rendell wishes to maximise the compensation payable in respect of the road-widening scheme which affects Barbara Ltd and minimise its losses in respect of its subsidiary, Vine Ltd.

(a) Barbara Ltd

Barbara Ltd is a wholly owned subsidiary of Rendell Ltd but, as a registered company, it is a separate legal person from its shareholder. Traditionally, a shareholder has no legal interest in the property of the company. Thus, in *Macaura v Northern Assurance* (1925), a shareholder was unable to claim on a policy of insurance which he had effected on certain of the company's assets and which had been destroyed by fire; one cannot insure another's property and the assets belonged to another — the company. Thus, the amount payable for the road-widening scheme would seem to be limited to an appropriate sum under the legislation necessary to compensate Barbara Ltd for its loss. However, the forfeiture of the land may also have an adverse affect upon other companies within the Rendell Ltd group resulting in greater loss than that which is payable to Barbara Ltd. Can Rendell Ltd claim that the veil of incorporation cloaking Barbara Ltd can be torn aside so that Rendell and Barbara are treated as one company for the purposes of compensation? There are some circumstances in which a court will ignore the separate legal personality of a company. This disregard of corporate legal status may be required by statute or, in exceptional cases, be decreed by the courts. One statutory situation is pertinent. The statutes which permit compensation for persons whose real property is subject to a compulsory purchase order allow a court to disregard the separate legal personality of individual companies within a group and consider the effect of the order on the business of the group as a whole. An example very similar to the facts of this case arose in *DHN Food Distributors v Tower Hamlets Borough Council* (1976).

(b) Vine Ltd

The situation in respect of this subsidiary is more complex.

(i) Turning to the first issue, is Rendell liable for the debts of its subsidiary? Once again the existence of the corporate veil shields the shareholder, Rendell, from the attentions of the disgruntled creditors of Vine Ltd. The situation is similar to that in *Salomon v Salomon & Co* (1897) in which S, who had converted his existing, successful, business into a limited company of which he was the managing director and principal shareholder was found not to be liable for the company's unpaid debts. This strict adherence to the separation of company (Vine) and its shareholders (Rendell) causes loss to creditors but as yet this position has not been ameliorated by the courts (see the somewhat caustic comment on this by Templeman LJ in *Re Southard & Co Ltd* (1979)). Hence, unless there is some reason to disregard the corporate personality of Vine, the creditors have no call upon Rendell. Grounds for lifting the veil include where a company is being used to conceal some fraudulent purpose as, for example, in *Jones v Lipman* (1962) where the defendant sought to evade a binding contract of sale between himself and the plaintiff by conveying the subject matter of the contract to a company he controlled — the corporate status of the transferee was disregarded by the court. There seems no evidence of fraud by the shareholder in Vine in this case. An alternative approach might be to claim that the company had engaged in wrongful trading and that the directors thereby incurred personal liability for the debts of Vine. If such liability arose (see below for a fuller discussion of this point) Rendell might also be liable if it could be regarded as a shadow director, ie a person in accordance with whose directions the directors of a company are accustomed to act (s 741). It seems probable that Rendell exercised this degree of control over at least some of the directors and the section might apply.

(ii) The contracts entered into by the reckless director are binding on the subsidiary even if not authorised by the objects clause of Vine Ltd because the validity of a company's contracts cannot be called into question simply because it lacked the capacity to enter into it (s 35). However, the directors of Vine can be held liable to the company if they permitted the company to over-step its legal capacity unless the default by them is ratified by special resolution (s 35(3)). Clearly, Rendell have a claim against the directors (it cannot be enforced by the creditors) but may not wish to exercise it or could choose to ratify the wrong-doing. While the contracts bind Vine, they are not enforceable against Rendell since to attempt to do so would disregard Vine's legal personality.

(iii) Liability may sometimes be imposed upon the directors in respect of corporate activities. A director can incur liability for the company's debts where he was knowingly a party to a company's fraudulent trading. Fraudulent trading occurs when a director allows his company to continue trading knowing that it cannot pay its debts at present and that there is no reasonable prospect that it will be able to pay them. Since fraud must be proved beyond reasonable doubt, actions for fraudulent trading are rarely successful (Insolvency Act 1986, s 213). It does not seem very likely here. It is wrongful trading, introduced by s 214 of the Insolvency Act 1986, which appears more likely to be the basis for the imposition of personal liability upon the directors of Vine Ltd and Rendell if it is a shadow director. However, wrongful trading is applicable only where a company has gone into insolvent liquidation which is not the case here. It might be worth Rendell propping up Vine Ltd to avoid insolvency and the possible imposition of personal liability which would mean the creditors of Vine would be paid. The sums must be done carefully to see which is most beneficial. Where, in the course of the winding up of a company, it appears that a director is guilty of 'wrongful trading', the courts, on the application of the liquidator, may declare him liable to make a contribution to the company's assets of such an amount as it thinks proper.

The power to make a declaration under s 214(1) applies in relation to a director if:

- the company has gone into insolvent liquidation;
- at some time before the winding up of the company, that person knew or ought to have concluded, that there was no reasonable prospect of the company avoiding insolvent liquidation; and
- he was a director at that time.

However, the court must not make a declaration if, after the person concerned first knew or ought to have concluded that there was no reasonable prospect of the company avoiding insolvent liquidation, he took every step to minimise the potential loss to the company's creditors as he ought to have taken. Section 214(4) provides that, for the above purposes, the facts which a person ought to have known, the conclusions he ought to reach and the steps which he ought to take are those which would be known, reached or taken, by a reasonably diligent person with the 'general knowledge, skill and experience that may reasonably be expected of a person carrying out the same functions as are carried out by that director' (ie the director potentially subject to an order) and with the 'general knowledge, skill and experience' of the director whom it is sought to make liable. This somewhat obscure provision seems to mean that what a director should have known or done is to be judged by reference to a theoretical director who possesses those skills that may 'reasonably be expected' of a director, unless the director is better qualified than this theoretical director when he is to be judged by reference to his own qualifications. The question is whether the directors of Vine Ltd have exercised sufficient skill — certainly the inactive directors might be at fault if, that is, some degree of activity or active supervision could be expected from them. In *Re Produce Marketing Consortium Ltd (No 2)* (1989) it was found that, once the directors should have concluded from the falling profitability and increasing debts of the company that liquidation was inevitable and they had failed to take all steps to minimise loss since the directors had not limited their dealings to running down the company's stocks (which action might have been justified as an attempt to minimise liability to creditors), they were required to contribute (£75,000) to the assets of the company, this being the loss which could have been averted by speedy liquidation.

(iv) Could the directors of Vine Ltd be liable to that company or Rendell Ltd or the creditors? Directors owe a duty to the company of which they are directors but not to any holding company. Consequently, the directors of Vine Ltd are not directly liable to Rendell for any default (*Lindgren v L & P Estates Ltd* (1967)) although any failure on their part as directors of Rendell may be actionable and it is hardly good policy for a director to upset the sole shareholder. Nor can they be liable to the creditors of Vine since no duty is owed to creditors of a company except, perhaps, when the company is already insolvent or on the point of collapse. Indeed, in *Kuwait Asia Bank EC v National Mutual Life Nominees Ltd* (1991), the Privy Council seemed unwilling to countenance even this possibility. However, as directors of Vine they do owe duties to that company. The enforcement of those duties is vested in the company itself but the company is controlled by its directors (by virtue of Table A, art 70) so that directors appear to be able to decide whether to pursue themselves in respect of any alleged wrong-doing on their part. However, the shareholders in a company can instruct the directors how to act (ie sue themselves) provided they do so by special resolution and, since Rendell can command such a resolution, there is no difficulty in bringing an action against the directors. Alternatively, Rendell could commence an action itself. In addition, whether or not the directors are in default, they can be sacked by ordinary resolution (s 303) although this may constitute breach of a service contract and prove to be expensive.

Merely because there is a plaintiff who could bring an action, it does not mean that the directors are in breach of duty. Apart from the director who engaged in speculative property dealings, which might be *ultra vires*, the directors who took no active part in management might be in breach of their duty of care and skill. The common law duty of care and skill borne by directors is traditionally very modest in that directors are merely expected to carry out their duties with an appropriate degree of care and skill. The traditional formulation of the nature and extent of this duty is that given by Romer J in *Re City Equitable Fire Insurance Co Ltd* (1925) in which he held that a director:

• need display only such skill as may reasonably be expected from a person of his knowledge and experience;

- need not give the affairs of the company continuous attention; and
- is entitled to leave the day-to-day running of the company to the officials of the company and is entitled to assume, in the absence of suspicious circumstances, that such officials are performing their duties honestly.

These propositions remain good law with regard to non-executive directors but executive directors will generally be constrained by their service contracts to devote a set percentage of their time to the affairs of the company. However, in *Dorchester Finance Co Ltd v Stebbing* (1977), two directors, who were qualified accountants, who left the running of the company to S doing little more than calling in periodically and signing blank cheques for S to use which cheques S converted for his own use, were negligent. The judge found that their complete failure to do anything in respect of the running of the company was, even for non-executive directors, negligent as well as in breach of several sections of the Companies Act. On this basis the directors might incur liability for failure to restrain actions by the active director.

Question 6

In May 1994, the shares of Large plc, a quoted international company, stood at £3.20. That month the company issued listing particulars in which the directors announced that the company was seeking finance to embark on gold mining in Siberia. The listing particulars contained a report by Bering Associates stating that the area over which Large had the mining concession was rich in easily mined gold and that enormous profits could be expected.

Midas read the listing particulars and subscribed for 5,000 £1 shares at a total cost of £15,000. On the last day of June, Midas sold half his shares at £3.80 each to Croesus, who had also read the company's listing particulars In early July, it was announced that a further survey revealed that, while there was gold in the area it was extremely difficult to mine, making the project barely profitable and the price of Large plc's shares tumbled to £1.80.

Advise Midas and Croesus as to any remedies which may be open to them.

Answer plan

Any answer to this question should differentiate between Midas, who will seek a remedy from the company and/or the directors and/or Bering Associates, and Croesus who might seek to pursue a claim against Midas. In respect of each complainant, the statutory and any common law remedies should be considered. It is assumed that any course will have concentrated upon the provisions of the Financial Services Act 1986, even where the relevant sections are not yet in force, rather than the provisions in the Companies Act which will be replaced.

Answer

(a) Midas

The Financial Services Act (FSA)

The remedy most easily available to Midas is that provided by the Financial Services Act 1986 which Act is based upon certain EC Directives (although criticism could be made of the adequacy of the implementation thus leaving open the question of whether an individual could rely on a Directive in preference to the Act). The FSA provides for both civil and criminal sanctions against those who fail to comply with the provisions of the Act or who induce subscription by false representations or engage in other improper practices. The first issue is whether there has been a false representation.

Section 146(1) of the FSA imposes a general duty of disclosure in respect of listing particulars (formerly prospectuses) and provides that the listing particulars must contain 'all such information as investors and their professional advisers would reasonably require, and reasonably expect to find there, for the purpose of making an informed assessment of (a) the assets and liabilities, financial position, profits and losses, and prospects of the issuer of the security...'. Further guidance is given on the information which might reasonably be expected in s 146(3). Is the information given to Midas about the mining operation etc information falling within sub-s (1)? It would seem so.

The second issue is who incurs liability in respect of this false statement. Section 146(2) states that the information to be included in the particulars is such information as is mentioned in s 146(1) 'which is within the knowledge of any person responsible for the listing particulars or which it would be reasonable for him to obtain by making enquiries'. Liability is imposed upon the person(s) responsible for the listing particulars by s 150 subject to certain defences contained in s 151 (s 148 which allows the non-disclosure of certain information does not apply here). The persons responsible are set out in s 152; they are:

- the company; and
- the directors; and
- each and every person who accepts (and is stated as accepting) responsibility for all or part of the particulars; and
- each other person who has authorised the contents of the particulars or any part of it.

Subject to s 151, there is little doubt that Large plc and its directors incur liability. Bering Associates would also appear to incur liability, that is for the parts of the particulars for which they were responsible if they have accepted responsibility for or authorised the contents. However, Bering will not be liable unless the misleading material included in the particulars appeared in substantially the form and context to which Bering had agreed. Are any of the parties, who would appear to be liable, exempt? Section 151(1) exempts any person 'if he satisfies the court that at the time when the particular were submitted ... he reasonably believed, having made such enquiries (if any) as were reasonable, that the statement was true and not misleading ...' provided that he continued in his belief until the time the securities were acquired or he continued in his belief until after dealings in the shares had begun and they were acquired after such a lapse of time that he ought reasonably to be excused. This can be called the reasonable belief exemption and it might apply here to Large and its directors — it seems unlikely to apply to Bering. Of greater relevance for Large and its directors is s 151(2). This sub-section exempts from liability those who relied upon a statement made by an expert (in this case Bering) provided that they can establish that they had reasonable grounds to rely upon the expertise of the provider of the misleading information (and the expert had agreed to its inclusion) and they continued to believe Bering was an expert until after the shares had been bought or they continued in that belief until after dealings in the shares had begun and they were acquired after such a lapse of time that they ought reasonably to be excused. Note that merely because Bering gave misleading advice does not necessarily mean that they are not competent. Even experts make mistakes. There are special rules where misleading information is corrected but these do not apply in the case of Midas. It should be noted that the onus of exempting themselves from liability fall upon those responsible for the particulars.

The third issue is the nature of any liability incurred. Section 150 provides that those responsible for misleading listing particulars are liable to pay compensation to Midas for the loss he has suffered, the measure of damages is thought to be that applicable in tort, ie restoration to his original position. Originally Midas had £15,000 and no shares, he now has two-and-a-half thousand worth £1.80 each (£4,500) and has received (it is assumed) £3.80 for each share sold to Croesus (£9,500) so that he needs £1,000 to restore him to his original position (plus any incidental expenses). If a contractual measure of damages was applicable, greater damages could be recovered (loss of expectation basis). It should be noted that Midas will not be able to claim compensation if he knew the relevant statement was untrue.

Other sources of liability

Midas should have no need to look beyond the FSA but other possible sources of compensation are the tort of deceit (where there is conduct akin to fraud), negligent misstatement either in tort or by virtue of s 2(1) of the Misrepresentation Act 1967 (the last of these would only be available against the company). Midas could not rescind the contract, it seems, because he has sold half the shares. The fact that he could not rescind would not now debar Midas from monetary compensation (s 111A reversing *Houldsworth v City of Glasgow Bank* (1880)).

(b) Croesus

The position of Croesus is not dissimilar from that of Midas in that he too may have a remedy under the FSA. The right to sue those responsible for the misleading listing particulars is not restricted to those who purchased the shares from the company. Now, anyone who has acquired shares who can show that he has suffered loss as a result of the misstatement has a *prima facie* case for compensation. Croesus will have to prove that there is a causal connection between the misstatement and the loss. Factors which will tend to negate such a connection are purchase after the true facts became known, which does not apply here, or such a lapse of time that the particulars can no longer be said to have any influence on the market. The gap between the publication of the misstatement and the purchase in this case does not seem so long as to debar Croesus from seeking compensation. Do any of those liable to Midas have a defence in the case of Croesus? The only possibility would seem to be that the company or directors could establish that Croesus bought the shares before it was reasonably practicable for them to bring a correction or inform people of the incompetence of the expert. The common law remedies seem unlikely to apply in this case except perhaps with regard to Midas.

Whatever the outcome of any claim under the FSA, Croesus has the usual common law remedies against Midas. Thus, if he can show that Midas knew the truth when he sold the shares he may have a remedy for misrepresentation but only if he relied upon an untrue statement made by Midas. If Midas knew the truth but kept quiet and made no statements there can be no liability on the part of Midas — he is obliged to refrain from lies but has no obligation to disabuse Croesus unless he stands in a fiduciary relationship to him.

Chapter 2

The Company and Insiders

Introduction

In this chapter, students are directed specifically to the internal relationships within a company. This involves the rights and duties of the members in their dealings with each other and with the company (see also Chapter 5). The articles of association are the primary source of the provisions determining these internal relationships. The status of the articles and their enforceability (which touches on the rule in *Foss v Harbottle*) is a standard area for questions, both problem and essay. Specific regard will also be paid to the appointment, payment and dismissal of officers of the company and the division of power between the shareholders and the directors. Such material can form the basis of a question or be combined with aspects of directors' duties, variation of class rights and s 459 or the external relationships of the company. Students should have at least background knowledge of the types of resolution and the majorities required and of the conduct of meetings and votes. Arguably the duties of the directors could form part of this chapter but it is such a large topic that they are dealt with separately. The employees of the company are also insiders but company law syllabuses rarely address issues relating to employees other than to say they have no *locus* to enforce the company's constitution and the duty owed to them by the directors.

Students must be familiar with the following areas:

- The nature of the articles and their legal effect
- Alteration of the articles
- The appointment, payment and dismissal of directors (disqualification might also be relevant)
- The division of power in a company

Students should be aware that related issues which could be linked to questions based on this area include:

- Variation of class rights, reduction of capital and s 459
- Directors' duties and their enforcement
- The ability of officers of a company to bind the company

Question 7

To what extent, if at all, does s 14 Companies Act 1985 give a shareholder enforceable contractual rights against a company. Does s 9 of the Companies Act 1985 render any such rights illusory?

Answer plan

Outline the contents of the memorandum and articles. Discuss the alteration of these documents. Assess the efficacy of the s 14 contract and the ability of the company to alter the contractual rights of a shareholder. Tie up the law by reference to the question.

Answer

The memorandum and articles of association are the key constitutional documents of a company. The minimum contents of the memorandum, which all companies must register, are set out in ss 1 and 2. A company cannot decline to comply with these sections, for example a company cannot have no-par value shares, although extra provisions can be inserted. The memorandum, broadly speaking, defines the position of a company *vis-a-vis* the outside world although its contents are subject to s 14, which *prima facie* also renders them enforceable internally. While all companies must have articles of association, a company limited by shares may use the statutory form of articles — Table A — and, unless and to the extent that, articles to the contrary are registered, Table A will apply automatically (s 8). The articles, again broadly speaking, define the internal relationships within a company — the division of power and the allocation of risk.

Section 14 provides that the memorandum and articles 'bind the company and its members to the same extent as if they ... had been signed and sealed by each member, and contained covenants on the part of each member to observe all the provisions of the memorandum and of the articles'. What does this rather peculiar provision mean? The first instance decision of Astbury J in *Hickman v Kent or Romney Marsh Sheepbreeders' Assoc* (1915) established that the memorandum and articles constitute a contract between the company and the members. Consequently, in *Hickman*, a provision requiring a member to refer any dispute with the company to arbitration was held binding on the member. The contract, despite the wording of s 14, is bilateral and binds both the company and the members; it is also binding between the members (*Wood v Odessa Waterworks Co* (1889)).

It is a contract with two unusual features. First, it is subject to the provisions of the Act; the provisions of the Act include s 9. Section 9 provides that a company may alter its memorandum by special resolution. Thus, one party, to the contract (the company) can alter that contract contrary to the wishes of another contracting party - a shareholder - provided that an appropriate majority of shareholders agree. Are shareholders in voting to amend the articles by special resolution entitled to vote with regard only to their own interests? Certainly there are dicta in the cases which suggest that, on a vote to change the articles, the shareholders must vote '*bona fide* for the benefit of the company' (*Allen v Gold Reefs of West Africa Ltd* (1900)) but this is probably overstating the position. It seems clear that, where the proposed change of articles is designed to appropriate the shares of the minority, the court will strike down the amendment unless it is objectively in the best interests of the company. In *Sidebottom v Kershaw Leese* (1920), the Court of Appeal upheld an amendment which permitted the company to require a shareholder who had an interest in a competing business (as S, who was a director of the company, did) to transfer his shares to nominees of the directors for a fair price. The court held that this was beneficial to the company thus indicating that had they not reached this view the judges would have struck the amendment down. In *Dafen Tinplate v Llanelly Steel* (1920), an amendment allowing any shareholder to be required to sell his shares was rejected by the court as going beyond that which was necessary to benefit the company. Whether there is a general requirement that shareholders vote on proposals to alter the articles in a manner which is objectively in the best interests of the company is uncertain. In *Greenhalgh v Arderne Cinemas Ltd* (1950), the majority shareholders in the company passed a special resolution in effect requiring any shareholder so directed to transfer his shares to a nominee of the majority shareholders at a fair price. G, who was the only shareholder likely to be affected by this scheme, objected and the Court of Appeal, while rejecting G's case, seemed to suggest that all shareholder resolutions were subject to the *bona fide* etc test. The test requires a voting shareholder to 'proceed on what, in his honest opinion is for the benefit of the company as a whole'. The Master of the Rolls, Lord Evershed, sought to explain what 'the company as a whole' meant by reference to whether the proposal was in the interest of a hypothetical member of the company not directly concerned in the contentious proposal. Given the uncertainty surrounding the nature of this test, and the fact that G was unsuccessful in his action, it is difficult to find much support for a general duty cast upon shareholders to act *bona fide* etc. However, limited support for such a duty can be found in two first instance decisions — *Re Holders Investment Trust* (1971) (majority to consider interests of minority in deciding whether to vary class rights) and *Clemens v Clemens Brothers Ltd* (1976) (majority not able to issue further shares to deprive minority of negative voting control). The statutory remedy for disadvantaged shareholders, s 459, seems likely to provide a more effective remedy than the somewhat elusive general principle relied upon in the *Greenhalgh* case to limit the power of the majority to use their statutory power to amend the articles.

Despite the use of the word 'may' in s 9, it is well established that the company is not bound by a provision in the articles or a shareholder agreement which purports to abolish the right to change the articles, ie 'may' means 'can' (subject to the appropriate number agreeing). The ability to alter a contract without the agreement of all other parties is unusual but not unique; clubs and societies are often empowered to amend their rules without the unanimous agreement of the membership. While it is not possible for a company to abrogate its right to change its articles, it is acceptable for the articles to provide that on a vote to alter the articles the shares of a particular member shall carry extra votes (*Bushell v Faith* (1970)). A weighted voting clause of this type could ensure that certain articles are entrenched. While a weighted voting clause in the articles is capable of change by special resolution, it could itself be entrenched by providing that class rights (which it would be) can only be amended with the concurrence of the relevant class. Alternatively, a weighted voting clause could be placed in the memorandum and class rights placed in the memorandum cannot be altered other than as provided for in the memorandum. Class rights placed in the memorandum are not subject to s 17 which, in other cases, provides that provisions placed in the memorandum, but not required to be so located by statute, can be changed by special resolution. In addition to the use of weighted voting clauses, a shareholder who wishes to protect himself from the effect of s 9 could enter into a shareholder agreement with his fellow members. Such an agreement would not bind the company and could not be used to prevent a change of the articles. It would, however, allow an action for breach of contract against fellow members who voted to change the articles.

It is the second feature of the s 14 contract which is more controversial. The ability of a shareholder (or the company) to enforce the contract which is contained in the articles is uncertain. The traditional view is that a shareholder can enforce the articles only insofar as the relevant article creates a 'membership' right, ie a right attaching to each and every share which relates to the holding of shares. This view also derives from the decision of Astbury J in *Hickman v Kent or Romney Marsh Sheepbreeders' Assoc* (1915) and would appear to preclude the enforcement of a right which does not fall into this obscure category. There are two difficulties with this decision. First, the precise nature of a 'membership right' is indistinct. It would seem that a right vested in only some of the membership (*Eley v Positive Life Ass Co* (1876), articles providing that E was to be company solicitor for life did not give E any contractual right of employment) or a right conferred, potentially, on all shareholders but relating to a shareholder in a non-member capacity is not such a right. For example, where the articles permit the reimbursement of promotion expenses, a member who, while acting as a promoter of the company incurred such expenses, could not rely on the articles to establish a contractual right to reimbursement (*Melhado v Porto Allegre Rly Co* (1874)) and, in *Beattie v E & F Beattie Ltd* (1938), a provision requiring members to submit disputes to arbitration did not apply to a dispute between the company and a shareholder in respect of his directorship. However, membership rights (or individual rights) are contractual rights and any attempt to ignore such a right is a breach of contract subject to legal action by the shareholder, ie membership rights are an example of a situation where the rule in *Foss v Harbottle* (1843), which restricts the right of a member to sue the company, does not apply. Examples of membership rights are the right to receive dividends and the right to participate on winding up.

The second, and more fundamental, objection to Astbury's view is that the section does not differentiate between membership and non-membership rights and powerful arguments have been raised against this interpretation of the s 14 contract. Lord Wedderburn in particular relies heavily upon the House of Lords' decision in *Quin & Axtens v Salmon* (1909), where a director-shareholder was held entitled to enforce an article which required his consent to the sale of company land, to advance the view that a shareholder has a personal right to require the company to act in accordance with its articles (subject to those matters of internal management, breach of which is ratifiable by ordinary resolution). Lord Wedderburn would even argue that a shareholder can enforce an article which benefits an outsider or himself in a non-membership capacity. If a court was prepared to disregard the conventional view on the s 14 contract and hold that all the articles constituted contractual rights (or that a member had a right to have the articles complied with), an outsider would still have to depend upon a member suing on his behalf. This would cause no difficulty where an injunction was sought but, where a member sued for damages on behalf of a third party, the rules of privity would seem to provide that any damages payable would reflect the member's loss and not that of the third party. Variations on Lord Wedderburn's argument would restrict the shareholder to having a right to ensure that the appropriate corporate body carries on the affairs of the company — on this analysis S succeeded in the *Quin & Axtens* case because the general meeting purported to take a decision which could only be taken by the board.

The precise scope of the s 14 contract is still far from clear; these difficulties may be explained by the fact that the wording of s 14 (and its predecessors) derive from provisions relating to unincorporated joint-stock companies which are legally an entirely different type of being. It is certainly possible to conclude that the combination of Astbury J's interpretation of s 14 and s 9 significantly diminish the rights of an individual shareholder. However, it could be argued that, at least in larger companies, it is entirely appropriate that the minority tail should not wag the majority dog. This is particularly true when an individual shareholder may be able to rely on s 459 to ensure that he is bought out of a company with which he is at loggerheads.

Question 8

'It is a basic principle of company law that all the corporators, acting together, can do anything which is *intra vires* the company' (*Cane v Jones* (1981), *per* Michael Wheeler QC).

Consider the efficacy of, and the problems caused by, 'shareholder agreements'.

Answer plan

Question concerning the control of companies by reference to non-statutory documents — shareholder agreements. This question simply requires a relatively factual description of the nature and function of such agreements in the context of company control. Some discussion of why shareholder agreements are used is also appropriate.

Answer

A company is an association of persons in pursuance of some common object, generally, but not necessarily for profit. Despite the immense complexity and size of the Companies Acts, forming a company is easy and relatively straightforward. All that the law prescribes by way of a corporate constitution is two documents — the memorandum of association and the articles of association. The contents of these documents are partly decreed by statute but derive principally from the choice of the founders of the company. Sections 1 and 2 provide that the memorandum must state: the name of the company; the situation of its registered office; the objects of the company; the amount of share capital and how it is divided up; and whether the company is public or private. The Act does not specify the contents of the articles although draft forms for different types of company are set out in Tables A to G. Tables A to G can be accepted or rejected as the founders of the company see fit, although the format of the Tables, ie numbered paragraphs, is compulsory (*Gaiman v National Association for Mental Health* (1971)). As can be seen there is considerable freedom in the drafting of the basic constitutional framework of a company. This freedom is reduced when it is sought to change the memorandum or articles.

After all, it is argued, a shareholder has acquired shares in a company on the basis that his rights and liabilities are as set out in the memorandum and articles and, while he knows from the outset that these rights and liabilities may be changed if a majority of shareholders so wish, the courts should be empowered to intervene to restrain the wish of the majority in certain cases. Others argue that where an appropriate majority has sanctioned a change in the memorandum and/or articles the courts should not intervene to restrain such changes however detrimental to the wishes of a shareholder because Parliament has decreed that the shareholders can amend their mutual rights and duties as they see fit.

There are some statutory restraints placed upon the powers of the majority to alter the constitution of the company and consequently to run the company as they wish. For example, ss 4 and 5 (alteration of objects) or ss 125 to 127 (variation of class rights) provide examples of specific restrictions or procedures on amendment of the company's constitution. In its way, the requirement that changes generally require a special resolution (75% majority) to implement them restrains the freedom of shareholders to amend the rights and liabilities of other shareholders. There are also rare examples of the courts requiring shareholders to exercise their right to vote in a manner which takes into account interests other than their own. For example, the court has determined that it can reject an alteration of the articles, which alteration complies with all statutory requirements, if the alteration is not 'bona fide for the benefit of the company' (*Allen v Gold Reefs of West Africa Ltd* (1900)), albeit this seems to operate only where an expropriation of shares is involved. However, any imposition of a fiduciary obligation on the majority contrasts with the normal position which is that shareholders, as owners of property, are permitted to do what they like with their property (shares) regardless of the wishes of others (*Welton v Saffery* (1897)). The ability of shareholders to do as they wish with their property may leave minority shareholders in a vulnerable position in that they may see their rights amended by the majority to their disadvantage with little they can do about it.

Where it is all the shareholders who wish to vary their mutual rights and duties, can there be any objection to them so doing? Obviously, the shareholders may choose to amend their respective interests by revision of the articles or the memorandum but, as indicated above, this may attract judicial intervention — although this is scarcely likely if all shareholders agree. However, it is not uncommon for shareholders to supplement, suspend or amend the memorandum or articles with 'shareholder agreements'. The majority may also use shareholder agreements, for example to provide a 'voting block' to retain control of the company or evade provisions in the articles designed to protect the minority. It is the shareholder agreement between all shareholders which the case of *Cane v Jones* addresses.

In *Cane v Jones*, two brothers, P and H, formed a company of which they were the 'life directors'; they were the only directors. All the shares were owned by close family members or trusts for such members. The articles provided that the chairman of directors had a casting vote at directors' and general meetings of the company. In 1967 all the then shareholders agreed that the chairman would not use his casting vote and that, where the director-brothers could not agree, an independent chairman (with a casting vote) would be appointed. The two sides of the family fell out and P's side claimed that P as chairman had a casting vote. H's daughter, the plaintiff, who was not a party to the 1967 agreement (although trustees acting for her were), sought to rely on that agreement and petitioned for a declaration that P's casting vote had been abrogated. Michael Wheeler QC determined that P's casting vote had disappeared and held that the 1967 agreement was in essence a general meeting which was effective to override the articles. The judge seemed to say that where all the shareholders agreed to amend the articles this could take effect as an alteration of the articles despite the failure to comply with s 9 (meeting and special resolution required) because s 9 was merely a way, but not the only way, of altering the articles. Whether this case should really be seen as an alteration of the articles can be doubted — if it was an alteration it would now be subject to the official notification procedure (s 42) so that the 'alteration' would only operate internally and would not bind third parties. Further, if it was an alteration of the articles, new shareholders would also be bound. This case should be treated as a shareholder agreement rather than an alteration of articles. What then is a shareholder agreement and can such agreements outflank the statutory requirements?

Shareholder agreements fall into two broad groups:

(a) agreements between all or some of the shareholders and the company; and

(b) agreements between all or some (a majority) of the shareholders which do not involve the company.

Shareholder agreements will generally constitute contracts, the consideration being the agreement of the other parties to be bound by the agreement. Such agreements may be positive, eg providing a method for the resolution of disputes between member and member or member and company, or negative, eg an agreement that the articles shall not apply or that non-compliance with the articles will not be actionable. In some cases, a shareholder agreement may be regarded as an informal equivalent to a resolution of the members in general meeting; if it is unanimous and in writing and Table A, art 53 expressly recognises the practice and treats such agreements as equivalent to formal resolutions. Where there is unanimous agreement to a proposal, there can be little objection to treating the agreement as binding between those who have agreed and as equivalent to a 'statutory' resolution, although official notification (s 42), when required, would be necessary to bind third parties. Is this also the case when the informal agreement conflicts with substantive statutory rules (as opposed to procedural rules) designed to protect members? This issue is unresolved. I would also argue that a shareholder agreement should not be treated as an informal resolution where the Acts provide a substantive rule to protect shareholders (even though they have all agreed). Many shareholder agreements cannot be treated as informal resolutions of the company, either because that was not the intention of the parties or, it seems, because the Acts may specify that the formal route is the *only* method of doing certain things. However, it should be noted that, in *Re Barry Artist* (1985), the court approved a reduction of capital to which all members had merely given informal approval despite s 135 which provides that a company may 'by special resolution reduce its share capital'. Where a shareholder agreement constitutes an informal resolution it may, it seems, bind subsequent transferees of shares (unlike a pure shareholder agreement) subject to the official notification rules.

An agreement between all shareholders (and perhaps the company), as predicated in the question, can be compared with the articles of a company. The agreement can be said to govern the internal workings of the company. However, unlike the articles, all aspects of such an agreement are, presumably, mutually enforceable and not merely those which create membership rights (provided the agreement is a contract), and the agreement cannot be changed without the agreement of all the parties to that agreement unless the agreement so provides. A further contrast with the articles is that the agreement creates personal rights which bind parties to the contract as such rather than as shareholders. Consequently, successors in title cannot enforce nor be bound by a shareholder agreement. However, it seems that a shareholder agreement, even if entered into by all the shareholders, cannot fetter the directorial discretion of a director-member (*Boulting v ACTAT* (1963)) or the ability of a company to change its articles (*Allen v Gold Reefs of West Africa Ltd* (1900)); such rights and/or duties are incapable of abrogation. In the case of the directors it is thought that their fiduciary duty outweighs any contractual right to bind their future conduct. In respect of alteration of the articles, the courts have almost unanimously held that s 9 which provides that 'a company may by special resolution alter its articles' means that a company cannot be restrained from altering its articles by special resolution even if the resultant alteration causes a breach of contract which may result in damages being payable (*Southern Foundries v Shirlaw* (1940)). What is uncertain is which provisions of company law cannot be abrogated by unanimous agreement of the shareholders. Where an agreement is held incapable of rendering a statutory provision inoperative, the agreement still binds the members — so that a shareholder could sue his fellow members for exercising their statutory rights even if he could not obtain an injunction to restrain them from so doing.

There is no doubt that shareholders can enter into a shareholder agreement which provides how they will vote in meetings of the company although it has been suggested that an agreement without limit of time may be invalid (*Greenhalgh v Mallard* (1943) but see *Russell v Northern Bank Developments Corpn Ltd* (1992) for a contrary view).

The House of Lords has considered the effect of shareholder agreements in *Russell v Northern Bank Developments Corpn Ltd*

(1992). In this case, the bank had lent money to two companies — TP Ltd, which company had incurred large losses, and TB Ltd, which company had proved extremely successful. As part of a restructuring agreement devised by the bank, it was decided that the shares controlling the two companies would be brought together in a new holding company, Tyrone, which would run both companies and which would be able to set TP's losses against TB's profits and thereby reduce the tax liability of TB. Four executives, including the plaintiff, were transferred from TB to run Tyrone and each of them was allotted 20 shares in Tyrone. The remaining issued shares (120) of Tyrone were allotted to the bank. One of Tyrone's articles (equivalent to Table A, art 32) allowed the company to increase its share capital but a shareholder agreement entered into by the bank, Tyrone and the four executives provided, *inter alia*, that no further share capital would be created or issued without the written consent of all parties to the agreement. Subsequently, the company sought to increase its share capital and the plaintiff, R, sought an injunction to restrain it from so doing on the grounds that this was a breach of the agreement.

Despite the agreement of all the shareholders, it was not argued that this was an informal alteration of the company's articles. The majority would not have accepted that this was an informal alteration (had it been argued) saying that such a finding would be inconsistent with the company being a party to the agreement. The respondent bank argued that, since the relevant statute (equivalent to s 121(2)(a)) permitted a company to increase its share capital provided its articles sanctioned such an increase, which Tyrone's articles did, a shareholder agreement which fettered the statutory power must be invalid. The House of Lords decided that the shareholder agreement was separate and distinct from the company's articles and was of a purely personal nature. It was open to the shareholders to make such an agreement. Lord Jauncey approved the famous dictum of Lord Davey in *Welton v Saffery* (1897): 'Of course, individual shareholders may deal with their own interests by contract in such a way as they see fit. But such contacts ... would create personal obligations against themselves only, and would not become a regulation of the company, or be binding on the transferees of the parties to it, or upon new or non-assenting shareholders.' Consequently, there was no objection to the shareholders making such an agreement as this, albeit it could not bind the company because that would fetter the company's statutory right to issue shares. While the court declared the power to issue shares to be an inalienable statutory power, the effect of upholding this agreement was to render the company incapable of issuing shares. This is the first case to treat the power to issue shares as inalienable even if the finding was nullified by the upholding of the shareholder agreement. The court did not provide any guidance upon which statutory powers are to be treated as inalienable and not subject to amendment or deletion even by unanimous agreement of the shareholders.

This case stressed the primacy of certain statutory rights but then allowed the parties freedom to negotiate between themselves how to run the company and could be seen as representing a non-interventionist approach by the court allowing those who risk their money to outflank the intention of Parliament. The case would appear to allow a majority to decide to stymie the statutory rights of a minority by informal agreement — perhaps a case for use of another statute, s 459!

Question 9

Sober Ltd was incorporated by Arnold in 1986 to import and sell non-alcoholic fruit drinks; he was the sole director of the company. Arnold held 90% of the issued shares and his wife, Helen, held 10%. The articles of the company named Helen as company secretary 'for life'. On Arnold's death his shares were inherited equally by his three sons who became the directors of the company.

The sons are proposing to amend the objects of the company, with consequential amendments to the articles, to permit the importation and sale of alcoholic drinks. Helen objects strongly to this proposal. Her sons tell her that they propose to employ a different company secretary and to insert a provision in the company's articles allowing the directors to require any shareholder whose statements or conduct is, in their opinion, detrimental to the company's future prosperity to transfer his or her shares to the directors at a fair price.

Advise Helen.

Answer plan

The issues that arise in this question are:

- can H prevent the alteration of the objects of the company;
- can H prevent any consequential amendments to the articles;
- is H entitled to be company secretary for life; and
- can H object to the article permitting compulsory acquisition of the shares.

The three later issues overlap.

Answer

It is not uncommon for a new generation which takes over a family company to have very different ideas on how the company should be run from their fathers. The law will not intervene to restrain the directors from pursuing a different policy or business even where it is a new venture in which the company has no expertise. For example, in *Re a Company* (1983), a minority shareholder in a company which was engaged in advertising failed in his attempt to stop the company using some of its surplus funds in opening a wine bar. However, where the change of policy necessitates a change of the memorandum or articles, there are appropriate statutory procedures which must be complied with and dissident shareholders may have the right to make their objections known to the court and sometimes to have the change struck down. The courts in considering applications by disgruntled shareholders have to balance the right of the majority of members to run the company (or have the directors run it on their behalf) as they wish and whether there is any necessity, especially where statute does not give a remedy, to protect the interests of individual shareholders even if this stymies the majority.

The first thing that the company wishes to do is to amend its objects clause permitting the company to trade in alcoholic as well as non-alcoholic beverages. The objects are the purposes which the company is empowered to pursue and are a statement to potential shareholders of the type of business in which their money will be expended. However, Parliament has permitted the alteration of the objects of a company (s 4) so that a shareholder may find he has invested in a company which he believes will pursue object X only to find that the company is now engaged in object Y. Parliament has provided that alteration must be by special resolution (passed by shareholders present or voting by proxy who command at least 75% of the votes). Since the Act lays down a procedure for qualified shareholders to object to the alteration, the courts have not thought it appropriate to impose further judicial barriers to alteration — if the majority of investors are happy, the court will not prevent the company following a new line.

Helen cannot block a special resolution nor is she eligible to rely on the statutory safeguard created by s 5 which provides that, unless a qualified shareholder objects, the alteration automatically takes effect after 15 days. Section 5 gives *locus* to a shareholder, or shareholders, who hold not less than 15% of a class of the shares of the company, who have voted against the resolution and object within 15 days. Helen with 10% of the shares will not have *locus* to petition the court to strike down the alteration. Once the objects have been altered the company must notify the Registrar of Companies to comply with the provisions of 'official notification' (s 42) and, until this is done, the company cannot rely on the amended objects clause against a third party.

Turning to any consequential amendments to the articles (the articles should not be altered first lest this introduce a conflict with the unamended memorandum which would potentially invalidate the new articles), s 9 provides that a company has the right to change its articles provided that the change is effected by special resolution and there is no way in which this provision can be excluded. In *Southern Foundries v Shirlaw* (1940), a director-shareholder sought an injunction to restrain a change of articles which would have the effect of dismissing him from his directorship in breach of his service contract. The House of Lords refused to grant the injunction holding that the right of those who own the company and whose money is hazarded thereby cannot be deprived of their right to change the internal constitution of the company. Thus, the company could change its articles but S was entitled to damages for breach of the service contract. Again, Helen cannot prevent the passage of a special resolution and there is no statutory procedure for challenging the alteration of the articles. However, Helen is permitted to petition the court for the striking out of the alteration if it is illegal, inconsistent with the memorandum or if the amendment is not *'bona fide* for the benefit of the company as a whole'. This judicial gloss, that the alteration must be *bona fide* etc, on the apparently unfettered right of the shareholders to amend the articles is a rare illustration of a fiduciary duty being imposed on shareholders; shareholders are normally entitled to vote without regard to any interest but their own (*Welton v Saffery* (1897)). This dictum which appears to place some limit upon majority power derives from *Allen v Gold Reefs of West Africa Ltd* (1900). However, it should be noted that in this case A's challenge to an alteration of the articles, which gave the company a lien over fully paid up shares in respect of any debt owed by a shareholder to the company, was unsuccessful. Allen was the executor of the only shareholder with fully paid up shares. While the Court of Appeal may have expounded this limitation on the power of the majority to change the rules of the company, the operation of the limitation has proved somewhat disappointing to minority shareholders.

Apart from any general consequential amendments to the articles, H is objecting to the particular change which permits the expropriation of shares of a member who expresses views etc held, by the board, to be detrimental to the company. These issues can be considered together. Does *Allen v Gold Reefs* assist Helen? It seems clear from later cases that, where the proposed change of articles is designed to appropriate the shares of the minority, the court will strike down the amendment unless it is objectively in the best interests of the company. In *Brown v British Abrasive Wheel* (1920), the company was in urgent need of capital which the majority of shareholders were willing to provide. However, 2% shareholders were not willing and the majority were willing to proceed only if they could buy out the 2%. The articles were changed to permit the acquisition of the objecting shareholders but was successfully challenged by one of them. The judge held that this alteration was for the benefit of the majority rather than the company. Even if one agrees with the idea that an alteration must benefit the company, this seems a strange application of the principle — the stymied majority, presumably, did not provide the needed capital and the company went into liquidation. *Brown* was distinguished in *Sidebottom v Kershaw Leese* (1920), in which the Court of Appeal upheld an amendment which permitted the company to require a shareholder who had an interest in a competing business (as S, who was a director of the company, did) to transfer his shares to nominees of the directors for a fair price. The court held that this was objectively beneficial to the company. Finally, in *Dafen Tinplate v Llanelly Steel* (1920), an amendment allowing any shareholder to be required to sell his shares was rejected by the court as going beyond that which was necessary to benefit the company. Consequently, if H can convince the court that this alteration is not for the benefit of the company she may succeed in having it struck down.

Whether there is a general requirement that shareholders vote on proposals to alter the articles in a manner which is objectively in the best interests of the company is less certain. In *Greenhalgh v Arderne Cinemas Ltd* (1950), the majority shareholders in the company passed a special resolution in effect requiring any shareholder so directed to transfer his shares to a nominee of the majority shareholders at a fair price. G, who was the only shareholder likely to be affected by this scheme, objected and the Court of Appeal, while rejecting G's case, seemed to suggest that all shareholder resolutions were subject to the *bona fide* etc test. The test requires a voting shareholder to 'proceed on what, in his honest opinion, is for the benefit of the company as a whole'. The Master of the Rolls, Lord Evershed, sought to explain what 'the company as a whole' meant by reference to whether the proposal was in the interest of a hypothetical member of the company not directly concerned in the contentious proposal. Given the uncertainty surrounding the nature of this test, and the fact that G was unsuccessful in his action, it is difficult to find much support for a general objective duty cast upon shareholders to act *bona fide* etc. However, limited support for such a duty can be found in two first instance decisions — *Re Holders Investment Trust* (1971) (majority to consider interests of minority in deciding whether to vary class rights) and *Clemens v Clemens Brothers Ltd* (1976) (majority not able to issue further shares to deprive minority of negative voting control). It seems improbable that H will be able to challenge the 'consequential amendments' which, even if the benefit of the company test applies, appear to be in the best interests of the company both subjectively and objectively. The statutory remedy for disadvantaged shareholders, s 459, may provide a remedy for H but the courts have set their face against using the section to provide a remedy for shareholders who object to the board's *bona fide* actions if they do not impinge upon the legitimate expectations of the shareholder; see, for example, *Re a Company* (1983), the wine bar case mentioned before, and *Re Saul Harrison & Sons plc* (1995). In the latter case, Lord Justice Hoffman accepted, however, that there are cases where the memorandum and articles do not represent the understandings upon which the shareholders are associated and, in such cases, it may be unfair to a shareholder for those who control a company to exercise the powers set out in the memorandum and articles if to do so denies the legitimate expectations of the shareholder. He gives an example: the widow of a joint venturer might have legitimate expectations about the benefits she should receive from the company founded by her deceased husband.

The final complaint put forward by H concerns her dismissal as company secretary. H will have considerable difficulty, as we have seen, in blocking an amendment of the articles to delete this provision; but she may have an action for damages if the amendment (or dismissal without the amendment) is a breach of contract. However, H may not have an enforceable contract — there is no difficulty if she has a service contract independent of the articles (which is improbable) but, if she wishes to rely on the articles as providing the contract, she faces two difficulties. First, a contract based on the articles changes if the articles are validly altered (*Read v Astoria Garage* (1952)) and, even if the articles are not altered, it is unlikely that they give H an enforceable contractual right. The traditional view (which derives from the decision of Astbury J in *Hickman v Kent or Romney Marsh Sheepbreeders' Assoc* (1915)) is that a shareholder can enforce the articles only insofar as the relevant article creates a 'membership' right, ie a right attaching to each and every share which relates to the holding of shares. It would seem that a right vested in only some of the membership is not such a right. For example, in *Eley v Positive Life Ass Co* (1876), where the articles provided that E was to be company solicitor for life, E was held to have no contractual right of employment as solicitor. There seems little comfort for Helen here.

In conclusion, one can advise H that, with the exception of the expropriation of shares, her only chance of blocking the dissipation of the traditional business of the company lies in s 459 but that even this seems a forlorn hope.

Question 10

In 1993, Robin, Swan and Turkey incorporated their existing printing business as Birdsong Ltd. They each hold 17% of the share capital and are the directors of the company. Four employees of the company each hold 5% of the share capital and the remaining shares are unissued.

The articles of the company depart from Table A in the following respects:

(a) Robin, Swan and Turkey are named as directors for life and may only be removed by special resolution.
(b) On a vote to remove a director, that director would be entitled to three votes per share.
(c) In the event of any additional shares being issued, such shares must be offered to existing shareholders in proportion to their then shareholding.

The directors have decided to restructure the business and many processes will, in future, require appreciably less staff than at present. In addition, machinery will be sold off. The employees are opposed to the re-structuring and consequent reduction in the workforce and consider the price proposed for the sale of machinery to be a gross undervalue. The directors propose to allot the unissued shares at a high price knowing that it is unlikely that the employees will have the funds to purchase them.

Advise the employees.

Answer plan

- Consider whether the shareholder employees can in law block the restructuring either as employees or as shareholders
- Can the shareholder employees question the sale of assets either as employees or shareholders
- Look at the terms in the articles relating to the directors — can they be sacked or can pressure be put on them to abandon the restructuring
- Finally appraise the proposed allotment

Answer

(a) *Locus*

The employees are seeking advice about the restructuring of their company. The first issue to consider is whether they have any *forum* for objection or *locus* to object either as employees or as shareholders in the company. While the Act requires the directors to have regard to the interests of employees in performing their functions as directors (s 309), the Act does not give the employees *locus* to object to decisions of the directors and shareholders. Obviously, the employees can make their feelings known but they have no status in company law. The employees who are also shareholders are in a different position; they are members of the company and can attend company meetings and vote on resolutions. However, a restructuring of the business by the board does not require approval by the shareholders unless it necessitates a change in the memorandum or articles for which a special resolution would be required. For example, if the restructuring needed a change in the objects of the company a special resolution would be necessary (s 4). The employees have sufficient votes to block a special resolution (20 out of the total issued of 71). If no shareholder approval is required it is likely that the restructuring falls within the general power to manage the company vested in the board by Table A, art 70. Can the employee-shareholders require a meeting to be held to discuss their objections? Section 368 permits members holding not less than 10% of the issued share capital to require the directors to call an EGM. On receipt of such a requisition, the directors have 21 days to call a meeting to discuss those matters specified in the requisition. Thus, the shareholder-employees can obtain a meeting. Can they do anything more?

(b) *Restructuring*

At the meeting, the shareholders can raise their objections to the restructuring but cannot block it nor have they the power to sack the board (simple majority required, s 303). They could argue that the proposals are unfairly prejudicial to them but the courts have been reluctant to use s 459 where there is a dispute between shareholders as to the policies of the company with no allied impropriety. For example, in *Re Saul Harrison & Sons plc*, a shareholder failed to prevent the directors of a company with substantial assets but a revenue deficit from continuing to operate the company rather than, as she wished, wind up the company and distribute its assets. The Court of Appeal held that unfairness for the purposes of s 459 was primarily governed by the memorandum and articles of the company and, if they have been complied with, the section was unlikely to be operative. Here the majority of shareholders (the directors) approve the new policies so the fact that it does not suit others is unlikely to give the disgruntled individuals a remedy. If, however, the directors are exercising their powers of management for an improper purpose, an action under s 459 might succeed.

(c) *Sale of assets*

The shareholder-employees could try to argue that the sale of an asset at an undervalue, if proven, might be evidence of impropriety and thus strengthen the s 459 claim. Is the proposed sale of an asset a breach of company law or in some way improper? Since the articles of the company incorporate Table A, and thus by virtue of art 70 the directors are the people who run the company, subject only to the direction of the general meeting by special resolution, there can be no doubt that the directors, *prima facie*, have the power to deal with the assets of the company. Wrongful dealing with the assets of a company by the directors is a breach of directors' duty. However, since this duty is owed to the company (*Percival v Wright* (1902)), a shareholder has no right to sue the directors for their action because it is well established that wrongs done to a company can be litigated only by the company (the famous case of *Foss v Harbottle* (1843)). Consequently, when, as here, the power to run a company is vested in the directors, it is the directors who must determine whether to initiate litigation for such wrongs. If the alleged wrong is a breach of duty by the directors, litigation is unlikely. Moreover, since the alleged wrongdoers are also the majority shareholders there can be no question of the shareholders using their residual power to instruct the directors to sue. It is this difficulty which has led to the possibility of a minority shareholder bringing an action in the company's name where the wrong done to the company is of the requisite type and the wrongdoers control the company. However, it is not very likely that the alleged wrong is of the appropriate type to permit a minority shareholder's action. If the allegation is that the directors are selling corporate assets at an undervalue, ie an allegation of negligence, it would seem that the case of *Pavlides v Jensen* (1956) (sale of mine for approximately one-fifth of its value, shareholders had no *locus* to sue in company's name) precludes a shareholder acting in the name of the company. A different conclusion might be reached if the majority directors were benefitting from the sale, for this would constitute equitable fraud. For example, in *Daniels v Daniels* (1980), a minority shareholder had *locus* to sue, on behalf of the company, a director who had sold an asset to herself which she later resold at a profit of £115,000. Unless there is an element of fraud, it seems that there is no remedy for the sale of the asset at an undervalue.

(d) *Articles of association*

Turning to the provisions in the articles relating to the terms of employment of the directors. First, the weighted voting clause which effectively renders a director impregnable unless all other shareholders vote to dismiss him (he has 51 votes and the rest of the issued shares could muster 54) using s 303. Despite powerful objections, it is well established that a weighted voting clause of this type is valid (*Bushell v Faith* (1970)), at least in companies of this type — small and private. Such a clause could be deleted using the procedure set out in s 9 which says that a company can change its articles by special resolution. However, this would require all the shareholders except a single director to vote in favour of the change which may be difficult to achieve. The court is even less likely to upset the clause than in *Bushell* since, even with the clause, s 303 is not nullified since all the shareholders together could dismiss any one director. Nor will the fact that the directors' service contracts exceed five years (contrary to s 319) aid the shareholders. It may be that the contracts were approved in advance by the shareholders in general meeting in which case they are unchallengeable but, even if this is not the case, the breach of s 319 does not automatically avoid the contracts. The effect of a breach of s 319 is thought to be that the service contract remains in place but becomes terminable by reasonable notice. This notice is given by the company and it is the directors of the company who determine the company's decision to give notice.

(e) *Allotment*

Finally, can the shareholder employees block the proposed allotment of shares? Whether it is the board or the general meeting which has the power to allot shares (s 80 vests the power in the general meeting unless and until revested in the board), the three directors between them can control the general meeting and so they, as the general meeting or the board, have the power to allot these shares.

Section 89 requires shares to be offered to existing shareholders in the proportion of their current holding; this the directors seem willing to do, confident that the shareholders cannot take up the offer. Even if the pre-emption right was ignored, the allotment would be valid and the disadvantaged shareholders would be limited to an action for damages. An alternative course would be for the directors to offer the shares in return non-cash consideration when the pre-emption right is inapplicable. However, the ability of the directors to allot shares is subject to the requirement that the directors, as fiduciaries, exercise their power *bona fide* for the benefit of the company and for a proper purpose (*Bamford v Bamford* (1970)). The so-called proper purpose test has been interpreted by the courts as giving the judges the power to determine the purpose for which a power has been allocated to the directors by the shareholders and to strike down any attempt to use the relevant power for other purposes. Thus in *Bamford v Bamford*, the Court of Appeal ruled that an attempt to block a take-over bid by allotting shares to associates was an improper use of directors' powers. In a case similar to this one, *Pennell v Venida* (1974), a rights issue which the directors knew could not be taken up by one impoverished shareholder was struck down as designed to emasculate the shareholder who objected to certain proposals by the board. While, *prima facie*, these cases seem to stymie the directors, there is no doubt that an act which is for a collateral purpose can be ratified by the company in general meeting by ordinary resolution (*Bamford*) and this they, the majority, could achieve. While ratification of the rights issue may be possible, it would seem to be an obvious case for an application under s 459. While a blatant attempt to emasculate one group of shareholders appears to be a clear case of unfair prejudice which would leave a court with an unfettered discretion to devise an appropriate remedy, it might be thought that the shareholders in this case were merely trying to impose their view of the company's future on the majority and, consequently, the s 459 application could fail. If an action were to succeed, the most likely remedy would be an order for the purchase, by the directors or the company, of the dissenting member's shares.

In conclusion, the position of the employees appears less than hopeful.

Question 11

(a) 'Corporate power lies with the board of directors.' Comment on this proposition.

(b) The shares of Rail Nostalgia Ltd are owned equally by its five shareholders, A, B, C, D and E. A, B and C make up the board of the company. The company needed to purchase iron chairs and agreed to buy them from Alpha Bros, a firm in which A is a partner. A disclosed to the board that he was a partner in Alpha Bros but did not reveal that he would receive a commission on the sale. On discovering the truth, D proposed to the board that the company should seek to rescind the purchase but the board refuse so to do. At a subsequent general meeting D and E vote to take legal action against A but the board have refused to act.

What is the legal position?

Answer plan

Two-part questions always call for effective time management if one part is not going to be squeezed for time. It is to be hoped that such questions allow for cross-referencing which should ameliorate the time problem.

Part (a) is essentially a description of the division of power within a company with a concluding paragraph to be added as comment.

Part (b) involves a possible breach of director's duty by A. As with any such question the general issue of *locus* arises, while the final issue is a specific question as to the in/ability of the general meeting to instruct the board to initiate litigation.

Answer

(a) The shareholders are the owners of a company and can, generally, do what they wish with their property. They are free to run the company as they see fit (subject to the rules of company law) either in person or by appointing representatives to act on their behalf. In practice, the shareholders appoint such representatives — a board of directors. The directors of a company may be co-extensive with the shareholders (for example in small family owned and run companies), be existing shareholders on appointment (majority or minority), acquire shares on appointment or own no shares in the company. When the shareholders in general meeting and the board are not co-extensive, even if there is an overlap in membership, there is potential for conflict. The issue that then arises is who makes the decisions for the company.

Early cases suggested that the power to run a company must be vested in its owners — the shareholders — but the Court of Appeal in *Automatic Self-Cleansing Filter Syndicate Co Ltd v Cunninghame* (1906) made it clear that the division of power between the board and the shareholders in general meeting depended on the articles of the company. Where the articles had vested power in the board it was the board, said the court, and the board alone that which ran the company. This view was affirmed by later cases including the House of Lords' decision in *Quin & Axtens v Salmon* (1909) and it is now well settled that, where the articles give the power to manage to the board, they have an exclusive power so to do subject only to the provisions of company law and any restrictions upon their powers contained in the articles themselves. This does not mean that the board's authority is inalienable; a power given in the articles can be amended or deleted by altering the articles. However, alteration of the articles requires a special resolution (s 9, three-quarters majority of those present and voting) so that changing the articles is not easy and, if the board members hold 25% or more of the votes, it is impossible without the agreement of the board.

Where the general meeting is unable to alter the articles, the drastic step of dismissing all or some of the directors and the substitution of more pliable office-holders might be possible. Section 303 provides that the general meeting can dismiss a director by ordinary resolution (at least 50% of those present and voting). While easier to achieve than amendment of the articles, dismissal of the directors, even where possible, will leave any new directors with the same powers of management as that possessed by the former board. Moreover, directors of small companies can effectively nullify s 303 by the use of a weighted voting clause which gives their shares extra votes where there is a proposal to dismiss a director (*Bushell v Faith* (1970)). Such a clause could be deleted using the procedure set out in s 9 but this requires a special resolution. Consequently, one can conclude that the board is not susceptible to the control of the general meeting *unless* the articles provide a method of control.

Since 1906, the majority of companies have adopted the relevant provision of Table A to determine the division of power between the general meeting and the board: the current provision is art 70. The current art 70 provides that 'Subject to the provisions of the Act, the memorandum and the articles and to any directions given by special resolution, the business of the company shall be managed by the directors who may exercise all the powers of the company'. Thus, it can be seen that the shareholders can give the directors instructions on how to manage but only in compliance with any particular provision in the articles or by special resolution. Where directions are given, they cannot invalidate any prior act of the directors (art 70) but can, presumably, instruct the directors not to implement that prior act if it is still executory. The wording of art 70 seems also to allow the shareholders to instruct the directors to undertake a course of action which the board had resolved not to pursue. It might be thought peculiar that the board can be sacked by ordinary resolution but cannot be instructed other than by special resolution particularly where the company is small or of the quasi-partnership type and it has been suggested that model articles for such companies might depart from art 70 and allow more day-to-day control over directors by the general meeting.

From the above discussion, it can be concluded that the board always runs the company but, where the board cannot or will not exercise the power vested in it, the general meeting regains, at least temporarily, the power to run the company. For example, in *Barron v Potter* (1914), the two directors of the company were not on speaking terms and board meetings could not be held — the power to conduct the company's affairs vested in the shareholders until an effective board was in place. Note that the default powers of the general meeting operate only where the board is completely incapable of acting and not when a minority of directors use their powers to block a decision by the majority of the board (see for example *Breckland Group Holdings v London & Suffolk Properties* (1989)) for, in the latter case, the board is precluded from acting by the operation of the articles, not an incapacity to act. Moreover, in a limited number of cases, it seems that a shareholder can commence legal proceedings on behalf of the company even if such is not the wish of the board (the fraud on the minority exception to *Foss v Harbottle*).

(b) Rail Nostalgia has articles in the form of Table A (s 8) so that the directors have the power to manage the company (art 70). The directors of the company, A, B and C, own 60% of the shares of the company and are, while united, immune from dismissal or the giving of directions as to how the company should be run. As directors, they owe duties of care and skill commensurate with their abilities and qualifications (if any), fiduciary duties and certain statutory duties; these duties are generally owed to the company and not to the shareholders (*Percival v Wright* (1902)). In this case, D and E are seeking to initiate litigation against A alleging that, in breach of his director's duty, he failed to make adequate disclosure of the circumstances surrounding the contract to buy iron chairs from Alpha. Any attempt to sue a director raises two issues: first who has the *locus* to sue; and, second, is there a breach of duty.

Since a breach of duty by a director is a wrong done to the company, the person who can sue the director is the company. The relevant body to determine whether to sue is the body with the power to run the company — in this case the board. Consequently, it might be concluded that, since the board is not in favour of litigation, A is immune from suit. Certainly, D and E cannot instruct the board how to act (only 40% shareholding, 75% required to give directions) nor could they sack A, B and C. Where the company is the appropriate plaintiff and it declines to sue, the rule in *Foss v Harbottle* (1843) generally precludes litigation by a shareholder. However, where a wrong done by a director who exercises control over the company can be categorised as 'fraud' the courts may permit a shareholder to bring an action on behalf of the company to vindicate the company's rights (a derivative action) since the wrongdoer is hardly likely to sue himself. If a derivative action is permitted it cannot be blocked by the directors and the litigant may be able to claim an indemnity for his costs (*Wallersteiner v Moir* (1975)).

A derivative action can be brought only where the wrongdoer has acted fraudulently but fraud in this context embraces a general lack of *bona fides* and an apparent lack of fair dealing in addition to legal fraud. For example, in *Daniels v Daniels*, a shareholder was given *locus* to sue a director who had sold land to herself at an alleged undervalue. Templeman J ruled that a director who was negligent might not be the subject of a derivative action but that a director whose negligence resulted in a profit of £115,000 to herself could be so liable. In this case, the 'wrongdoers' control the company (both by virtue of art 70 and their 60% shareholding). In *Smith v Croft (No 2)* (1988), Knox J further refined the notion of control by ruling that the crucial issue is whether the plaintiff being 'improperly prevented from bringing these proceedings on behalf of the company?' He then concluded that, where an independent organ of the company rather than a wrongdoer was blocking litigation, the shareholder had no right to drag the company into litigation — the denial of proceedings was entirely proper. This does not seem to apply here and presumably a derivative action could be brought. What then is the 'wrong' committed by A and ignored by B and C?

A, as a director, has a fiduciary duty to ensure that there is no conflict between his duty to the company and his own personal interest. One area where the possibility of such conflict arises is when a director benefits either directly or indirectly from a contract made by the company of which he is a director. In *Aberdeen Rly Co v Blaikie Bros* (1854), the House of Lords ruled that a director cannot benefit from a contract entered into by the company even if the contract is perfectly fair. This strict approach was extended to indirect contractual benefits, as in this case, by *Imperial Mercantile Credit Assn v Coleman* (1871). However, directors are not trustees and they are not prohibited from benefitting from their directorship *provided* that any benefit is revealed in advance to the shareholders or, where permitted, other relevant body. Where there is no disclosure, the transaction is voidable at the company's option (*Hely-Hutchinson v Brayhead* (1970)). This company has adopted

Table A, art 85 which provides that the contractual benefit to a director will be valid if disclosed to the board. Statute has limited this principle by declaring that disclosure must additionally comply with s 317. Here, A has declared his interest to the board in compliance with art 85 but has failed to comply with s 317 in that he has not declared the nature of his interest. Unfortunately, the effect of such non-compliance is obscure — certainly A is liable to a fine and the traditional view is that the relevant contract is voidable albeit at the option of the company (ie the board can ratify and A can vote). In addition to a possible breach of s 317, the transaction might, though on the facts this seems unlikely, be a substantial property transaction in which case A must comply with s 320, ie disclose interest to the general meeting, or run the risk that the transaction will be invalidated by s 322.

In conclusion, it seems that D and E may have *locus* to sue in the company's name but that, should they seek so to do, A, B and C will simply ratify the disputed transaction leaving no wrong in respect of which litigation could proceed.

Question 12

Christie Ltd was incorporated in 1989. The articles of the company contain the following provisions:

(a) So long as he remains a member, Marple shall be entitled to be a director of the company and to be the company secretary.

(b) Marple shall be paid such remuneration as a director as the board shall determine and he shall be paid not less than £20,000 per annum as company secretary.

Marple holds 15% of the issued shares of the company, the remainder being held by his brothers, Battle and Poirot. The three brothers are the only directors of the company but Poirot takes no active part in management. Marple quarrels with Battle over the future of the company: Battle enters into an agreement with Poirot whereby, in consideration of a payment of £10,000, Poirot agrees to vote with Battle at all board and general meetings. After appropriate notice an Extraordinary General Meeting is held and art 1 is deleted by special resolution.

The remuneration of the directors has never been fixed; Marple received about £75,000 in total for the years 1989-1992 'for services rendered'. He has received no money in 1993 for his services as a director of the company but has always been paid for his work as company secretary. The company is profitable but has never declared a dividend.

Marple is worried about his position and seeks your advice. Advise him.

Answer plan

Marple has, presumably, a number of concerns. First, the deletion of the article by virtue of which he had a right to be a director and to be the company secretary. Second, has he any entitlement to be paid while he continues to act as director and/or company secretary and has he any claim for the period prior to the amendment of the articles. Third, is the voting agreement between Battle and Poirot valid.

In addition to any specific remedy open to Marple, consideration should also be given to overall remedies, for example use of s 459 or, less likely, s 122(1)(g) Insolvency Act 1986.

Answer

In advising Marple (hereafter M), consideration must be given to his specific concerns relating to the change of articles but also to the possibility of a more general remedy being open to him.

(a) *Deletion of art 1*

Companies have an unfettered right to amend their articles by special resolution (s 9). M lacked a sufficient shareholding to block the passing of a special resolution to amend the articles of the company so that the deletion of art 1 appears unchallengeable. However, shareholders in voting to amend the articles may not have an unfettered right to cast their votes with regard only to their own interests. There are dicta in the cases which suggest that, on a vote to change the articles, the shareholders (Battle and Poirot, hereafter B and P) must vote *'bona fide* for the benefit of the company' (*Allen v Gold Reefs of West Africa Ltd* (1900)). Could this apply in this case so that M could seek the re-instatement of art 1? There are two objections to such a proposal. First, the scope of this dictum is uncertain although it is clear that, where the proposed change of articles is designed to appropriate the shares of the minority, the court will strike down the amendment unless it is objectively in the best interests of the company. For example, in *Dafen Tinplate v Llanelly Steel* (1920), an amendment to the articles allowing any shareholder to be required to sell his shares in the company was rejected by the court as going beyond that which was necessary to benefit the company. However, whether there is a *general* requirement that shareholders vote on proposals to alter the articles in a manner which is objectively in the best interests of the company is uncertain. In addition, B and P could argue that this proposal *is* in the best interests of the company.

A further argument of which M should be apprised is that the deletion of this article may not affect his rights in that art 1 gave him no rights! B and P could then argue that, since M was no worse off, there could be no objection to the deletion of art 1. Certainly, despite art 1, M could have been sacked by ordinary resolution (s 303). Where dismissal using the statutory format constitutes a breach of contract, the sacked director would be entitled to compensation. However, if art 1 did not give M any enforceable contractual rights as a director, M would be no worse off if he was dismissed by ordinary resolution before or after the deletion of art 1. M might try to argue that art 1 created a contract between himself and the company, which entitled him to be both a director and to be company secretary, because s 14 provides that the articles constitute a contract between the shareholders and the company. However, the scope of the s 14 contract and the ability of M to enforce it in his capacity as director/secretary is likely to disappoint him. The traditional view is that a shareholder can enforce the articles by virtue of s 14 only insofar as the relevant article creates a 'membership' right, ie a right attaching to each and every share and which relates to the holding of shares. This view derives from the decision of Astbury J in *Hickman v Kent or Romney Marsh Sheepbreeders' Assoc* (1915) and would appear to preclude the enforcement of a right which does not fall into this category. In this case it is difficult to see that a right conferred on M to be a director or to be company secretary could be regarded as a membership right. For example, in *Eley v Positive Life Ass Co* (1876), where the articles provided that E was to be company solicitor for life, E was held to have no contractual right of employment as solicitor and, in *Beattie v E & F Beattie Ltd* (1938), a provision requiring members to submit disputes to arbitration was held not to apply to a dispute between the company and a shareholder in respect of his directorship.

(b) *Entitlement to be paid*

While M continues to act as company secretary, he is entitled to be paid for this work. If he has a service contract that will define his entitlement. If M had an express service contract in respect of his role as company secretary the deletion of art 1 would have no effect on that contract and any attempt to dismiss him in breach of the independent contract would allow M to sue for damages. Any amendment of art 2 could not affect a separate service contract or any entitlement already earned *(Swabey v Port Darwin Gold Mining Co Ltd* (1889)). Section 9 could be used by B and P to amend the articles (eg change the salary in art 2) even if the amendment resulted in breach of M's service contract although damages would then payable *(Southern Foundries v Shirlaw* (1940)). If the terms of M's service contract are expressed to be as set out in the articles, any amendment of the articles would amend the service contract *(Read v Astoria Garage Ltd* (1952)). If he has a service contract whose terms on the relevant issue (in this case pay) are deficient or non-existent, the articles may be treated as implied terms of the contract and, as terms, the articles would be enforceable under the normal rules of contract. If this applied here, M could rely on art 2 to claim £20,000 a year. In such a case, it would seem that amendment of the articles does not change the service contract because the usual rule in contract is that contract terms cannot be changed without the agreement of all parties to the contract. If M has no separate contract but is relying upon s 14 to provide a contractual right to remuneration he will be disappointed — see *Eley v Positive Life Ass Co* (above) - in that the s 14 contract does not apply to rights which are not membership rights.

While M remains a director, has he any entitlement to be paid? If he has an express service contract his rights are parallel to those outlined above in respect of his role as company secretary. If M has a service contract, the terms of which are expressly based on the articles (terms subject to change using s 9) or a service contract into which the articles are implied (terms subject to change only with M's consent), his entitlement to remuneration is determined by art 2. In *Re New British Iron Co ex p Beckwith* (1898), the directors were held entitled to claim the sum specified in the articles as remuneration because the relevant article was 'embodied in and formed part of the contract between the company and the directors'. This case was approved, *obiter*, by the House of Lords in *Guinness plc v Saunders* (1990). If M does not have a service contract, he cannot rely on s 14 to confer a contractual right based on art 2 (see the arguments above). However, even if M can claim that the article gives him a contractual right, his right is limited to that provided by the contract which, in this case, is what the board decide. Thus, if the board decide to pay M nothing he will receive nothing. Further, the House of Lords in *Guinness v Saunders* (1990) held that, where a provision in the articles was the implied contract term as to pay, the contract term was the exclusive definition of a right to pay even if, as in that case and here, it effectively deprived the director of any remuneration.

(c) *The voting agreement*

M may challenge the validity of any decisions by B and P acting as directors or shareholders in that B has bought P's votes and that P has exercised no independent judgment in voting. It has been repeatedly laid down that votes are proprietary rights which the holder can do with as he wishes and there seems little doubt that as a shareholder P can bind himself to vote in a particular way (*Alexander Ward & Co Ltd v Samyang Navigation Co Ltd* (1975)). However, in a limited number of cases, the courts have held that this freedom to deal with ones assets (votes) as one sees fit must be restricted in the wider interests of company law. However, the situations where a shareholder is subject to an inalienable duty are mainly concerned with expropriation of company property or the shares of other members and do not seem to apply here. It can be concluded that in respect of the decision to delete art 1 P's decision to sell his shareholder votes to B is unchallengeable.

The situation is different when M seeks to challenge P's sale of his votes as a director. P as a director owes fiduciary duties to the company. One duty is to act in good faith in the best interests of the company which requires the director to be free to vote at board meetings as he wishes; the director must be 'left free to exercise his best judgment in the interests of the company' (*Boulting v ACTAT* (1963)). Presumably an agreement to fetter one's directorial discretion is a fraud on the minority thus allowing M, a minority shareholder, to litigate. While the agreement between B and P can be challenged by M it would appear to be binding as between B and P themselves (*Dawson International v Coats Paton plc* (1989)).

(d) *General remedies*

Given the uncertainty of the remedies which apply to the specific difficulties faced by M, it would be wise to advise him of the possibility of pursuing a general statutory remedy. The statutory remedies open to shareholders are to apply for a just and equitable winding up under s 122(1)(g) of the Insolvency Act 1986 or to seek a declaration of unfair prejudice under s 459. The just and equitable winding up route will be open to the court where the company is of the appropriate type — traditionally called a quasi-partnership company — and it is plain that there is such a breakdown in the relationship of the corporators that the company cannot function as intended.

In *Ebrahimi v Westbourne Galleries Ltd* (1973), the House of Lords ordered the winding up of a small company where one of the founder members was, lawfully, excluded from management. As in this case, the clear intention of the parties was that all would participate in running the company and all profits were paid as directors fees and not as dividends so that dismissal of one director from his post meant that the underlying assumptions on which the company was founded were destroyed and winding up was necessary. Of course, winding up is a very drastic remedy and M might prefer to use s 459. In *Re Kenyon (Swansea) Ltd*, the court held that an attempt to exclude from management a director who had the legitimate expectation that he would continue to be involved in management was unfair prejudice. Perhaps the same could apply here, especially given the conduct of B and P on voting, and the court could award a remedy — possibly the exclusion of B from management or an order for the company to buy M's share at a fair price.

Chapter 3

The Company and Outsiders

Introduction

A company if it engages in any business at all must necessarily have dealings with persons who are not members of the company and may have dealings with members in a non-member capacity (eg many shareholders in Sainsburys buy their groceries from the company). It is the ability of the company to deal with outsiders and the legal implications of such dealing that this chapter addresses.

There are two main issues. First, what is the company entitled to do in its capacity as a company and, if there are restrictions on its power to operate, what is the effect of overstepping these constraints. Second, since a company exists only as a matter of law and must necessarily act through human agents, what is the position where the human agent engages in an activity on behalf of the company which the company was authorised to do but which the agent was not authorised to transact on the company's behalf?

In both these areas, there has been a considerable amount of statutory tinkering with the common law rules. With respect to the first issue (the powers of the company) this has simplified the law but, in the second (the ability of individuals to bind the company), the law is something of a dog's dinner.

Students should be familiar with:

- The rules relating to the determination of the powers of a company and the consequences of non-compliance with any limitations on these powers (*ultra vires*)

- The rules relating to the ability of representatives of the company (or those purporting to represent the company) to bind the company

The latter issue overlaps with the provisions pertaining to the liability of a director for breach of his director's duty.

Question 13

'In the light of the reforms contained in the Companies Act 1989, the requirement of a statement of objects in every company's memorandum is nothing more than a waste of paper.'

Comment on this assertion.

Answer plan

A question of this type requires an analysis of the purpose of the objects clause, the reforms of 1989 which might affect the objects clause and a conclusion as to effect of these reforms. It does *not* require a detailed discussion of the *ultra vires* rule from Victorian times until the present although reference to the pre-1989 position will be relevant in addressing specific points.

Answer

Every registered company must have a memorandum of association which document must be submitted to the Registrar of Companies prior to registration. The Act specifies the minimum content of the memorandum in s 2. Section 2(1)(c) provides that the memorandum must state the 'objects of the company', a provision which has been present in company legislation since 1856. The model memoranda in the Tables, designed to provide a pattern for company promoters, show that the intention was that the objects should be few and should specify the business which the company intended to pursue but not the means by which the business was to be run. Thus, the Tables did (and do) not envisage a listing of such things as 'this company can borrow money' or 'enter into leases' or 'purchase items necessary to facilitate the achievement of our specified object'. The legal effect of the objects clause was determined by the House of Lords in the famous case of *Ashbury Carriage Co v Riche* (1875), in which R sued the company for money owing to him in respect of his supervision of a project entered into by the company to build a railway in Belgium. The company sought to deny liability for this debt by pointing out that the objects of the company were to build railway rolling stock and not railways and asking the court to hold that the objects clause defined the contractual capacity of the company thus denying the company the capacity to engage in contracts relating to building railways. The House of Lords accepted the company's argument and held that since the company did not in law have the ability to enter into a contract to build a railway it could have no capacity to employ R to supervise such a project — it was beyond the powers of the company, ie it was *ultra vires*. Consequently, R had no contract and no contractual right to be paid. The rationale behind this decision was that shareholders and creditors must know what they were putting their money into; if you invested in a company which said it was going to build railway carriages you were entitled to expect the money to be used for that purpose alone.

While this might be true of shareholders, although one might argue they would have no objection to their money being used in non-authorised but profitable purposes, it is difficult to see how this rule protects creditors. One could say that creditors whose debts are incurred in the company pursuing authorised purposes are protected by the inability of the company to waste its money on paying debts incurred on unauthorised business but this is a somewhat remote benefit. In addition, creditors, like Riche, whose debts are disallowed as being contracted in pursuance of unauthorised activities and who are not paid did not feel protected by the rule. Interestingly enough, the decision in *Ashbury* was no more popular with companies than it was with Riche and means were soon adopted to try and evade the effect of the decision. This unpopularity stemmed from the fact that a company might expand into new areas without realising the need to amend its objects so that the company, or others who had financed the change of direction, would find that they had entered into a series of unenforceable transactions. In addition to the problems of the *ultra vires* rule proper, the courts further clouded this area of law by failing adequately to distinguish between a situation where a company had entered into an unauthorised transaction (*ultra vires* and company not bound) and the situation where the directors of the company had caused the company to enter into an authorised transaction which they had subverted for improper ends (company bound but directors liable). However, the Court of Appeal in *Rolled Steel Ltd v British Steel Corpn* (1986) had attempted to explain the distinction between these two situations. The difficulties of the rule itself were compounded by the doctrine of constructive notice which meant that the objects clause, once registered, was constructively (ie in law) notified to everyone so that a person who had dealt with a company could not claim not to know that a transaction was not within the company's objects since, in law, he knew the contents of the objects clause. In addition, the courts created innumerable problems in respect of charitable giving even at one period holding that charitable giving was *ultra vires* when the objects of the company expressly allowed such giving unless the donation was beneficial to the company (a heresy laid to rest in *Re Horsley and Weight Ltd* (1982)).

Companies sought means to evade the effect of the rule. This self-help approach generally took the form of adopting extremely long objects clause embracing everything the founders of the company and their advisors could think of with a view to authorising every conceivable activity. The judicial attitude to such self-help was mixed. In *Cotman v Brougham* (1918), the House of Lords accepted, with reluctance, the validity of an objects clause authorising the company to do almost everything. However, in later cases such as *Re Introductions* (1970), the Court of Appeal held that a list of registered 'objects' could be divided by the courts into 'true' objects and mere powers; the latter authorised activities only insofar as they were in pursuance of a true object. The situation was a mess. The rule existed but companies sought to evade it — sometimes with success and sometimes without. Parliament ameliorated the effect of the *ultra vires* rule in the European Community Act 1972 but the position before 1989 was that the rule remained in modified form. Hence, a company was only authorised to engage in activities which were designed to achieve its registered objects although, by virtue of the statutory amendment, a party dealing with a company could, in some circumstances, enforce an *ultra vires* contract.

What then did the 1989 Act do in this area? Despite the recommendations of the Prentice Report, it did not abolish *ultra vires* either wholly or in part. Instead, an approach was adopted to mitigate and marginalise the rule. There are four sections which were inserted into the 1985 Act which are relevant. First, s 3A, which could ultimately render the *ultra vires* rule obsolete for all but charitable companies. This section provides that a company can adopt as its object 'to carry on business as a general commercial company' and then says that, in such a case, the company has as its object 'to carry on any trade or business whatsoever'. This section, which overturns case law which had rejected similar objects clause, is strangely worded but it clearly allows a company to adopt a general object so that a company which has such an object can be authorised to do practically anything. This general objects clause cannot be adopted by non-commercial companies, eg charities. Section 3A then confirms the common law by adding that such a company 'has power to do all such things as are incidental or conducive to the carrying on of any trade or business by it' (s 3A(b)). Section 3A appears to be couched in objective terms so that companies using s 3A may register an additional object allowing the pursuance of activities which the directors believe to be incidental to the carrying on of trade or business. While retaining the *ultra vires* rule, this section allows trading companies to adopt an object which authorises the pursuance of any lawful activity so rendering the rule moribund.

Second, the new s 4 allows a company to change its objects, eg to that authorised in s 3A, by special resolution. Unlike previous sections which had allowed a change of objects, the proposed change does not have to be for a reason authorised by Parliament. A change of objects is subject to confirmation by the court if qualified shareholders dispute the change of objects. The procedure for objection is set out in s 5 and *locus* to object is granted only to a shareholder or group of shareholders who can muster 15% of the votes of any class of shares. This simplifies the previous scheme for the alteration of objects and encourages existing companies to move to the new all-purpose objects clause.

Thirdly, the new s 35 provides for the enforcement of *ultra vires* transactions if certain conditions are satisfied. Section 35(1) provides that: 'The validity of an act done by a company shall not be called into question on the ground of lack of capacity by reason of anything in the company's memorandum.' This section, if it stood alone, would have given companies legal capacity comparable to that enjoyed by natural legal persons of full age and understanding; unfortunately, as we shall see, it does not stand alone. While the wording of s 35(1) says that the validity of an act done by a company cannot be called into question on the grounds of lack of capacity by reason of anything in the memorandum, it is thought to extend to an action not mentioned by the memorandum, ie an act not restricted by the objects clause but not authorised by it either. Further, it is assumed that the section also covers a decision not to act by the company despite the reference to an act done. Turning to the restriction on the operation of s 35(1): s 35(2) allows a member of a company to restrain the company from doing an act which, but for s 35(1), would be beyond the company's capacity. For example, if the objects of the company do not authorise the company to buy property, a member can, it seems, restrain the directors from buying property on behalf of the company. However, s 35(2) is itself restricted in that it only permits a member to restrain the directors from a proposed action; once a legal obligation arises, the lack of capacity on the part of the company cannot be used by a member to restrain an action entered into by the directors on behalf of the company. Thus, a shareholder can stop a contract which it is proposed shall be entered into but cannot stop the carrying out of a contract which has been entered into. This limitation is designed to preserve an element of the rationale of the *ultra vires* rule — the ability of shareholders to know where their money is going. Section 35(2) also reinforces that element of the common law which permitted a member to restrain the *ultra vires* activities of his company (this was one of the areas where the rule in *Foss v Harbottle* (1843) did not apply).

Perhaps to reinforce the idea that a member should have some control over the use of his money, s 35(3) provides that the shareholders can by special resolution ratify a transaction which would be beyond the capacity of the company but for s 35(1). This allows shareholders to decide whether to authorise, albeit retrospectively, the company to spend their money on *ultra vires* activities. If the shareholders do not ratify a transaction entered into by the company, s 35(1) still protects the person dealing with the company so that this aspect of s 35(3) is applicable only where the company has not yet entered into a transaction and s 35(2) would allow a shareholder to seek a restraint order. Section 35 is subject to a qualification contained in s 322A but this is primarily concerned with the situation where the directors exceed their powers rather than the company so doing. Section 35(3) also considers the liability of a director who authorises an *ultra vires* transaction but this is a different issue from that with which we are concerned.

Finally, s 711A (when implemented) will abolish constructive notice so that the mere fact that the objects clause is contained in a registered document will not give constructive notice of its contents. This provision is of limited relevance given the enforceability of *ultra vires* transactions under s 35(1) but is of considerable importance in determining whether a third party can enforce a contract etc within the powers of the company which has been negotiated by a director without the power so to do (see s 35A). However, there is some doubt as to whether this section will now be brought into force.

These statutory changes have not rendered the objects clause a meaningless piece of verbiage but they have reduced the effect of the objects clause in a way which self-help could never achieve. However, a recent case — *Halifax Building Society v Meridian Housing Association Ltd* (1994) — reminds us that statutory companies (and registered charitable companies) are not subject to ss 3A and 35. The objects clause of a such companies will continue to be judged by reference to their own rules on capacity.

One minor area where the objects clause, theoretically, retains some life is the *substratum* rule. This rule allows a shareholder to wind up the company where the company can no longer achieve its registered object (*Re German Date Coffee Co* (1882)). Since companies now adopt very long objects clause setting out a mass of objects and have the option of using the s 3A object, it is difficult to imagine this rule ever operating unless the world comes to an end.

Question 14

Tentfamily Ltd was a wholly owned subsidiary of World Travel plc; it had been dealing, rather unprofitably, in budget holidays for families. Alice, Belinda and Chloe, who worked for the company, believed they could make it profitable by specialising in skiing holidays and limiting operations to Scandinavia. They borrowed money from their parents and bought Tentfamily from World Travel. Each of them holds 30 shares and is a director of the company; the remaining 10 shares are owned by Chloe's partner. Each director entered into a two-year service contract with the company which contract was expressed to be automatically renewed on identical terms at the end of the two-year period. The contracts provided for the payment of a monthly salary to the directors for the exercise of designated management functions.

On taking control, they changed the articles of the company to provide that a contract giving rise to a corporate obligation exceeding £1,000 in value could be entered only with the approval of the other directors. This article was stated to be alterable only with the unanimous approval of all the directors. They have decided to change the name of the company to Skiscand Ltd and, at the request of their parents, to amend the objects of the company to limit the activities of the company to skiing holidays. The company would like to sponsor the British Ski team to provide publicity for its new venture.

Before any of the proposals were implemented, Alice broke her leg on a fact-finding tour in Norway and, with the agreement of Belinda who was with her, hired at a cost of £3,000, charged to the company's account, an aeroplane to fly her home. Alice has announced that she will be away from the company for several months to recuperate from the accident. Chloe, who has been managing the company, is not happy about this expenditure and feels that Alice cannot expect her usual salary while she is away from work.

Comment on the legal implications of what is proposed and what has occurred.

Answer plan

This question addresses a number of issues:
- a change of corporate direction and the in/validity of the amendments to the articles;
- the proposed change of name;
- the proposed change of objects;
- payments to the ski team;
- the validity and enforceability of the service contracts; and
- the accident and its consequences.

Answer

(a) *The change of direction*

The company was originally dealing in general holidays of a budget variety. The directors, who also control 90% of the shares have, as is their right, chosen to alter its sphere of activity (Table A, art 70 gives the directors the power to manage the company). The only restraint upon the power of the directors to change corporate direction is the requirement that a company should only engage in activities authorised by its objects clause. It seems highly likely that the objects of the company permitted it, expressly or impliedly, to deal in skiing holidays. Indeed, it is hard to imagine the original objects clause allowed the company to sell holidays but specifically excluded ski trips. Thus, the proposed narrowing of the sphere of activity is probably *intra vires*, ie it is within the objects of the company registered in the memorandum (in compliance with s 2). If the change of direction is not within the objects of the company any change in the articles would be invalid insofar as the changed articles were inconsistent with the objects clause. In addition, the new activity would be *ultra vires* (beyond the powers of the company) and void as, for example, in the famous case of *Ashbury Carriage Co v Riche* (1875). While the *ultra vires* principle remains good law it has been outflanked and rendered largely impotent by statute. Section 35 (substituted in 1989) provides that for *ultra vires* activities, transactions can be enforced both by the company and the person with whom the company was dealing if certain conditions are satisfied. Hence, a person dealing with the company, eg the owners of the aeroplane, could not be defeated by a claim that skiing holidays and matters related thereto were not authorised activities. Section 35(1) provides that 'The validity of an act done by a company shall not be called into question on the ground of lack of capacity by reason of anything in the company's memorandum.' This is thought to allow the enforcement both of corporate activities apparently prohibited by the memorandum and also those not expressly authorised by it.

It may be noted that even though the amended article is stated to be unalterable without the approval of all the directors, such a provision cannot bind the company. In *Russell v Northern Bank Development Corpn Ltd* (1992), the House of Lords refused to uphold an agreement by which the shareholders agreed not to enforce a statutory right conferred by the Companies Act. Thus, a company cannot contract out of its right to change its articles (s 9). The directors could enforce this agreement among themselves and seek to restrain a fellow contract-party from voting to change the articles of the company to delete this provision. However, the agreement could not bind future shareholders or other non-parties to the agreement.

(b) *The change of name*

The name of the company can be changed by passing a special resolution (s 28) and informing the Registrar of Companies who will then issue a new certificate of incorporation. A change of name does not terminate any liabilities owed by the company so that the debts of Tentfamily remain payable by Skiscand (see *Oshkosh B'Gosh Inc v Dan Marbel Inc Ltd* (1989)). As on first incorporation there are restrictions on the choice of name a company may adopt. However, this name does not fall foul of any of the normal restrictions on company names so that the only objection would be if there is an existing company with the same or a similar name. Even if the name is registrable, Skiscand could be liable for the tort of passing off if there is another established business trading under a similar name in the same field.

(c) *The change of objects*

A company may seek to change its objects for any purpose it sees fit provided the new object is lawful. Such a change is sanctioned by s 4 and, provided a change is implemented by special resolution (which the directors can obtain by their own votes), the modification of the objects is automatic unless a qualified shareholder dissents. Section 5 provides that any objection must be made within 21 days and by a shareholder or shareholders with at least 15% of any class of shares who did not vote for the alteration — there can be no-one in this case who satisfies s 5. The outsiders, who put up the money for the shareholders, have no right to impose a change of objects and, as non-shareholders, have no power to complain about any failure by the company to implement the change.

(d) *Payments to the ski team*

There can be no objection to the company making payments to the ski team if such a payment is authorised by the objects of the company. The company may have an express power to make gratuitous payments in which case they can be made even though akin to charitable donations and whether or not the payments benefit the company (*Re Horsley and Weight Ltd* (1982)). However, if the company is not expressly authorised to make such payments they will be *ultra vires* unless falling within the implied powers of the company; this is the case even if the payments are made *bona fide* (see *Hutton v West Cork Railway Co* (1883)). Such payments will be within implied powers if made *bona fide* and for the benefit of the company. It would seem that the publicity gained by the sponsorship deal would benefit the company and would be within its implied powers — at least once the objects have been changed. If the payments were *ultra vires*, the directors who authorised them would be liable to reimburse the company unless their breach of duty was approved by the company by special resolution.

(e) *The service contracts*

Section 319 prohibits any term whereby a director is to be employed for a period exceeding five years without such contract being terminable unless the term has first been approved by the shareholders in general meeting. However, the directors in this case have contracts for a fixed term of two years albeit a period which is automatically renewed at the end of this and every two-year period. Does such a contract infringe s 319? It seems so. Section 319(1) provides that where a contract stipulates that a director's employment is to continue or may be continued for more than five years the section applies. This contract, by providing for automatic renewal, seems to be capable of continuing for more than five years without any intervention on the part of the director or company since it re-generates every two years. Thus, the term which violates the section is void and the directors' contracts should be treated as for a fixed term of two years. The fact that a majority of shareholders clearly approved the contracts will not satisfy s 319 which requires contracts exceeding five years to be approved at a general meeting.

Since the contract with the company benefits the directors they should ensure that they make adequate disclosure of their interests in their respective contracts before entering into them. While failure to do might seem a minor breach, and one which time would ratify, there is the risk that the company might go into liquidation, or be taken over, in the near future and the liquidator or new owner could seek to disclaim any contract not adequately disclosed (see *Neptune (Vehicle Washing Equipment) Ltd v Fitzgerald* (1995) for such a disclaimer where a single director had failed formally to disclose his interest to the board, ie himself).

(f) *The accident*

Three issues arise. First, whether the contract to hire the aeroplane binds the company. Second, whether Alice is entitled to be paid while she is absent from the company and finally whether failure to attend to the affairs of the company gives rise to liability.

Alice, with Belinda's approval but without consulting Chloe, has hired an aeroplane, ie has entered into a contract without the unanimous approval of the directors contrary to the newly adopted articles. This breach of the articles is actionable by the company unless ratified by the company but it would seem that Alice and Belinda between them have sufficient votes to ratify such action. Whether the contract binds the company depends upon the authority of Alice and Belinda to obligate the company. Since a company is an artificial legal person its decisions and actions have to be taken by natural persons acting on its behalf. While the power to run a company is vested (generally) in the board that does not mean that the board has the exclusive jurisdiction to enter into a contract on behalf of the company. Whether a particular person (or persons) can bind a company is essentially a question of agency — the principal (the company) is bound by acts entered into on its behalf by a person with actual, usual or ostensible authority so to do. For the company to be bound, the third party must establish that Alice had authority to enter into this contract. Alice does not have express authority. She will have the usual authority that a person exercising her functions within a company would possess — we are not sure of her exact executive role but she seems not to be managing director (a post which carries wide usual authority). If, however, she can be said to have usual authority by virtue of whatever post she does hold the company cannot rely on the restriction in the articles to deny liability (s 35A). The question is whether her capacity in the company cloaks her with the authority to hire aircraft is a matter of fact.

Alternatively, Alice may have ostensible authority to hire the air craft. Ostensible authority arises when those with actual authority within a company hold out a person as having authority to bind the company. A holding out by Alice and Belinda would not do since one cannot hold oneself out as authorised to act on behalf of a third party. However, if the aircraft company had had prior dealings with Alice in which dealings she had dealt in planes (as part of her role with the company) she might be invested with ostensible authority if the company had always honoured previous contracts she had negotiated. The clause in the articles requiring unanimity could be ignored by virtue of s 35A provided the other party acted in good faith.

Alice's absence from management might be thought to comprise negligent conduct unless she is incapable of acting as a director because of the broken leg; this seems improbable. She seems to be proposing to take an inordinate time to recover from the accident. It is true that a non-executive director is not required to give the company his or her undivided attention. The common law provides that a director must exercise such care, skill and diligence in the exercise of his or her directorial function as might reasonably be expected in the circumstances. Certainly it is accepted that a non-executive director need not attend board meetings on a regular basis so that such absence is not itself negligent. For example, in Re Denham & Co (1883), a four-year absence from board meetings was not actionable and in The Marquis of Bute's Case (1892), the Marquis (there were 50 directors) was not negligent and not liable for thefts carried out by officials of the bank despite having attended only one board meeting in 47 years. Whether Alice was entitled to director's fees for the period she was absent from the company would depend upon the articles of the company and the shareholders in general meeting. However, Alice also seems to have a management role within the company and her ability to take extended leave with or without payment would depend upon the company and the terms of her employment as an executive. A speedy recovery is advised.

Question 15

Domusfecit Ltd was incorporated in 1993, its objects being 'to engage in the maintenance of domestic property and any business incidental or conducive thereto'. The company has three directors, who each own 25% of the company's shares, all of whom are active in the business. One of these directors, Brick, generally acts as managing director although he has not been formally appointed to the position. Brick has long thought that the company should expand into the refurbishment of commercial premises and in 1995 he successfully tendered for such a contract on behalf of the company.

Brick has just revealed to his fellow directors, Fletton and Commons, that he has entered into the commercial refurbishment contract and that he has ordered new equipment for the work from Equip Ltd. Fletton and Commons think the company will lose money on the contract for refurbishment, which they wish to evade, Equip wishes to enforce the sale of equipment.

Advise Fletton, Commons and Equip.

Answer plan

Three main issues arise
- what right, if any, have the relevant parties to seek to evade or enforce the contracts;
- is the contract/sale beyond the powers of the company and if so can it be enforced by the third party;
- has the contract/sale been negotiated by a person who has the authority to bind the company to such a transaction and if not can it be enforced by the third party.

Brick's liability to the company or shareholders or third parties can also be touched on.

Answer

The company is seeking to escape from the commercial refurbishment contract and the equipment purchase contract negotiated by Brick. It will try to do so on two grounds. First, that the company does not have the capacity to enter into such contracts and second, that even if the company had the necessary capacity, Brick did not have the authority to bind the company to such a transaction. If the latter argument is successful, the third party with whom Brick has contracted may be able to sue him for breach of warranty of authority.

Right to litigate

Fletton and Commons constitute a majority of the board of the company and are shareholders in the company. Since they would appear to be able to pass an ordinary resolution (majority of those present and voting) they can seek to dismiss Brick as a director (s 303) and, as a majority of the board, they can instruct Brick not to act as managing director or appoint a new managing director. Brick's dismissal would not affect the validity of any contract entered into by him. As a majority of the board of a company which has Table A, art 70, Fletton and Commons have the power to run the company and can seek to deny liability on behalf of the company (probably unsuccessfully as shown below) or initiate litigation against Brick for acting improperly or negligently. Liability for negligence is unlikely given the limited obligation directors bear in this area. As shareholders rather than directors, Fletton and Commons can seek to raise the alleged *ultra vires* nature of the contracts but this would not preclude a third party enforcing the contracts under s 35. Since Brick's ability, if any, to bind the company is based upon the holding out by Fletton and Commons that he is the managing director with the powers of a managing director, it would seem odd if, acting as shareholders, they could sue Brick for exceeding his authority. Presumably, there is no objection to them initiating litigation on behalf of the company against Brick but they too might be liable for allowing him to act without any board control.

Can the company be bound

There is no doubting the legality of these contracts so that the contracts cannot be challenged on that ground. However, Domusfecit, in common with all registered companies, is required to register a memorandum of association which includes an objects clause (s 2(1)(c)) which clause has been held to define a company's contractual capacity. The objects clause can be changed by special resolution (s 4) but it has long been the case that a company lacks the capacity to enter into a contract not expressly or impliedly envisaged by the objects of the company. For example, in the famous case of *Ashbury Carriage Co v Riche* (1875), R sued the company for money owing to him in respect of his supervision of a project, entered into by the company, to build a railway in Belgium. The company successfully denied liability by taking the point that the objects of the company were to build railway rolling stock and not to build railways. The House of Lords held that since the company did not in law have the capacity to enter into a contract to build a railway it could have no capacity to employ R to supervise such a project. Thus, R had no contract and no contractual right to be paid. Consequently, at common law the court would have to decide whether the contract of refurbishment fell within the purview of the objects clause in that it was expressly or impliedly authorised. If the contract was not authorised Fletton and Commons, acting on behalf of the company or in their own right, could obtain a declaration that the contract was void in that it was beyond the powers of the company, ie *ultra vires*. The contract to purchase equipment might be authorised by the objects clause even though it is bought to carry out the refurbishment contract. This would be the case when the equipment could be properly used in the authorised business of house refurbishment and Equip did not know that the director with whom he negotiated intended to subvert the equipment for an unauthorised business (*Rolled Steel Ltd v BSC* (1986)).

However, even if one or both the contracts were beyond the powers of the company, s 35 provides that an *ultra vires* contract is enforceable, both by the company and by the third party, if certain conditions are satisfied. Fletton and Commons must be told that 'The validity of an act done by a company shall not be called into question on the ground of lack of capacity by reason of anything in the company's memorandum' (s 35(1)). Section 35(2) might seem to assist their cause in that it allows a member of a company to restrain the company from doing an act which but for s 35(1) would be beyond the company's capacity. However, s 35(2) is itself limited in its effect in that a shareholder cannot restrain an act which would be in fulfilment of an existing legal obligation of the company. In consequence, Fletton and Commons as individuals cannot prevent the carrying out of a contract which has been entered into by the company. In this case the legal obligation has arisen and the company cannot escape liability on either contract on the basis that it was not authorised to enter into such a contract. There is no question of ratification in this case.

Can Brick bind the company

Since a company is an artificial legal person its decisions and actions have to be taken by natural persons acting on its behalf. Whether a particular person (or persons) can bind a company is essentially a question of agency - the principal (Domusfecit Ltd) is bound by acts entered into on its behalf by a person with actual, usual or ostensible authority so to do. In this company it is the board of directors who have the actual authority to make the decisions as to how the company is to operate (Table A, art 70). However, merely because the board could have entered into contracts does not mean that the board has the exclusive jurisdiction to enter into a contract on behalf of the company. The question of who has the power to bind a company is one where the law has ambled down several different paths most of which met at the same point. To this confusion of common law has been added a series of statutory reforms which supplement but do not replace or codify the common law.

The company, we assume, wishes to escape liability on two contracts entered into by Brick, a single director who acts as the company's managing director. For the company to be bound, the third party must establish that Brick had authority to enter into these contracts and bind Domusfecit. Domusfecit, if not bound, could choose to ratify these contracts but this does not seem to be what Fletton and Commons want. Brick has not had actual authority bestowed on him by the board nor can he claim to have the usual authority which is vested in a managing director since he has not been appointed to such a post. However, it is well established that where a person (Brick here) is held out by those with actual authority (the board in this case) as occupying a particular post the body which does that holding out cannot rely upon any internal irregularity in the appointment of the person held out to claim that his acts cannot bind the company (*Royal British Bank v Turquand* (1856)). Where those with actual authority hold out a person as occupying a particular post, they are also deemed to hold that person out as having an ability to bind the company which is co-extensive with the usual authority which a properly-appointed holder of such a post would possess, ie the authority of such an agent is determined by reference to what a holder of the post would usually be expected to have. Brick in this case would have the equivalent of the authority usually possessed by managing directors since he has been held out as such and his actions could be relied on by a third party acting in good faith. A leading case is *Freeman & Lockyer v Buckhurst Park Properties Ltd* (1964), in which the Court of Appeal ruled that a person who was allowed to act as managing director of a company with the apparent consent of the other three directors had, subject to any restrictions known to a third party or the circumstances being such as to put the third party on inquiry, power to bind the company to a contract under which the plaintiffs were employed in connection with the refurbishment of the company's property. The precise extent of the usual or ostensible authority of a managing director is not clear but it can be hazarded that any transaction which the board would have had the power to negotiate could be negotiated by a managing director (or person acting as such) unless of such magnitude that a reasonable third party would be put on inquiry. These contracts do not seem so outside the scope of a managing director's authority that the relevant third parties would have been put on inquiry. If there are suspicious circumstances, the third parties will not be able to claim that they relied upon the authority which the board appeared to have bestowed on Brick unless they 'made such inquiries as ought reasonably to be made' (*Underwood Ltd v Bank of Liverpool* (1924), bank liable to reimburse company when director signed cheques drawn on company's account in his own favour). Since Brick seems to have been held out as having the powers of a managing director in that the rest of the board, Fletton and Commons, allow him to act as such the company is bound. Section 35A which deals with restrictions on the powers of the board does not apply here because, even if the section applies to the acts of a single director, it merely removes a restriction upon the authority of a director. The section does not confer authority and the critical issue here is whether Brick has authority. Nor is s 285 applicable since it validates the acts of defectively appointed directors who would, but for the defective appointment, have authority.

Question 16

The articles of Fish Ltd state that:

(a) the board of directors may delegate all or any of its powers;
(b) any transaction with a value of £40,000 or more must have the prior approval of the company in general meeting;
(c) company cheques must be signed by two directors.

The board recognising the company is in need of new business, appoints Shark to the board with particular responsibility for marketing and instruct him to 'make things happen'. Without reference to the rest of the board, Shark immediately organises a 'sales conference' for potential clients at a luxury hotel in the Bahamas, at a total cost of £50,000. Shark pays a deposit of £5,000 to the hotel by means of a company cheque which he alone signs having forged the signature of a second director since he is keen to book the conference before the hotel implements a proposed price rise.

Shark has just reported his actions to the board. The board horrified by proposed expenditure wish to dismiss him from his post of Marketing Director, terminate his directorship and intend to cancel the conference.

Advise Shark and the luxury hotel.

How, if at all, would your answer differ if the board had organised the conference without reference to the shareholders and the shareholders objected to the cost?

Answer plan

Shark and the luxury hotel have different concerns. Shark does not want to be dismissed from either his executive post or his office of director or at least wants compensation for loss of office. The luxury hotel is concerned with the enforceability of the contract negotiated by Shark — issues of agency and effect of forgery arise. In the alternative situation, the hotel is looking at the enforceability of a contract negotiated by the board — the impact of the articles on enforceability and s 35A are in point.

Answer

Shark's directorships

Shark should be advised that in forging a signature on the cheque he has committed a serious criminal act for which he could be prosecuted. Even if prosecution, conviction and imprisonment ensued this would not automatically terminate his non-executive directorship although it might well terminate his executive directorship since he would be unable to act as an effective marketing director from prison. Whether prosecution or imprisonment arise, Shark should be informed that he has broken the terms of his executive directorship by acting as he has and that it is likely to be a breach which entitles the company to terminate his contract of service. If this is so, there is no requirement to pay compensation so that even if there is more than four years of the service contract to run there will be nothing, other than salary already earned, to pay Shark for termination of his executive role. The power to dismiss Shark from his executive post is vested in the company; as in most companies, this means the power is vested in the board of directors (Table A, art 70).

As to his non-executive role this would continue unless and until terminated by the company. The articles of the company do not give the board power to dismiss a director (there is nothing in Table A to this effect) so for the board to try and do so would be ineffective. However, there is no reason why the shareholders should not dismiss Shark by using s 303. Section 303 allows the shareholders to dismiss a director by ordinary resolution provided appropriate notice of the meeting has been given and the director has had the chance to put his case to the shareholders and to speak at the meeting. The shareholders can use their powers under s 303 even if a director has done nothing wrong and they just feel like a change — it is not a power which must be exercised for a proper purpose. Termination of office using s 303 does not entitle the director to any compensation for loss of office.

The luxury hotel

Regardless of who negotiated the contract with the hotel (H) there is little doubt that Fish Ltd had the contractual capacity to enter into such a contract. Surely the ability to organise a sales conference

falls within the implied powers of the company since all companies
have implied powers to undertake activities conducive or
necessary to the pursuance of their objects. Consequently, the
contract cannot be rejected on grounds of *ultra vires* and, even if
such was the case, the contract would be enforceable by H by
virtue of s 35. However, simply because the company has the
capacity to contract does not mean that the contract is binding on
Fish. Since Fish Ltd is an artificial legal person its decisions and
actions have to be taken by natural persons acting on its behalf.
These acts and decisions may fall to be taken by the board or the
shareholders in general meeting or by agents or employees of the
company. Whether a particular person (or persons) can bind the
company to this contract is essentially a question of agency — the
principal (Fish Ltd) is bound by acts entered into on its behalf by a
person with actual, usual or ostensible authority so to do. In this
company it is the board of directors who have the power to make
the decisions as to how the company is to operate (Table A, art 70)
subject to the need for approval from the general meeting for
contracts valued over £40,000. Does this mean that Shark's
agreement cannot bind the company?

(a) Contract negotiated by Shark

The hotel wants the contract entered into by Shark, a single
director, to be binding on Fish Ltd. In order to enforce the contract,
H must establish that Shark had authority to enter into this contract
and bind Fish. Alternatively, Fish would be bound if it ratified an
unauthorised act but it seems plain that the board has got cold feet
about Shark's activities and has made it plain that it does not wish
to ratify Shark's contract. Has Shark authority to bind the
company?

Plainly Shark has not got express authority to enter into this
transaction unless the instruction to 'make things happen' confers
express authority to do anything on Shark. Nor can H rely on the
articles to claim that Shark was impliedly authorised by the articles,
in that the board could have delegated power to him, since the
cases seem to accept such reasoning only where the third party has
read the articles (*British Thomson-Houston Co Ltd v Federated
European Bank Ltd* (1932)). This would raise difficulties for H since,
if it had read them, it would know of the restriction on Shark's

powers albeit H might be able to argue that it was entitled to
assume the general meeting had given permission in accordance
with the principle enunciated in *Royal British Bank v Turquand*
(1856). It is unlikely that H has read Fish's articles.

More promising for the hotel is the possibility that Shark has
usual authority to enter into this transaction. The extent of Shark's
usual authority to enter into a transaction is determined by
reference to the position which he holds — he has the powers
which the holder of such a post within a company would usually
possess. For example, a company secretary has usual authority to
run the administrative side of a company's affairs. This could
involve purchasing office equipment, hiring staff and generally
ensuring the smooth running of the support side of a business. In
Panorama Developments Ltd v Fidelis Furnishing Fabrics Ltd (1971), the
usual authority of a company secretary was held to include the
hiring of cars to transport visitors to the company's premises so
that the company was liable for the car-hire charges even when the
secretary had used the cars for his own purposes. The question for
H in this case is what is the usual authority of a 'marketing
director'. If it includes the organisation of a sales conference then
Fish is bound even though it did not actually authorise Shark to act
as he did. Shark is a properly appointed director so the problems of
de facto appointments do not arise. There are no cases on the usual
authority of a marketing director so one can merely speculate on
the scope of his usual authority. It can be assumed that Shark has
authority for matters concerning marketing but at some point the
magnitude of the transaction might indicate that board approval is
required — the sums involved in this case do not seem so large (but
see the articles) that H should instantly be suspicious nor do there
seem to be any suspicious circumstances which should have put it
on its guard. If there are suspicious circumstances H will not be
able to claim that it relied upon Shark's usual authority unless it
'made such inquiries as ought reasonably to be made' (*Underwood
Ltd v Bank of Liverpool* (1924), bank liable to reimburse company
when director signed cheques drawn on company's account in his
own favour). Even if, *prima facie*, Shark has usual authority, H has
deemed notice of the limitation on the powers of individuals
contained in the articles because registration of the articles is
constructive notice of their contents to the whole world
(constructive notice is prospectively abolished by s 711A but this is

not yet in force). However, if H can rely on s 35 (see below) the restriction on Shark's power contained in the articles does not bind it. In addition to usual authority an agent may have ostensible authority whereby an agent of the company is held out by those with authority (eg the board) as having wider powers than that normally possessed by an agent of that type (ostensible authority also has other meanings) but there seem no question of Shark possessing such authority. The scope of ostensible authority, if any, would also be curtailed by the articles unless H could rely on s 35A to abrogate the restriction on Shark's authority. It is not clear if s 35A applies to an action decided upon by a single director rather than one entered into by the board. The wording of the section seems to suggest that it applies only to actions by the board.

The act of forgery committed by Shark should not destroy his usual authority provided that he was simply carrying out an authorised task (conference organising) in an unauthorised way (contra the case of *Ruben v Great Fingall Consolidated* (1906)). However, even if Shark is found to have authority to enter into the hotel contract, Fish is not criminally liable for the forgery committed by Shark.

Thus, H could enforce the contract against Fish only if not bound by the restriction in the articles.

(b) Contract negotiated by the board

There is no doubt that if the board had decided to embark on organising a sales conference for less than £40,000 the company would have been bound. Even if such a decision had been a breach of directors' duty, for example if it had not been made *bona fide* or for a proper purpose, that would not affect the validity of the transaction as far as the third party was concerned. However, in this case the board has exceeded its powers by not referring the contract to the shareholders. The validity of appointment of the board of Fish has not been raised so it can be assumed that the board are all *de jure* directors.

At common law the third party, H, would have had constructive notice of the need for prior shareholder approval although H might have been able to rely on the case of *Royal British Bank v Turquand* (1856) to enforce the agreement. *Turquand* established that where the board (or an individual) appeared to have authority to act, the company could not rely upon some internal irregularity in its own procedures to deny that liability. However, H can rely on s 35A if it wishes to enforce the conference contract despite the wishes of the shareholders. Section 35A(1) provides that 'in favour of a person dealing with a company in good faith, the power of the board of directors to bind the company ... shall be deemed to be free of any limitations under the company's constitution'. In interpreting this section, s 35A(2) provides some guidance. A person 'deals with a company' if he is a party to a transaction or other act to which the company is a party — H has no difficulty in satisfying this test. Section 35A(2) then provides that it is assumed that a person dealt in good faith unless the company proves the converse. Cases on earlier versions of s 35A, which would probably remain applicable, ruled that good faith was a subjective test. Nourse J in *Barclays Bank Ltd v TOSG Trust Fund* (1984) stated that 'A person acts in good faith if he acts genuinely and honestly in the circumstances of the case'. There seems no evidence of any lack of good faith on the part of H in this case and H would appear to be protected by s 35A. Moreover, s 35B provides that while H is not under a duty to enquire as to whether the directors are exceeding their powers in entering into the disputed contract (ie failure to inquire is not bad faith).

Thus, H can be advised that its contract with Fish is enforceable against the company.

Question 17

Mansfield Park Ltd was incorporated in 1993. The objects of the company provide that Mansfield Park Ltd is to purchase a specific stately home, Mansfield Park, and convert it into luxury flats for rent and that the company can also purchase and convert similar properties. The articles of the company include the following provisions:

(a) the qualification to hold office as director shall be the holding of shares in the company to the nominal value of £100;

(b) the board of directors may delegate all or any of their powers or functions to any director or directors;

(c) any contract to purchase land for the company's use must be approved by the company in general meeting.

At the outset the company had three shareholders, Austen, Bingley and Collins, who each held 25% of the company's share capital. Austen and Darcy were appointed as directors; Darcy has always acted as managing director but has never been formally appointed to the position. In 1994, Elton was appointed to manage the flats at Mansfield Park. In early 1995, Elton ordered a car costing £25,000 in the company's name to be used by him primarily for company business. Elton, in conjunction with Austen, has just negotiated the purchase, at a price of £500,000, of another property for conversion, Kellynch Hall, which belongs to his brother.

Darcy does not wish the purchase of the car or Kellynch Hall to proceed and wishes to dismiss Elton and restrict Austen to a non-executive role in the company.

Advise Darcy, Bingley and Collins.

Answer plan

First it must be established whether Darcy, who has not taken any qualification shares, has any *locus* to act on his own account or on behalf of the company or, if he does not have such *locus*, whether he acts in conjunction with Bingley and Collins in respect to these issues. The second issue is the ability of a manager to enter into a contract which can bind the company (car) and whether he can be sacked. Third, can Elton and Austen together bind the company to purchase Kellynch and if they can does the fact that it belonged to Elton's brother affect the validity of the contract.

Finally, have Bingley and Collins any rights of their own without acting through Darcy.

Answer

The first thing to note is that Darcy, who acts as managing director, has not, in breach of the articles, acquired any qualification shares. Consequently, he can have no rights as a shareholder. Does this failure on his part affect his ability to enforce the rights of the company, assuming he has such a right, and is he in breach of his director's duty in failing to acquire the shares?

The power to run a company, which includes the right to sue

errant directors, dismiss employees and seek to evade contracts, is determined by reference to the articles. This company has Table A, art 70 so that it is the directors who decide whether to exercise legal rights on the company's behalf. The directors of this company are, *prima facie*, Austen and Darcy. However, Mansfield Park has retained the rather outmoded requirement that the directors acquire qualification shares. Section 291 provides that if such shares are not acquired by a director within two months of his appointment the errant director has to quit his office and is not eligible for reappointment until the shares are acquired. Thus, it seems that Darcy is not a director of the company and that the power to run the company is vested in Austen. Consequently, Darcy cannot act for the company or initiate litigation and is himself liable to a fine for acting as a director without acquiring shares. If he acquires the shares he can be re-appointed.

Until Darcy acquires the shares, Austen is the sole director of the company and he may not wish the company to try and back out of the car contract given that he appears to be allied to Elton and is, it can be assumed, in favour of the purchase of Kellynch. Bingley and Collins cannot instruct Austen in how he runs the company because such instructions are operative only if given in the form of a special resolution which they cannot muster (they hold 50% of the share capital or 66% if only 75% issued). However, Bingley and Collins do have sufficient voting strength to obtain an ordinary resolution which would enable them to dismiss Austen (s 303, which would terminate both the non-executive and executive roles). Should they do so they may then seek to appoint new directors (or reappoint Darcy), or run the company themselves (they would then be treated as the directors even if not formally appointed, s 741) or reappoint Austen with limited powers.

While Austen remains in charge the shareholders cannot engage in legal activity on behalf of the company because the famous case of *Foss v Harbottle* (1843) provides that the power to act on behalf of the company is vested in the directors. There are cases where *Foss* does not apply; one being when the company has acted *ultra vires*. However, *ultra vires* is limited to cases where the company has exceeded its powers and is not in issue when the company itself is authorised but the particular human intermediary was not authorised to act. The purchase of a car and the purchase of Kellynch clearly fall within the express or implied powers of the company so that these contracts cannot be called *ultra vires*. Another exception to *Foss* arises when there is 'fraud on the minority', ie an unratifiable wrong has been done to the company and the wrongdoers control the company so that there is no effective champion of the company's rights. If the purchase of the car or Kellynch is such a wrong then Bingley and Austen have power to initiate litigation in the name of the company by means of a derivative action. This looks a remarkably long-winded way of outflanking Austen whom they can sack and it is difficult, although not impossible, to see why justice (a factor relevant in determining whether shareholders should be given *locus* to pursue the company's claims, see *Barrett v Duckett* (1995) for an example) should allow Bingley and Collins to act for the company while ignoring their alternative remedy. However, Bingley and Collins might argue that it was more appropriate for them to sue rather than sack if sacking Austen might jeopardize the existence of the company in that Austen's dismissal could trigger a claim by him for just and equitable winding up. Section 122(1)(g) Insolvency Act 1986 allows such an action if the company has the hallmarks of a 'quasi-partnership' company and the relationship of the parties has irretrievably broken down. This could well apply here.

If Bingley and Collins dismiss Austen (or persuade him to fall in with their views), they may seek to pursue the remedies sought by Darcy — to evade the car and Kellynch contracts. Since there is no doubt that a company such as this has an implied power to purchase a motor car for a senior employee, even if he also uses it for non-company business, the company is bound by this contract unless it can establish that the person who negotiated the contract, Elton, had no power to bind the company to a contract of this type. Since Mansfield Park is an artificial legal person its decisions and actions have to be taken by natural persons acting on its behalf.

Whether Elton can bind a company is essentially a question of agency — the principal (the company) is bound by acts entered into on its behalf by a person with actual, usual or ostensible authority so to do. Elton does not appear to have actual authority to enter into this contract but he may have usual authority, ie the authority that can be assumed to arise from the position he holds within the company. A senior manager must have some ability to bind his company but there is little case law on the usual authority of senior employees. It is a moot point whether a third party is entitled to allege that he was entitled to assume that Elton had the power to buy a car of relatively high value on behalf of the company. Alternatively, Elton may have possessed ostensible authority. Ostensible authority allows a person to bind the company because those with actual authority, the board, have indicated to the world that Elton possesses such power, ie they have given the impression that he has the relevant power and the car dealer has no reason to doubt the impression the board has given him. The fact that the directors can delegate all or some of their powers does not mean that a third party is entitled to assume that a power has been delegated; there must be some indication by the board that Elton has the authority to bind Mansfield Park.

If Elton does not have usual or ostensible authority it seems that the company is not bound by the car contract and it should be noted that s 35A would not affect this. Section 35A merely permits a restriction, which would limit an authority which would otherwise exist to be ignored, it does not confer authority where none existed previously.

Elton can be sacked by his employer, the company, provided the decision to sack him is taken by the appropriate organ of the company — the board. The consequences of this will depend upon whether he was in breach of his contract of employment which would allow dismissal without compensation or whether there was no such breach so that the company would have to compensate him on normal legal principles.

Finally, have Bingley and Collins either as the new board (or a new set of directors appointed by them) or as shareholders, any power to challenge the purchase of Kellynch? The question of authority again arises — can Austen (the sole legitimate director) and Elton (a manager) bind the company. Clearly, the company has the ability to undertake such a purchase since the objects of Mansfield Park permit the purchase and conversion of other properties of a similar type to Mansfield Park itself. Kellynch would appear to be such a property. Whether Bingley and Collins can prevent the contract of sale proceeding to completion without exposing the company to an action for breach of contract depends upon the authority possessed by the negotiators and the effect, of any, of the close relationship of the vendor with one of these negotiators. Plainly, neither Austen and Elton together or singly had actual authority to bind the company. While a manager must be regarded as having some usual authority by virtue of his position (see above) it cannot extend to a transaction of this magnitude (*Armagas Ltd v Mundogas SA* (1986)) so that the company is bound only if Austen has usual authority or Austen and/or Elton had ostensible authority.

Generally the usual authority of a single director who is not a managing director is very limited and in this case Darcy, however improperly, has been acting as managing director so that Austen cannot be regarded as filling that post. Perhaps it could be argued that since Darcy is not a director (no shares) then Austen is the board and that, since the board could negotiate this contract, Austen could bind the company by virtue of being the only director or that Austen, as the board, could hold himself out as able to bind the company. If Austen has no authority he cannot bind the company, if he has authority the vendor of the land may still appear to be defeated by art 3. Article 3 provides, in effect, that the purchase of land without the approval of the general meeting cannot bind the company. However, section 35A(1) provides that 'in favour of a person dealing with a company in good faith, the power of the board of directors to bind the company ... shall be deemed to be free of any limitations under the company's constitution'. The vendor of Kellynch falls within the section especially since s 35A(2) then provides that it is assumed that a person dealt in good faith unless the company proves the converse. Cases on earlier versions of s 35A, which would probably remain applicable, ruled that good faith was a subjective test. Nourse J in *Barclays Bank Ltd v TOSG Trust Fund* (1984) stated that 'A person acts in good faith if he acts genuinely and honestly in the circumstances of the case.' Thus, the fact that the vendor is related to an employee of the company (even one who was involved in negotiations) does not mean that there is a lack of good faith on his part in this case and the vendor might well be protected by s 35A. It should be mentioned that s 35B provides that a third party is not under a duty to inquire as to whether the directors (or director) are exceeding their powers in entering into the disputed contract (ie failure to inquire is not bad faith).

Entry into the land transaction is breach of director's duty on the part of Austen (and breach of his duty as employee on the part of Elton) but this simply gives the company a remedy against Austen and does not allow it to disregard the contract if it is rendered enforceable by s 35A.

Chapter 4

The Directors

Introduction

There are few aspects of company law which do not, in some way, involve a discussion of the directors and their powers. Every company must have at least one director (two in the case of a public company) and they have a multifaceted role within a company. The directors may be employees, they have duties as directors and they generally act on behalf of the company in its dealings with the outside world (ie as agents). This variety of functions means that any question can include an aspect relating to the directors – a question on shares might raise issues of the power to allot (s 80), a question involving litigation might touch on division of power within the company, almost any transaction might be challengeable as an improper use of directorial power and, as discussed in Chapter 3, the validity of a company's contract can turn on the authority of the director who purported to act on behalf of the company. In addition, questions might raise, although rarely as the only issue, issues of the validity of the appointment, the amount of remuneration or the legitimacy of a dismissal of a director.

The most likely area for questions solely on directors is that of the extent of their duties. Students must not become too narrow-minded in addressing the issue of directors duties. For example, a question may require consideration of a contract between a director and the company – obviously the usual rules on disclosure, the nature of the disclosure and the effect of non-disclosure (including possible ratification) arise but students must also consider the nature of the contract. Ask yourself is the transaction a substantial property transaction (s 320) or does it involve a loan etc (ss 330–342) or a service contract (s 317). Entry into a contract may also be attacked as an improper use of directors power. Any question on directors duties may raise the issue of locus; is the person seeking to sue the director authorised so to do. Locus involves the case of *Foss v Harbottle* and its exceptions and it may be that a litigant denied locus on behalf of the company has an alternative remedy under s 459 or s 122(1)(g) Insolvency Act 1986.

Linked to questions of directors' duties may be questions about the liability of third parties who have been involved in misappropriating corporate property. The ambit of constructive trusteeship in respect of third parties arises in such cases.

Question 18

The combination of *Percival v Wright* (1902), *Foss v Harbottle* (1843) and Table A, art 70, effectively frees directors from any risk of litigation for breach of duty being brought by minority shareholders or creditors.

Discuss.

Answer plan

Discuss first what the decisions and statutory provision provide then turn to the effect of the law on potential actions by minority shareholders or creditors. Sum up by determining whether directors are right to feel fearless.

Answer

All companies are required by law to have at least one director (s 282), public companies must have at least two and Table A provides that all companies shall have at least two directors unless the company determines otherwise by ordinary resolution (art 64). When a company is registered the shareholders of the company possess the authority to determine how the company will operate and be operated and they are not required to bestow all or any of their powers on the board of directors. The shareholders generally give away their power to run the company in the articles but the degree of delegation is a matter for the shareholders to determine either in the articles or subsequently. In practice, most companies adopt Table A, art 70 which effectively gives the power to operate the company, which would otherwise be vested in the shareholders in general meeting, to the directors. Consequently, the shareholders (majority or minority) cannot complain if the directors exercise the powers which have been delegated to them unless the articles of the company, or other provision giving power to the directors, restrict the apparently unfettered use of such powers. The articles can, of course, be changed by special resolution (s 9) but this will not avail a minority shareholder (who will be unable to muster the requisite number of votes) or a creditor (who has no right to attend company meetings). Directors who upset their shareholders can be dismissed by ordinary resolution (s 303) but a minority shareholder may find even this lowered hurdle too high to scale. Table A, art 70 contains a provision permitting the shareholders to instruct the board how to act provided that such directions are given by special resolution – this is of little practical value to minority shareholders and none at all to creditors. It can be concluded that in most companies the directors have a relatively unfettered right to run the company although their right to do so is hedged by fiduciary and statutory obligations.

A minority shareholder or a creditor might seek to restrain the proposed acts of the board or sue in respect of past acts alleging breach of a fiduciary or a statutory duty. Potential litigants have two case with which to contend, *Percival v Wright*, which provides that the board in exercising its powers (or duties) is generally responsible to the company and not to individual shareholders or creditors (or the employees) and *Foss v Harbottle*, which held that a breach of duty owed to a company can be litigated only by the company. Since the power to litigate on behalf of the company will normally reside in the board (by virtue of art 70 or its equivalent) the directors would appear to be able to determine whether to sue themselves in respect of wrongs which they have done to the company. While the board might be willing to sue a director (or former director) with whom the majority had fallen out it is difficult to imagine a united board voluntarily agreeing to sue itself. The issues which must be considered are whether *Percival v Wright* precludes a director owing a duty to a shareholder or creditor and whether *Foss v Harbottle* is subject to exceptions.

In *Percival v Wright* (1902), the directors of a company were privy to confidential information which, once released, was likely to increase the value of the company's shares. Percival, a shareholder, offered to sell his shares to the directors who accepted his offer. When the confidential information was released, P sought to have the contract of sale set aside and to recover the shares on the ground that the lack of disclosure was a breach of fiduciary duty by the directors. Swinfen-Eady J, in rejecting P's claim, held that the directors did not, simply by being directors, owe a fiduciary duty to an individual shareholder; they did owe such a duty to the company but they had not broken it. This case remains the law despite being the subject of fierce criticism. Hence, a director owes fiduciary and other duties to his company by virtue of his office but owes none to a shareholder or creditor on that basis. However, it does not preclude a director being found to have chosen to undertake some responsibility to a shareholder (fiduciary or contractual) on a personal level, ie the duty arose because of an arrangement between two people who happen to be a director and shareholder (or creditor). For example, in *Allen v Hyatt* (1914), the directors induced the shareholders to give them options to purchase shares without disclosing the possibility that the directors would be able to re-sell the shares at a profit. The Privy Counsel found that the directors had by their words and actions made themselves agents for each shareholder and owed the usual obligations of an agent to his principal. These obligations include a duty to account for any benefits accruing from the agency so that the directors had to account for the profits they had made on the exercise of the options and the subsequent re-sale of the shares. However, in most cases there is no question of the directors undertaking responsibility to an individual shareholder so that *Percival v Wright* is the norm. The fiduciary obligations owed to the company can be summarised as a duty to act in the best interests of the company even if this is not in the best interests of the director. It is the fact that the directors should act in the interests of the company which has allowed some mitigation of the effect of *Percival v Wright*. The interests of the company are generally concurrent with the economic interests of current and future shareholders but not any particular shareholder. However, when the company is the subject of a take-over bid the interests of the company have been treated as concurrent with the interests of current shareholders so that directors have a duty to give them honest advice about the merits of the bid (first established in *Gething v Kilner* (1972)). The New Zealand courts have gone further and have expressed the view that a director can incur liability to an individual shareholder without the need for agency and in circumstances other than that of a take-over bid. In *Coleman v Myers*

(1977), Woodhouse J held that whether liability could arise depended 'upon all the surrounding circumstances and the nature of the responsibilities which in a real and practical sense the director has assumed towards the shareholder'. In *Coleman*, the managing director of a family owned and run company, who had persuaded shareholders to sell him a majority shareholding on the basis of the published valuation of the company's assets, was required to account to those shareholders when the assets were sold at a price substantially above book value. The English courts have not been prepared, as yet, to follow *Coleman*.

What then of creditors? There are *dicta* which suggest that directors should have regard to the interests of creditors. It should be noted, however, that the *dicta* which suggested that directors owe a duty to creditors may be incapable of support following the decision of the Privy Council in *Kuwait Asia Bank EC v National Mutual Life Nominees Ltd* (1992). In this case the appellant bank, which was registered in Bahrain, was a major shareholder (holding approximately 40% of the shares and nominating two out of five directors) in a New Zealand money-broking company (AICS) which had gone into insolvent liquidation. The respondent company NMLN was, in accordance with New Zealand law, trustee for AICS's depositors and had incurred considerable liabilities and expense in connection with the insolvency. NMLN was seeking a contribution to its liabilities from a number of defendants including the directors of AICS. The Privy Council, in considering whether the New Zealand courts had jurisdiction over the bank, advised that a director does not owe a duty to the creditors of his company simply by virtue of his office although he may by agreement or representation undertake such a responsibility. Lord Lowry in his speech relied upon a number of 19th century decisions (none in the House of Lords) in support of this view but, somewhat surprisingly made no reference to the more recent cases (including one in the House of Lords) which had appeared to acknowledge the possibility of such a duty existing. None of the recent cases appear to have been cited by counsel. If this case is construed literally it would appear to be strongly persuasive to the effect that directors cannot incur liability to corporate creditors. However, its effect may be restricted to a denial of a duty of care *in tort* being owed to creditors (despite not being

expressly so confined) leaving open the development of a *fiduciary*
duty in accordance with such cases as *Winkworth v Edward Baron
Development Co Ltd* (1986).

Thus, shareholders and creditors may then find that the
directors have the power to run the company (art 70) and owe their
duties to the company and not to them (*Percival v Wright*). A further
difficulty facing shareholders who wish to sue directors is that even
where a wrong has been done to the company the proper plaintiff
is the company (you cannot sue to enforce another person's rights
or remedy their wrongs) so that, as indicated above, it is the
company (the operation of whose powers are vested in the board)
which decides whether to sue the board or a director (*Foss v
Harbottle* (1843)). However, there are a limited number of cases
where a shareholder, but not a creditor, has locus to sue to enforce
the rights of the company (a shareholder can always sue a director
to enforce his own rights, if any) – such an action is called a
derivative action. For a shareholder to bring a derivative action is
somewhat unattractive, the shareholder has to pay for the litigation
(although the courts have the power to order the company to
indemnify the shareholder – *Wallersteiner v Moir* (1974)) and any
remedy which is ordered accrues to the company and not the
shareholder. Moreover, it is not that easy to establish that an
exception to *Foss* has arisen. To do so the shareholder must
establish a *prima facie* case of fraud on the part of those in control of
the company and unless such a case is established the shareholder
must be denied locus (*Prudential Assurance v Newman Industries*
(1981)). Fraud in this context extends beyond legal fraud to
embrace an apparent lack of probity (equitable fraud). Hence, in
Daniels v Daniels (1978), where legal fraud was not alleged, a sale of
a corporate asset to a director at a price which appeared to be
substantially below its market value was held to fall within the
exception in that, while simple negligence could not form the basis
of an exception to *Foss*, a sale at an undervalue which had benefited
a director to the extent of £115,000 could be treated as equitable
fraud. Even when 'fraud' and control by the wrongdoers (which
embraces effective as well as legal control) have been established,
the courts have a discretion to deny locus to a shareholder. Denial
of locus has arisen when the shareholder has himself behaved
improperly (*Nurcombe v Nurcombe* (1985)), the shareholders or

(margin annotation: derivative action)

directors who are not party to the wrongdoing have indicated that they do not wish an action to proceed (*Smith v Croft (No 2)* (1988)), or the shareholder is acting for an ulterior motive rather than to enforce the company's rights (*Barrett v Duckett* (1995)). The logic underpinning these cases is that if the company is not going to benefit from the action it is foolish to allow it to be dragged into litigation against its will. Hence, where a case could be brought but a majority of independent shareholders are against it for a *bona fide* reason, for example the unlikelihood of any real benefit to the company, their views should prevail over those of a minority shareholder.

As the previous paragraphs illustrate a director can indeed assume that while he retains the support of his fellow directors he will be free of litigation in respect of his running of the company. However, s 459 is likely to prove a more troublesome provision for directors than anything in the rest of company law. Section 459, which allows a shareholder to litigate if he has been unfairly prejudiced by some act or proposed act of the company, gives locus to a single shareholder (but not creditors) who, if successful, obtains any remedy awarded by the court although there is no question of the company being required to fund such an action.

Question 19

Directors of companies have onerous fiduciary and statutory duties imposed upon them which makes their limited liability for negligence all the more puzzling.

Comment.

Answer plan

A straightforward question requiring a synopsis of the fiduciary and statutory duties imposed on directors with a comment as to whether these duties can be classified as onerous, followed by a similar synopsis on the liability of a director for negligence with a comment as to whether it is 'limited'. A concluding paragraph should be added to link up the arguments on the relative weight of directorial burdens.

Answer

All companies must have at least one director (s 282, two in a public company). There are few statutory restrictions upon who is eligible to be a director, youth is no bar, a day-old baby can be a director, nor is age (subject to s 293 in respect of public companies), nor is there any entrance examination. The only automatic bar to a directorship is being an undischarged bankrupt. Most companies adopt Table A, art 70 which effectively gives the power to operate the company, otherwise vested in the shareholders in general meeting, to the directors although their right to do so is hedged by fiduciary, statutory and common law obligations. What then is the nature of these duties and to what extent is there an imbalance between those imposed by common law and the rest and is this disparity, if proven, justifiable?

1 *Fiduciary and statutory duties*

As Lord Porter put it in *Regal (Hastings) Ltd v Gulliver* (1942), 'Directors, no doubt, are not trustees, but they occupy a fiduciary position towards the company whose board they form'. As a fiduciary each director is individually subject to equitable duties – fiduciary duties – which require him to exercise his powers in a way which has regard to the interests of the person to whom the duties are owed and not to abuse his position of trust and influence within the company. Indeed, in respect to corporate property the director's fiduciary duty goes further and, in common with a trustee, a director cannot, without the unanimous approval of the shareholders, derive any benefit from the use of corporate property. Fiduciary duties are owed to the company, that is current and future shareholders as a body, and not to individual shareholders (*Percival v Wright* (1902)) although a director may voluntarily undertake a fiduciary duty towards a shareholder by acting as his agent (*Allen v Hyatt* (1914)).

Fiduciary duties can be sub-divided into the general and the applied. The general duties cast on a director consist of an obligation to act *bona fide* in exercising his powers and a requirement that certain powers are used only for 'proper purposes'. The obligation to act *bona fide* is subjective so that provided a director honestly believes he is acting properly in deciding how to operate the company he is not in breach of this duty (*Re Smith & Fawcett Ltd* (1942)). Since a director must make decisions on the basis of his own honest belief in what is best for the company, it is a breach of fiduciary duty for a director to fetter his freedom to exercise his powers. Consequently, an agreement by a director that he would always vote for proposals put forward by X would be a breach of fiduciary duty. However, a director must exercise his powers not only honestly but also for a purpose consistent with that for which the powers were conferred on him. A leading case in point is the Privy Council decision in *Howard Smith Ltd v Ampol Petroleum Ltd* (1974). In *Ampol* the directors of HS, a company in need of further finance, issued shares to members who held a minority interest in the company but offered none to the majority shareholder (A) who had made an unwanted take-over bid. The effect of the issue was to reduce A's shareholding to below 50%. This allotment of shares was challenged by A as an improper use of the directorial power to issue shares. The Privy Council ruled that when the use of a power is challenged, the court should first consider the nature of the power, ie why was this power conferred on the directors whose exercise thereof is in question, and then examine the substantial purpose for which it was exercised. If, considering the issue objectively, the power was not exercised for the proper purpose the exercise of the power is void. The court ruled that the power to allot shares is given to directors to raise funds for the company and that while the directors intended this allotment to raise capital the primary purpose of the issue was to defeat A's bid and not to raise money. Consequently, this allotment was void – the facts of this case could now also fall within ss 80–96. Other cases on this area have held that an improper use of directorial power can be ratified by ordinary resolution (*Bamford v Bamford* (1970)). It is uncertain which powers must be exercised for proper purposes.

In addition to the general obligations a director is also subject to the requirement to put the interests of the company before his own interests. This responsibility has given rise to a number of areas of litigation some of which have been supplemented by statutory provisions. An obvious source of conflict between corporate duty and personal interest concerns corporate contracts which directly or indirectly benefit the director. The House of Lords in *Aberdeen Railway Co v Blaikie Bros* (1854) ruled that a director could not benefit directly or indirectly from a contract made by his company. This has been modified to provide that a director cannot benefit from a contract between himself and his company or between his company and a third party without making adequate disclosure of his own interest in that contract. Disclosure should be to the shareholders unless the articles allow disclosure to the board; Table A, art 85, permits disclosure to the board. Section 317 provides rules for the nature of the disclosure to the board. It can be argued that disclosure to ones fellow-directors is not an onerous duty. Failure to make adequate disclosure in compliance with the common law or the articles allows the company to rescind the contract (where the director has received a direct benefit) or make the director liable to account (indirect benefits). The effect of failure to comply with s 317 is obscure but it may render the contract voidable. Perhaps because disclosure to the board might allow a cosy cartel among directors certain sections impose further obligations in respect of particular contracts upon directors. Section 319 places restrictions upon the service contract which a director can make, s 320 affects 'substantial property transactions' and s 330 prohibits a company from making loans to directors. The general thrust of these provisions is not to prohibit contracts between directors and their companies but rather to ensure that such contracts are valid only if affirmed by the shareholders in general meeting.

The general duty to put corporate interest above private profit is augmented in respect of corporate property; in common with a trustee, a director cannot, without the unanimous approval of the shareholders, appropriate (even innocently) corporate property. If he does so appropriate he is liable as a constructive trustee. It is obvious that if a director appropriates the company's tangible property he will be liable to return the property to the company. The same is true of appropriation of intangible corporate assets, for example the benefit of a contract possessed by the company. This liability for misappropriation is extended to commercial opportunities which are within the company's grasp. For example, in *Cook v Deeks* (1916), a company, X, was about to sign a contract to build a railway when the railway company was persuaded by some of the directors of X to award the contract to a new company which they had formed. The directors were held liable to hold the benefit of the contract as constructive trustees for X.

Misappropriation of corporate assets is an unratifiable breach of directors duty. Difficulties can arise in determining what is corporate property in the area of corporate opportunities. Further, because of the onerous obligations in respect of corporate property the courts have distinguished between misuse of property and misuse of the position of director and the line between the cases can be hard to draw. In most cases where a director has benefitted from his position, for example by using information received in a corporate capacity, liability is imposed not for breach of a trustee-like duty but rather for breach of a lesser fiduciary duty. This fiduciary duty provides that a director should not benefit from his position as director, which duty extends after the ending of the directorship, at the expense of the company. This is not an absolute prohibition so that a director can benefit from his position if there is no real conflict of interest. A recent decision in this area is to be found in *Framlington Group plc v Anderson* (1995). In this case A, C and L had all been employed by the plaintiff group as private client fund managers and had been directors of companies within the group. A, C and L agreed to take up employment with R plc and the plaintiff company negotiated a sale of the business represented by the clients who would move their business to R plc when A, C and L moved; A, C and L were not party to these negotiations and had been specifically told not to be become involved in any negotiations on behalf of the plaintiff group. Subsequently, A, C and L entered into contracts with R plc which entitled them to shares in R plc (in addition to their salary) in proportion to the amount of business transferred by Framlington clients on their change of employer. The plaintiffs, who had not been aware that share benefits would be payable to A, C and L, claimed to be entitled to the shares transferred to them alleging that such shares were secret profits arising from their directorships of companies within the plaintiff group. Blackburne J found no conflict between the duty owed by the directors and their own interests. What, he said, is the specific interest of the plaintiff which is in conflict with A, C and L negotiating for themselves a generous remuneration package at the time that another director within the plaintiff group was negotiating with R plc? A, C and L were free to leave the plaintiff group at any time and were able to solicit clients if they left, hence their deal with R plc was a sale of an asset (client goodwill and their freedom to exploit it) in return for shares and a salary. There is no obligation on a director leaving a company to take up other employment to reveal to his current company the nature of his remuneration package, nor is there any duty as a fiduciary not to compete with the company with which one has previously been connected. While the decision may be justified on the basis that there was no real conflict between personal interest and fiduciary duty, the notion that since the directors were not party to the negotiations between the plaintiff group and R plc they were free to arrange a deal for themselves which might be adverse to their current company seems somewhat surprising.

If a director does benefit from his position and there is a conflict of interest the profit made by the director can be retained if the company by ordinary resolution so decrees. It is not clear whether a company can absolve a director from liability in advance, rather than relieve him from the consequences of breach thereafter, although *dicta* in *Regal (Hastings) Ltd v Gulliver* (1942), would suggest not. The uncertainty over this issue and over the borderline between ratifiable and unratifiable breaches of directors duty is widely felt to be unsatisfactory. What is clear is that fiduciary duties are extensive and pervasive.

2 *Care and skill*

In contrast the common law duty of care and skill borne by directors was traditionally very modest. However, it must be noted that directors can incur liability for wrongful trading by virtue of s 214 Insolvency Act 1986 irrespective of any common law liability but only if the company goes into insolvent liquidation. At common law directors are expected to carry out their duties with an appropriate degree of care and skill. The traditional formulation of the nature and extent of this duty is that given by Romer J in *Re City Equitable Fire Insurance Co Ltd* (1925) in which he held that a director:

(a) need display only such skill as may reasonably be expected from a person of his knowledge and experience;

(b) need not give the affairs of the continuous attention; and

(c) is entitled to leave the day-to-day running of the company to the officials of the company and is entitled to assume, in the absence of suspicious circumstances, that such officials are performing their duties honestly.

These propositions remain good law with regard to non-executive directors but executive directors will generally be constrained by their service contracts to devote a set percentage of their time to the affairs of the company. The most important aspect of a director's duty of care relates to the amount of skill he must exercise. Directors are not subject to the Supply of Goods and Services Act 1982 which requires service-providers to display reasonable care and skill. It is plain that a director who does his honest best may be held to have exercised sufficient care and skill to evade liability for negligence – the test of liability is subjective and not objective. Certainly a director need possess no particular skill on appointment (*Re Brazilian Rubber Estates & Plantations Ltd* (1911)). Each case turns on its own facts and the issue is did the relevant director, given his qualities, display adequate care and skill? The courts are beginning to be a little more robust in determining the standard of care which a company can expect. In *Dorchester Finance Co Ltd v Stebbing* (1977), the company had three directors S, P and H; S and P were chartered accountants and H had considerable accounting experience. P and H left the running of the company to S doing little more than calling in periodically and signing blank cheques for S to use; no board meetings were held. The issue before the court was a claim by the company against all three directors for negligence. Foster J in determining the appropriate degree of care and skill to be expected from S, P and H took into account their experience of accountancy and business. The judge found that the complete failure by P and H to do anything in respect of the running of the company was, even for non-executive directors, negligent as well as in breach of several sections of the Companies Act. Signing blank cheques was also negligent in that, allied to their lack of control, it allowed S to run the company as he pleased. In addition, S ran the company without any care and skill and was plainly in breach of this duty and he was also liable for breach of fiduciary duty (misapplication of corporate assets). This change of emphasis can also be seen in *Norman v Theodore Goddard* (1991), in which a chartered surveyor B, who was a director of a Jersey-based company had been tricked by a co-director Q, a solicitor, into authorising the payment of the company's money to a company controlled by Q. Q's partners were liable to reimburse the money and were seeking a contribution from B alleging that he had failed to display sufficient care and skill as a director. Hoffman J found on the facts that B's conduct in trusting Q was reasonable and that B had not been negligent. However, he held, *obiter*, that the duty of care and skill at common law was co-extensive with that imposed by s 214 Insolvency Act 1986, ie that a director should display such care when carrying out functions in relation to the company as would reasonably be expected from a person carrying out those functions. This seems to have a more objective ring about it that the Romer J view which assessed a director's conduct by reference to the relevant director's abilities and not by reference to those of *a* person carrying out directorial functions. Cases on s 459 have also held that gross negligence by a director may be unfairly prejudicial to the shareholders (*Re Macro (Ipswich) Ltd* (1994)).

3 *Conclusion*

Despite recent developments, there is little doubt that the fiduciary and statutory duties of directors greatly outweigh the duties of care and skill. Perhaps it is not inappropriate that we can demand honestly and fair dealing from our directors but cannot necessarily expect skill, equally it could be argued that people should not allow shareholders to entrust money to their care without exercising some degree of care in looking after it.

Question 20

Epsom is a director and employee of Ludlow Ltd and is a shareholder in two other companies. He holds 10% of the shares of Aintree Ltd and 15% of the shares of Newbury Ltd. He is also owed £2,000 salary by a former employer, Fontwell Ltd. All these companies are connected with the racing industry.

He seeks your advice about the following:

(a) Fontwell Ltd is incompetently managed and is apparently moving towards insolvency.

(b) The directors of Ludlow have proposed an allotment of shares to their employees and hope thereby to defeat a hostile take-over bid.

(c) The board of Aintree decided that it had no immediate need of a substantial piece of land which it owned and, being unable to sell it, leased it to the company's managing director at market rates. He intends to use the land to develop a new business unconnected with racing.

(d) Newbury Ltd has five directors but management of the company was carried on by two of them and the rest took no interest in the running of the company and rarely attended board meetings. One of the executive directors has recently absconded with some of the company's money.

Answer plan

A large number of issues are raised which allows little scope for lengthy discussion of any one issue. After general introductory comments two issues arise in respect of each company:

(a) has Epsom (E) *locus* to bring an action in respect of these activities; and

(b) are the actions, or proposed actions, of the directors of the relevant companies a breach of their duties as directors.

Answer

It can be assumed that the acts about which E seeks advice are not beyond the powers of the company concerned, ie are not *ultra vires*. Two issues arise in respect of each company – first, has E has the ability to litigate either on his own account or on behalf of the company (the *locus* point) and second, is there a cause of action open to him.

(a) *Fontwell*

E is owed money by Fontwell Ltd (F), he is a creditor of the company. A creditor of a company has no right to intervene in the running of the company and has no locus to complain about the alleged inefficiency of the management either on his own account or on behalf of the company. E has no rights under s 459 which confers rights only on shareholders. E has the usual remedy open to a creditor owed more than £750, that is to make a statutory demand for the sum and if it is unpaid to seek to wind up the company on the ground that it is unable to pay its debts (s 122(1) Insolvency Act 1986). A threat of liquidation may galvanise the company into trying to pay E's debt although such a payment could be set aside if the company went into liquidation within six months and the payment was found to be a 'preference' (s 239 Insolvency Act 1986). If the company was to go into liquidation before E had enforced his claim he would be a preferred creditor for the first £800 of his debt (ie would take priority over all other creditors except those with a fixed charge) and an unsecured creditor for the balance in respect of which he would rank behind anyone holding any charge over the assets of the company. E's position does not look promising unless he moves swiftly or is confident that there will be assets available to satisfy his debt if the company goes into liquidation.

(b) *Ludlow*

As an employee of Ludlow, E has no *locus* to challenge or to enforce the proposed allotment of shares either on his own account or on behalf of the company. Section 309 provides that the directors must have regard to the interests of the employees in performing their functions but this section confers no locus upon employees who wish to claim that the directors are not paying due regard to their interests. In addition there is no evidence that this allotment is not in the interests of the employees. If any offer to allot shares is accepted by E he is a party to a contract and as such would seem to have the usual contractual remedies if the company failed to keep its side of the bargain and he will have to pay for the shares. However, if the allotment of shares is in some way improper, for example if it is made for an improper purpose, the contract may be unenforceable and the directors (including E), by proposing to make such an allotment, might be in breach of their fiduciary duty. However, only a shareholder or the company could raise the invalidity of the allotment and such an allotment can be ratified by the company in general meeting (the disputed shares cannot be voted). There is no question of E being forced to buy the shares.

The directors should be warned that in issuing shares they must comply with the provisions of the Act and their own fiduciary obligations. Section 80 provides that the power to allot shares can be exercised by the directors only if they have been authorised so to act either in the articles or by a resolution of the shareholders which authorisation can be for an indefinite period in the case of a private company which has so determined by elective resolution (s 80A). If an allotment is not authorised, it is still valid (s 80) but the directors are liable to a fine. The directors of Ludlow Ltd (L) should comply with s 89 (pre-emption) in allotting shares, unless they are to be held under an employee share scheme, but failure so to do does not invalidate the allotment. The directors who breached s 89 and L would be liable to compensate those shareholders who were no offered the shares for any loss thereby suffered (s 92). L, being a private company, may have chosen to exclude the right of pre-emption (s 91). If the proposed allotment to employees is at a discount or otherwise not fully paid the allotment remains valid but the allottees would be liable to make up the discount (s 112 although an allottee can be relieved of liability by the court, s 113) and the directors and L would be liable to a fine (s 114).

However, the most likely challenge to the allotment of shares would be the potential take-over bidder. An outsider cannot challenge the validity of the allotment but a shareholder could do so on the basis that the directors, in making the allotment, were not acting for a proper purpose (*Bamford v Bamford* (1970)), ie in breach of fiduciary duty. If the challenge was successful the allotment would be invalid but capable of ratification by the shareholders in general meeting (*Bamford v Bamford* (1970)). A leading case on the improper use of directorial power is the Privy Council decision in *Howard Smith Ltd v Ampol Petroleum Ltd* (1974) which concerned the allotment of shares. In *Ampol* the directors of HS, a company in need of further finance, issued shares to members who held a minority interest in the company but offered none to the majority shareholder (A) who had made an unwanted take-over bid thereby reducing A's shareholding to below 50%. This allotment of shares was challenged by A as an improper use of the directorial power to issue shares. The Privy Council ruled that when a use of power is challenged, the court should first consider the nature of the power, ie why was this power conferred on the directors whose exercise is in question, and then examine the substantial purpose for which it was exercised. If the power was not exercised for the proper purpose the exercise of the power is invalid. The court stated that the decision as to whether the power was properly exercised is determined objectively. In this case the court ruled that the power to allot shares was given to directors to raise funds for the company and that while the directors intended this allotment to raise capital the primary purpose of the issue was to defeat A's bid and not to raise money. Consequently, this allotment was invalid and A, the majority shareholder had no desire to ratify the allotment. This would seem to apply here. Thus, whether E can enforce any contractual right to the shares will depend upon whether the validity of the allotment is challenged and if it is whether the shareholders ratify the actions of the directors.

(c) *Aintree*

E is a minority shareholder in Aintree Ltd (A) and as a shareholder he can enforce any rights conferred upon him as a shareholder. Unfortunately, as a shareholder he would seem to have no individual right to complain about the conduct of the board in letting property to one of their number because, even if it is a breach of fiduciary duty, the directors owe their duty to the company and not to individual shareholders, that is current and future shareholders as a body (*Percival v Wright* (1902)), although a director may voluntarily undertake a fiduciary duty towards a shareholder, for example, by acting as his agent (*Allen v Hyatt* (1914)). There seems no question of E being owed a fiduciary duty as an individual. Section 322 provides that if a transaction between a director and a company is a substantial property transaction it is voidable unless approved by the shareholders in general meeting (a director-shareholder could vote on a resolution to ratify). Approval of such a transaction can be informal, see *Niltan Carson Ltd v Hawthorne* (1988), where knowledge and acquiescence by the majority shareholders was held to constitute approval of the activities of the director. A transaction is a substantial property transaction if a director acquires an interest in a non-cash asset the value of which is over £100,000 or 10% of the asset value of the company (subject to its value exceeding £2,000) which seems likely to be the case here. However, the section provides that an unapproved substantial property transaction is voidable at the instance of the *company*. Thus it seems that E has no *locus* to challenge the lease. If the lease is perceived as in some way a device to defraud the company E might, as an exception to *Foss v Harbottle* (1843), be able to bring a derivative action on behalf of the company but since the lease is at market value the conduct of the board seems unimpeachable. Section 459 might prove a more effective statutory remedy for E if he can establish that the conduct of the directors is unfairly prejudicial to the shareholders. E would seem to have no cause of action in respect of the managing director taking up another business either. Even if such conduct was in breach of the director's service contract, E as a minority shareholder has no right to litigate the matter although he could raise it at a meeting of the company.

(d) *Newbury*

As a minority shareholder in Newbury Ltd (N), E has no *locus* to complain about any lack of care and skill on the part of those members of the board who failed to attend meetings either on his own account or on behalf of the company. The duty of care and skill is not owed to individual shareholders and a want of care and skill does not form an exception to *Foss* in order to allow E to bring a derivative action on behalf of the company. Indeed it can be said that the conduct of the non-executive directors may well not constitute a breach of the duty of care and skill owed by directors. The traditional formulation of the nature and extent of this duty is that given by Romer J in *Re City Equitable Fire Insurance Co Ltd* (1925) in which he held that a director is entitled to leave the day-to-day running of the company to the officials of the company and is entitled to assume, in the absence of suspicious circumstances, that such officials are performing their duties honestly. Consequently, failure to prevent fraud by the absconding director, unless the circumstances gave rise to suspicion which was not followed up, is unlikely to be actionable even by the company. The absconding director is liable to reimburse the company and any director who knowingly assisted his acquisition of corporate assets would be liable to the company. Such conduct, were it to present, would be an unratifiable breach of a director's duty thus allowing E to sue on behalf of the company.

Question 21

Murphy Motors Ltd has a share capital of £1,000 £1 shares (of which 960 have been issued) and its net assets have never exceeded £50,000. Its directors are Alice and Bashir who between them hold 470 shares and Corin who holds 490 shares.

The company wished to extend its premises in order to develop the sales side of the business and duly purchased land from Alice for this purpose. Alice, who had owned the land for some years, made a profit of £75,000 on the sale.

As part of its business Murphy Motors provided chauffeur driven limousines for weddings and other functions. Bashir, who was a member of the local council, heard at a council meeting that the council had decided to dispose of the Mayor's car and rely on a hired limousine service when required. Bashir persuaded Murphy Motors to sell him one of its older limousines (for market value) and successfully negotiated a contract to provide a limousine service for the Mayor.

In early 1995, Corin sold his shares to a friend, Devinder, who, on discovering these transactions protested to Alice and Bashir. Alice and Bashir then allotted the remaining shares to themselves and passed an ordinary resolution approving their actions.

Advise Devinder.

Answer plan

As usual in questions involving alleged wrong-doing by directors there are two issues. First, has D any locus to complain about these incidents and second, are the actions of the directors in breach of duty.

Answer

Originally A, B and C were the shareholders and directors of this company. C, and now D, was a majority shareholder capable of passing an ordinary resolution on his own while the last 40 shares remain unallotted. A and B or C (or D) all have the power to block a special resolution but no-one can pass such a resolution on his or her own. If A and B have validly allotted the remaining shares to themselves they can pass an ordinary resolution (but not a special resolution) and D can no longer do so. Hence one complaint made by D could involve the allotment of shares. In addition D has already raised the question of the sale of land to the company by a director and the actions of Bashir in providing limousine services for the mayor. First, can D bring an action against the directors either on his own behalf or on behalf of the company?

(a) Can Devinder sue?

D can sue in his own right if the directors owed him a duty which they have broken. Potential litigants such as D have two cases with which to contend. *Percival v Wright*, which provides that the board in exercising its powers (or duties) is generally responsible to the company and not to individual shareholders (or creditors or the employees) and *Foss v Harbottle*, which held that a breach of duty owed to a company can be litigated only by the company. In *Percival v Wright* (1902), the directors of a company were privy to confidential information which, once released, was likely to increase the value of the company's shares. Percival, a shareholder, offered to sell his shares to the directors who accepted his offer. When the confidential information was released, P sought to have the contract of sale set aside and to recover the shares on the ground that the lack of disclosure was a breach of fiduciary duty by the directors. Swinfen-Eady J, in rejecting P's claim, held that the directors did not, simply by being directors, owe a fiduciary duty to an individual shareholder; they did owe such a duty to the company but they had not broken it. This case remains the law despite being the subject of fierce criticism. Hence, a director owes fiduciary and other duties to his company by virtue of his office but owes none to a shareholder or creditor on that basis. Since A and B do not seem to have undertaken any personal duty towards D he has no locus to complain as a shareholder other than by using the statutory remedies contained in ss 459 and s 122(1)(g) Insolvency Act 1986.

Should D seek to sue on behalf of the company, *Foss* becomes crucial since it provides that the proper plaintiff to enforce the rights of the company is the company itself. Since the power to litigate on behalf of the company will normally reside in the board (by virtue of art 70 or its equivalent) the directors would appear to be able to determine whether to sue themselves in respect of wrongs which they have done to the company. A and B, for example, are unlikely to sue themselves. If, However, D exercises his power to sack the board (s 303) he can then appoint new directors, for example himself, and the new board could pursue A and B for their alleged wrong-doing. If the allotment of shares is valid then D cannot sack A and B and if he wishes to pursue them on behalf of the company he must bring himself within an exception to *Foss*. Such an action is called a derivative action. For D to bring a derivative action is an unattractive proposition, he would to pay for the litigation (although the courts have the power to order the company to indemnify the shareholder – *Wallersteiner v Moir* (1974)) and any remedy which is ordered accrues to the company and not D. Moreover, it is not that easy to establish that an exception to *Foss* has arisen. To do so D need to establish a *prima facie* case of fraud on the part of those in control of the company and unless such a case is established he must be denied locus (*Prudential Assurance v Newman Industries* (1981)). Fraud in this context extends beyond legal fraud to embrace an apparent lack of probity (equitable fraud). Hence, in *Daniels v Daniels* (1978), where legal fraud was not alleged, a sale of a corporate asset to a director at a price which appeared to be substantially below its market value was held to fall within the exception in that, while simple negligence could not form the basis of an exception to *Foss*, a sale at an undervalue which had benefited a director to the extent of £115,000 could be treated as equitable fraud. There is also a problem establishing control in this case since D has a majority shareholding unless the allotment is valid. Even if A and B do have control has their conduct been fraudulent?

(b) *The conduct of the directors*

When a company is registered the shareholders of the company possess the authority to determine how the company will operate and be operated and they are not required to bestow all or any of their powers on the board of directors. The shareholders generally give away their power to run the company in the articles but the degree of delegation is a matter for the shareholders to determine either in the articles or subsequently. In practice, most companies adopt Table A, art 70 which effectively gives the power to operate the company, which would otherwise be vested in the shareholders in general meeting, to the directors. Consequently, the shareholders (majority or minority) cannot complain if the directors exercise the powers which have been delegated to them unless the articles of the company, or other provision giving power to the directors, restrict the apparently unfettered use of such powers. The articles can, of course, be changed by special resolution (s 9) but this will not avail D since even if the allotment is bad he cannot pass a special resolution. There are, however, restrictions upon the ability of the board to run the company as they see fit and directors who upset their shareholders can be dismissed by ordinary resolution (s 303) which, as already mentioned, D could achieve if the allotment is ruled to be invalid.

Fiduciary duties can be sub-divided into the general and the applied. The general duties cast on a director consist of an obligation to act *bona fide* in exercising his powers and a requirement that certain powers are used only for 'proper purposes'. Thus A and B must exercise their powers not only honestly but also for a purpose consistent with that for which the powers were conferred on him. A leading case in point is the Privy Council decision in *Howard Smith Ltd v Ampol Petroleum Ltd* (1974) in which an allotment of shares made principally for a non-proper purpose (beating off a take-over rather than raising capital) was held to be invalid. This would seem to suggest that D could have the allotment set aside and even though such an allotment is ratifiable he can block ratification. If the allotment is invalid D can sack the directors but this does not help the company in any quest for compensation. Note in passing that the power of A and B to allot shares must have been specifically conferred upon them by the articles or a special resolution (s 80) but even if they lacked this power the allotment is not invalidated – A and B would be liable to a fine.

In addition to the general obligations A and B are required to put the interests of the company before his own interests. This responsibility has given rise to a number of areas of litigation some of which have been supplemented by statutory provisions. An obvious source of conflict between corporate duty and personal interest concerns corporate contracts which directly or indirectly benefit the director. The House of Lords in *Aberdeen Railway Co v Blaikie Bros* (1854) ruled that a director could not benefit directly or indirectly from a contract made by his company. This has been modified to provide that a director cannot benefit from a contract between himself and his company or between his company and a third party without making adequate disclosure of his own interest in that contract. Disclosure should be to the shareholders unless the articles allow disclosure to the board; Table A, art 85, which this company has, permits disclosure to the board. Section 317 provides rules for the nature of the disclosure to the board. Thus, if A disclosed her interest in the land which she sold to the company in accordance with the articles and s 317 the sale appears to be valid. Perhaps because disclosure to the board might allow a cosy cartel among directors certain sections impose further obligations in respect of particular contracts upon directors. The relevant section in this case is s 322. Section 322 provides that if a transaction between a director and a company is a substantial property transaction it is voidable unless approved by the shareholders in general meeting (a director-shareholder could vote on a resolution to ratify). The transaction is clearly a substantial property transaction since A, a director, sold to the company a non-cash asset which exceeded in value 10% of the asset value of the company. But shareholder-approval of such a transaction can be informal, see *Niltan Carson Ltd v Hawthorne* (1988), where knowledge and acquiescence by the majority shareholders was held to constitute approval of the activities of the director. Thus, even if this transaction is a substantial property transaction A, B and C might have informally approved it. It should also be noted that the purchase of lands to develop sales could, but is unlikely to be, *ultra vires*, in which case the board exceeded its powers in buying the land and s 322A renders the purchase voidable. B's purchase of the car could be subject to similar analysis to the land sale albeit it could not be *ultra vires*.

Turning to B. The general duty to put corporate interest above private profit is augmented in respect of corporate property; in common with a trustee, a director cannot, without the unanimous approval of the shareholders, appropriate (even innocently) corporate property. If he does so appropriate he is liable as a constructive trustee. It is obvious that if a director appropriates the company's tangible property he will be liable to return the property to the company. The same is true of appropriation of intangible corporate assets, for example the benefit of a contract possessed by the company. This liability for misappropriation is extended to commercial opportunities which are within the company's grasp. For example, in *Cook v Deeks* (1916), a company, X, was about to sign a contract to build a railway when the railway company was persuaded by some of the directors of X to award the contract to a new company which they had formed. The directors were held liable to hold the benefit of the contract as constructive trustees for X. Misappropriation of corporate assets is an unratifiable breach of directors duty. Could the possible contracting out of mayoral transport of which B, as a councillor, becomes aware be regarded as a corporate opportunity – it seems unlikely since there was no question of Murphy's being about to get the contract. There is further fiduciary duty. This fiduciary duty provides that a director should not benefit from his position as director at the expense of the company. This is not an absolute prohibition so that a director can benefit from his position if there is no real conflict of interest. However, B did not become aware of the new opportunity by virtue of being a director but because he was a councillor. Perhaps it can be said that he had a duty to pass on relevant information to the company, however he acquired it, where there was an obvious conflict of interests between personal interest and company profit. Such a view would seem to be consistent with *dicta* in *IDC v Cooley* (1972). If B can be said to have benefitted from his position the profit made by him can only be retained by him if the company by ordinary resolution so decrees (*Regal (Hastings) Ltd v Gulliver* (1942)).

In addition B's conduct in acting as a rival to Murphy's is a clear breach of his duty as a director. Again his actions seem to be ratifiable.

Undoubtedly, D's best course of action is to get rid of A and B and seek to recover damages or an account of profits from A and B. He might also be advised not to buy shares from C again.

Question 22

The board of Kington Ltd, which consists of Cecil, Dot and Dash, have authority to issue shares and the articles of the company exclude the right of pre-emption. Cecil is also a non-executive director of Pembridge Ltd, a company in the same line of business as Kington which owns 14% of Kington's shares. Anson plc purchased 26% of Kington's shares from the founder of the company on the understanding that if any further shares were created they would be allotted to Anson to facilitate its eventual acquisition of the company. The remaining 60% of the Kington shares are owned by the James family who proposed Dot and Dash as directors. Kington is short of work and the board hope to sell its business to Pembridge. If the deal goes ahead Dot and Dash would join the Pembridge board, but 50% of the Kington workforce would be made redundant. The board recommended acceptance of a take-over bid by Pembridge and members of the James family who hold 30% of the Kington shares have agreed to sell out to Pembridge. The directors of Kington propose to create a further ordinary shares and allot them to Pembridge for cash thus giving Pembridge 53.3% of Kington's share capital; Anson's shareholding would be reduced to 21.6%.

Advise Anson.

Answer plan

Anson would oppose the plan for two reasons, first the reduction in their shareholding to a figure below that capable of blocking a special resolution and second, the destruction of its hopes of taking over Kington. Anson has a number of lines of attack. Consider:

(a) the allotment of shares – improper purpose, variation of class rights, s 459;

(b) the role of the Kington board;

(c) the non-supporting members of the James family.

Try to marry practical as well as legal advice.

Answer

Anson (A) has three choices open to it when faced with the proposals made by the board of Kington (K). It could launch a rival bid to that made by Pembridge (P), offer to sell its shares to P or try to destroy or modify the current proposals. Even if it was to launch a rival bid there is no guarantee that it would be successful and there may be practical reasons not to proceed with such a plan, for example lack of funds. An offer to sell shares to P might be rejected and may not be in line with A's business plans. It should be noted that P have no right to force A to sell. However, if P had made an offer for all the shares in K and its offer had been accepted by holders of 90% of the shares, ss 428–430F permit P to acquire the remaining shares compulsorily and these sections also give a right to the holder of the unpurchased shares to be bought out. Where shares are purchased under the provisions of ss 428–430F the price payable is that offered to those who have accepted the offer. Obviously P cannot obtain 90% of the shares without A's agreement. If A does not wish to make a counter offer or to sell its shares it may wish to oppose the proposed scheme, can it do so?

(a) *The allotment of shares*

A company which has issued its full complement of shares can increase its share capital, if authorised by its articles (Table A, art 32 so authorises), in accordance with s 121. Section 121 permits a company to increase share capital by ordinary resolution, thus A cannot block the creation of further shares. In issuing shares, directors must comply with the provisions of the Act and their own fiduciary obligations. Section 80 provides that the power to allot shares can be exercised by the directors only if they have been authorised so to act either in the articles or by a resolution of the shareholders which authorisation can be for an indefinite period in the case of a private company which has so determined by elective resolution (s 80A). Hence, the board of K have the necessary authority. K has excluded the right of pre-emption, which as a private company it is permitted to do (s 91), so that shares do not have to be offered to existing shareholders. The proposed allotment is for cash at, it is assumed, a non-discounted price. The requirements of the Act appear to be satisfied.

The validity of the allotment is more likely to be questioned on the basis that the directors, in making this allotment, were not acting properly. Directors are not required to obtain the highest possible price for any shares allotted (provided there is no discount) but in choosing to allot shares the directors are subject to the fiduciary duty – to exercise the power for a proper purpose (*Bamford v Bamford* (1970)). An improper allotment is invalid and capable of challenge by A even though such an allotment is ratifiable by ordinary resolution (contra *Foss v Harbottle* (1843)). If the allotment is ratified before any court action is brought, the court would refuse to hear A's application. Is the allotment by the director's of K in breach of their fiduciary duty? Consider the Privy Council decision in *Howard Smith Ltd v Ampol Petroleum Ltd* (1974) which concerned the allotment of shares. In *Ampol* the directors of HS, a company in need of further finance, issued shares to members who held a minority interest in the company but offered none to the majority shareholder (A), who had made an unwanted take-over bid, thereby reducing A's shareholding to below 50%. This allotment of shares was challenged by A as an improper use of the directorial power to issue shares. The Privy Council ruled that when a use of power is challenged, the court should first consider the nature of the power, ie why was this power conferred on the directors whose exercise thereof is in question, and then examine the substantial purpose for which it was exercised. If the power was not exercised for the proper purpose the exercise of the power is invalid. The court stated that the decision as to whether the power was properly exercised is determined objectively. In this case the court ruled that the power to allot shares was given to directors to raise funds for the company and that while the directors intended this allotment to raise capital the primary purpose of the issue was to defeat A's bid and not to raise money. Consequently, this allotment was invalid and A, the majority shareholder had no desire to ratify the allotment. This would seem to apply here with the proviso that A, without the help of at least some of the James family, cannot block ratification. On a vote to ratify, the disputed shares do not vote. The fact that the employees of K would be adversely affected by the take-over would tend to support the impropriety of the allotment (s 309) although an attempt to allot shares to preserve, *bona fide*, workers jobs has been held to be improper (*Hogg v Cramphorn Ltd* (1967)).

If A cannot block the allotment of shares by raising the validity of the director's acts it may seek to do so on the basis that it had an agreement that any new shares would be allotted to it and that failure to do so is breach of contract or a variation of its class rights. If there is a valid contract between Kington and Anson relating to the allotment of shares it would seem to give A a contractual right to the new shares but it is described as an understanding and it may be difficult to enforce as a contract. The understanding might be deemed to be a class right and where a company proposes to vary the rights attaching to a class of shares it must comply with its own internal procedures and the provisions of ss 125–127. A faces two difficulties. First, can its parcel of ordinary shares be regarded as a class distinct from the other ordinary shares and second, is the dilution of its shareholding and the disregard of its understanding a variation of any class right. In *Cumbria Newspapers Group Ltd v Cumberland and Westmoreland Herald Ltd* (1987), Scott J postulated three situations. First, where there are rights attaching to a particular group of shares, second where rights were conferred on a shareholder in his capacity as a shareholder (as in the *Cumbria* case), and third, where rights were conferred on a particular individual. Only the first two categories create class rights – applying this case A might have class rights if the understanding could be called a right conferred on A in its capacity as a shareholder. If this is not the case the mere fact that there are two opposing groups of shareholders is unlikely to be regarded as creating two classes of share (see the Court of Appeal decision in *Greenhalgh v Arderne Cinemas* (1946)). Indeed, even if A can be treated as constituting a separate class of ordinary shareholder, the diminution in voting strength is unlikely to be seen as a variation of class rights. In *Greenhalgh v Arderne Cinemas* (1946), G's ordinary shares had been sub-divided into 5 thereby quintupling his votes. The company then proposed similarly to sub-divide the rest of the ordinary shares thereby affecting the efficacy of G's votes and, as here, depriving him of negative voting control. The Court of Appeal held that provided the rights attaching to G's shares remained the same (they did, he was not losing votes) there was no variation of his class rights notwithstanding the fact that the result was to alter the voting equilibrium of the shareholders. *Greenhalgh* was distinguished by Foster J in *Clemens v Clemens Bros Ltd* (1976) on non-existent grounds. In *Clemens*, the majority shareholder

(55%), who was the dominant director, authorised the allotment of shares to other directors thereby depriving the minority shareholder (45%) of her negative voting control. The judge set the allotment aside. While this case has parallels with A's position, there is an important distinction. In *Clemens* the disputed allotment was made by the majority shareholder and the judge felt able to classify the allotment as a breach of the fiduciary duty imposed on a shareholder. A should be warned that it is unlikely that *Clemens* will be followed here. If there is no variation of class rights ss 125–127 do not apply. A should argue that the understanding does create a separate class of shares and that the allotment is a variation which must be approved by the appropriate majority of the relevant class (in compliance with s 125). Since A is the sole member of the class the majority will not be forthcoming.

A will be best advised to challenge the validity of the allotment under s 459. This section provides that a shareholder can seek an order that a proposed act of the company would be unfairly prejudicial to him and, if successful, the court can make such order as it thinks fit (s 461). There has been something of a torrent of case law on this provision and it has proved a flexible tool in judicial hands for the righting of injustice to minority shareholders. Section 459 provides a remedy independent of the existence (or lack) of any other remedy provided there has been unfair prejudice although remedy is at the court's discretion. Cases have shown that an attempt to dilute the voting strength of a shareholding may be unfairly prejudicial (see *Re OC (Transport) Ltd* (1984)) even if, as in this case, not in breach of company law. A court would consider the basis on which A acquired its shares – did A have a legitimate expectation that it would retain negative voting control, if so any dilution is likely to be unfairly prejudicial – or had A done anything to justify deprivation of negative voting control. If unfair prejudice is proven the court could order A to be bought out at a fair price, could require shares to be allotted to A to preserve the voting equilibrium or could allow A to take K over, although the last remedy is unlikely.

(b) *The conduct of the directors*

A may feel aggrieved by the conduct of the board of K. Cecil is a director of P already and Dot and Dash are to join the board of

Pembridge and all three have recommended acceptance of the P bid. Surprisingly, being a director of two rival companies (P and K are in the same field) is not a breach of director's duty (*London & Mashonaland Exploration Co Ltd v New Mashonaland Exploration Co Ltd* (1891)) but it is clear that rival directorships are not a breach of duty by a director only when the director is not involved in management at all. In the recent case of *Conran* (1993), the court held that it would be difficult to envisage a situation where a person who was a director of two competing companies would not be in breach of his duty of loyalty and good faith if he took any part in running either company. However, this potential breach of fiduciary duty by Cecil is actionable by the company and not by A (*Foss v Harbottle* (1843)).

The directors of K in recommending P's take-over bid probably owe a duty to individual shareholders and not, as is usual, merely to the company. Whether this is because the directors by offering advice have voluntarily undertaken a duty towards shareholders (akin to *Allen v Hyatt* (1914)) or whether it is because directors automatically owe a duty to current shareholders as the manifestation of the company in a take-over context in not clear. The duty seems to be one of honesty and fair dealing – putting the case for the bid fairly (*Gething v Kilner* (1972)) and there is no requirement to support the highest bid (*Dawson International plc v Coats Paton plc* (1988)) although the board should do nothing to prevent members getting the best possible price (*Heron International v Lord Grade* (1983)). If the duty is owed to the shareholders is broken the breach is actionable by the shareholders; in *Gething* the judge ordered the withdrawal of a misleading circular issued to shareholders but in other cases it has been suggested, *obiter*, that damages could be awarded. If the directors of K could be said to be in a special relationship with their shareholders it would be possible to impose liability under *Hedley Byrne v Heller* (1964) but the assessment of damages in the case of a private company would be difficult.

(c) *Conclusion*

Apart from the legal advice offered to A, it would be well-advised to seek to mobilise the James family to block the allotment of shares and promise that if it is not yet in a position to make a bid it will soon do so at a price better than that of P (not that such a promise would be enforceable). Alternatively, sell out to P if the price is right rather than risk being a minority shareholder in a hostile environment.

Question 23

Sell-U-Home Ltd, which operates a chain of estate agents, has a subsidiary, Fix-U-Up Ltd, which offers financial services to homebuyers. Julian, a director of Sell-U-Home, asks Fix-U-Up to enter into the following transactions:

(a) To lend Julian £75,000 to enable him and his wife to purchase a holiday home;

(b) To pay Julian's monthly account at a local hotel (where he frequently entertains clients) on the understanding that Julian will repay Fix-U-Up in respect of any private use of the hotel;

(c) To guarantee a hire-purchase contract under which Julian's son, Sandy, is to acquire a car.

Advise the directors of Fix-U-Up, which is in a shaky financial state, as to whether it may comply with Julian's requests and, if so, with what conditions must it comply.

Answer plan

A question which would only be set for students with access to the relevant statutory material, in which case it is relatively straightforward. Statutory interpretation is all that is required and the question could even be tackled by a student who had done no revision on this area but knew there are statutory provisions on loans. Consider:

(a) any general points on director's duties; and

then in respect of the three situations, consider:

(b) is the proposal prohibited?

(c) if so, does an exception apply?

(d) what are the conditions for the operation of an exception?

(e) consequences of no exception or non-compliance with conditions in (c)

Answer

The directors of the subsidiary company, Fix-U-Up (F), have an unfettered discretion to run the company as they see fit. However, they are, in law, required to comply with instructions given to them by their shareholders by special resolution, and, in practice, may feel it prudent to comply with the wishes of a director of their (one assumes) major shareholder, Sell-U-Home (S). In exercising their powers, the directors of F must comply with the usual duties imposed upon directors particularly the obligation to act *bona fide* in the interests of F and to exercise their powers for proper purposes. Failure to comply with these fiduciary duties could result in action by F, but since F is controlled by S this is unlikely unless Julian was acting without the approval of S or the remainder of its board. If F were to go into liquidation the Liquidator would also have the power to sue the directors of F for breach of fiduciary duty (eg acting for an improper purpose in making these 'loans') and it would be no defence to an action that they complied with the unofficial instructions of Julian although this might allow the court to relieve them from the consequences of their actions (s 727). Indeed these loans might be seen as wrongful trading by the directors and if F were to go into insolvent liquidation, the Liquidator could seek contribution from the directors to swell the company's assets (s 214 Insolvency Act 1986).

In addition to the general duties imposed on directors, ss 330–346 has specific provisions dealing with loans and related transactions. These sections restrict the ability of a company to make loans (or guarantee a loan) to a director of the company, or a director of a holding company, or to a shadow director (s 330(1)). Further, where the company is a relevant company the prohibition is extended to quasi-loans and credit transactions (or guarantees thereof) to the same people or to a person 'connected' to such a person (s 330(2)). A company is a relevant company is either a public company or is a member of a group one of whose members is a public company (s 331). F and S are not public companies (both bear the name Ltd) but it is possible that there is a further company in their group which is a public company so that the possibility that F is a relevant company cannot be excluded even though it seems unlikely. A connected person includes a spouse and children under the age of 18 (s 346) of a director of a company so that Julian's son may be a connected person. Perhaps the purchase of a car would tend to suggest a child who may be over 18 and, consequently, not connected. Julian's wife (see (a)) is a connected person. J may also be deemed to be a shadow director of F since he seems to be a person on whose instructions the board of F are accustomed to act and the rules on loans apply to shadow directors.

Turning to the three proposals to be considered by the board of F.

(a) *The loan to Julian and his wife*

Section 330 provides that a company shall not make a loan to a director of a holding company. Julian is such a director and his wife is a connected person so the loan, unless it falls within an exception, is prohibited. The consequences of such a loan are that the transaction would be voidable at F's behest unless restitution of money or any asset which is the subject of the transaction is impossible, or the company has been indemnified, or restitution would affect the rights of a *bona fide* purchaser for value (s 341). This would allow F to recover the money, if lent, from Julian and his wife. Section 341 also provides that a director (or connected person) who authorised the loan must account to the company making the loan for any gain made as a result of the loan and indemnify the company against loss. Thus, if the loan was made, the holiday home bought and then resold at a profit, the profit would be payable to F. There are exemptions from liability – one which might apply here is s 341(5) which exempts from liability any director or connected person did not know the circumstances which constituted a contravention of the Act. This applies to persons who do not know the *circumstances* which were the contravention, not knowing about the relevant law is not a defence. There are also criminal penalties (fine and or imprisonment) for breach of s 330 but only where the lending company is a relevant company. The criminal penalties apply to the company, to the directors of the company or any person (Julian here) who procures the illegal transaction.

Section 330 provides that a loan to a director may fall within one of the exemptions in ss 332–338. The only section which might be relevant is s 338. This provides that a loan made by a money-lending company may be exempted from s 330. Section 338(2) defines a money-lending company as a company whose ordinary business includes the making of loans. F is a company which offers financial services to homebuyers and as such it may make loans. However, if it organises loans from third parties, for example, building societies, and arranges security for loans, for example, endowment policies, it would seem not to be *making* loans but facilitating loans and not a money-lending company. Even if F is a money-lending company, the loan is not exempt unless s 338(3) is complied with – the loan must be made in the ordinary course of business (this seems unlikely here) and the loan must be on the same terms as that which would be made to a non-director applicant of the same financial standing as Julian (one could be called 'standard loan terms'). A non-relevant company can lend an unlimited amount under this provision but a relevant company is limited to loans of up to £100,000 unless it is a banking company (which F is not). The second condition set out in s 338(2) (the 'standard loan terms') does not necessarily apply where the money is lent for the purchase or improvement of a house (s 338(6). However, this derestriction will no apply to Julian since it is limited to loans for the purchase etc of the director's only or main residence.

An exempt transaction must be revealed in the accounts of the company.

(b) *Julian's monthly account*

Payment of Julian's monthly account is not a loan and is, thus, not prohibited at all under s 330(1) although it may be a breach of fiduciary duty by the director's of F to enter into such a transaction. In addition, there will be tax to pay on the benefit received by Julian. If F is a relevant company, the payment may be prohibited by s 330(2) which provides that a relevant company cannot make a quasi-loan to a director of a holding company. A quasi-loan is defined in s 331(2) to include an agreement whereby a person (F in this case) agrees to pay a sum to a third party (the hotel), expenditure incurred by another (Julian), for which the company will be reimbursed. Thus, Julian's private usage of the hotel which the company pays for and which he has agreed to reimburse is a quasi-loan. The business usage of the hotel would not be a quasi-loan since Julian has not agreed, and is not liable, to reimburse F for this sum although s 337 would apply. Section 337 provides that providing a director with funds to meet business expenses (or reimbursement thereof) does not fall within s 330 provided that there is adequate disclosure in advance of the provision of funds (matters to be disclosed are set out in the Act) and the transaction is approved by ordinary resolution. Failure to make adequate disclosure or failure to approve results in the money being repayable by the director. Relevant companies are limited in the amount of expenditure outstanding at any one time which it can reimburse (currently £20,000). Should F be paying for Julian to entertain clients of S anyway – perhaps there is an improper purpose issue here? The consequences of making a prohibited quasi-loan are the same as for a loan (see above) but since liability can arise only if F is a relevant company, the criminal penalties may be issue.

The quasi-loan will be exempt from s 330 if an exception applies. Section 332 states that a quasi-loan which (including any other quasi-loan) is for less than £5,000 and which is repayable within two months of it being incurred – this seems likely to be the case here. Arguably s 338 would also apply if F was a money-lending company (see above).

An exempt transaction must be revealed in the accounts of the company.

(c) *Guarantee of the hire-purchase contract*

If Sandy is over 18 he is not a connected person and whether the transaction should be approved by the board of F depends upon the power of F to guarantee hire-purchase contracts (ie it is a question of *ultra vires*), the ambit of the powers of the board, and whether this a proper purpose. If S is a connected person, the guarantee of a credit transaction (which includes a hire-purchase contract, s 331(4)) is prohibited if F is a relevant company (s 330(4)). This seems improbable but not impossible. The usual penalties apply in such a case unless the guarantee is exempt. There seems to be one section which could exempt the guarantee – s 335 (s 338 does not apply to guarantees of credit transactions, s 334 only applies to loans of small amounts to directors). Section 335 provides that s 330(4) does not apply a transaction entered into by the company in the ordinary course of business and it is made on the same terms as would be offered to an applicant who was not connected with the company. It seems unlikely that F's business ordinarily includes the guaranteeing of such contracts as this.

(d) *Ability to sue*

Failure to comply with these statutory duties could result in a civil action. However, since the power to sue is vested in F, and F is controlled by S, such an action is unlikely unless Julian was acting without the approval of S. If F were to go into liquidation the Liquidator would also have the power to sue the directors of F for breach of the Act and it would be no defence to an action that they complied with the instructions of Julian although this might allow the court to relieve them from the consequences of their actions (s 727).

Question 24

Certain persons, notably directors, are in a position to gain valuable information about a company. To what extent, if at all, does the law prevent such persons from using that information for their own personal profit?

Answer plan

A general question requiring a student to select information carefully and not simply reproduce vast amounts of information. It is important to consider both the civil and the criminal law in this context.

Answer

While this question is not limited to directors it is obvious that directors are a group well placed to acquire valuable information about their company so that it is directors who are primarily considered. All companies are required by law to have at least one director (s 282), public companies must have at least two and Table A provides that all companies shall have at least two directors unless the company determines otherwise by ordinary resolution (art 64). A single director cannot also be the company secretary. Limitations on the ability of a director (or others) to use information gained by virtue of his connection with the company fall into two principal categories – criminal sanctions and civil penalties – although there are other minor constraints.

Criminal law

Information about companies is an important factor in determining the value of company shares, such information is available to those closely connected with the company giving them the opportunity to deal in the shares of the company before that information is generally known. Use of inside information (insider dealing) is generally regarded as reprehensible. First, in that it lowers investor confidence in the Stock Exchange (though not all condemn insider dealing on this ground). Second, because insider dealing may constitute fraud on the shareholders, for example if they are persuaded to sell their shares to the directors at an undervalue relative to the value of the shares once the information known to the directors is widely known. Where fraud is provable, which is difficult, directors who defraud shareholders can be prosecuted. More importantly, the Criminal Justice Act 1993 (which replaces earlier legislation) makes insider dealing a criminal offence. While fraud is difficult to prove it is wider in its scope than the Criminal Justice Act (hereafter the CJ Act) which does not apply to unlisted securities, ie shares in private companies and shares in unquoted public companies, or face-to-face, as opposed to market, dealings.

The CJ Act provides that if a person deals in securities (the Act covers dealings in things other than shares, eg gilts) listed on a regulated market, for example the Stock Exchange, he is guilty of an offence if he is -

(a) an insider (or a tippee); and
(b) privy to specific and precise information which relates to the shares themselves or the state of the company which issued them; and
(c) the information has not been made public; and
(d) the information is of the sort which, if it had been made public, would be likely to have had a significant effect on the share price; and
(e) the dealing is intended to make a profit or prevent a loss.

The definition of insider includes directors and a tippee is a person who has obtained information, directly or indirectly, from an insider. Liability under the CJ Act is entirely criminal and no civil remedy is available to shareholders who have sold shares little knowing that the purchaser was privy to inside knowledge which might have affected the share price. Experience of the previous provisions concerning insider dealing suggest that a rush of criminal cases cannot be anticipated. The rules requiring a director to disclose any interest in the shares of the company aid any investigation of a director's share dealing.

In addition to the criminal penalties under the CJ Act, the Stock Exchange Code for Securities Transactions, which forms part of the Listing Agreement, limits the right of a director a company to deal in its shares and requires disclosure of all authorised dealings.

Civil law

Directors, and possibly senior employees, have a fiduciary relationship with their but are not to be equated with trustees. As Lord Porter put it in *Regal (Hastings) Ltd v Gulliver* (1942), 'Directors, no doubt, are not trustees, but they occupy a fiduciary position towards the company whose board they form'. As a fiduciary each director is automatically, individually subject to equitable duties – fiduciary duties – which require him to exercise his powers in a way which has regard to the interests of the person to whom the duties are owed and not to abuse his position of trust and influence within the company. In addition to this automatic fiduciary duty which attaches to a director in all he does and at all times (*IDC v Cooley* (1972)), a director may, in particular circumstances, incur further duties. For example, a director-employee owes to the company the duty of loyalty and good faith which is imposed on all employees and in respect of corporate property the director's duty can be equated with that of a trustee, a director cannot, without the unanimous approval of the shareholders, derive any benefit (even innocently) from any use of corporate property. Fiduciary and other duties are owed to the company, that is current and future shareholders as a body, and not to individual shareholders (*Percival v Wright* (1902) a case on use of insider information). In *Percival v Wright* (1902), the directors of a company were privy to confidential information which, once released, was likely to increase the value of the company's shares. Percival, a shareholder, offered to sell his shares to the directors who accepted the offer. When the confidential information was released, P sought to have the contract of sale set aside and to recover the shares on the ground that the lack of disclosure was a breach of fiduciary duty by the directors. Swinfen-Eady J, in rejecting P's claim, held that the directors did not, simply by being directors, owe a fiduciary duty to an individual shareholder; they did owe such a duty to the company. This case remains the law despite being the subject of fierce criticism but it does not preclude a director being found to have chosen to undertake some responsibility to a shareholder (fiduciary or contractual). For example, in *Allen v Hyatt* (1914), the directors induced the shareholders to give them options to purchase shares without disclosing the possibility that the directors would be able to re-sell the shares at a profit. The Privy Council found that the directors had by their words and actions made themselves agents for each shareholder and owed the usual obligations of an agent to his principal. These obligations include a duty to account for any benefits accruing from the agency so that the directors had to account for the profits they had made on the exercise of the options and the subsequent re-sale of the shares.

To what extent do the duties imposed on directors and owed to the company impinge upon their ability to use information obtained by virtue of their position for their own profit? The civil law, unlike the CJ Act, makes no distinction between public and private companies nor is the law limited to market dealings in the shares of a company. Consider three categories:

(a) obligations akin to trusteeship;
(b) fiduciary duties;
(c) director-employee duties.

(a) *Trusteeship*

In common with a trustee, a director cannot, without the unanimous approval of the shareholders, use corporate property to make a personal profit. A director who does use corporate property to make such a profit is a constructive trustee of any benefit derived for the company. This constructive trusteeship can also be imposed on a third party who has knowingly received, or knowingly assisted in the misuse of, corporate property. It is obvious that if a director appropriates the company's tangible property, however innocently, he will be liable to return the property to the company. The same is true of appropriation of intangible corporate assets, for example the benefit of a contract entered into by the company. This liability for misappropriation has been extended to commercial opportunities which are within the company's grasp. For example, in *Cook v Deeks* (1916), a company, X, was about to sign a contract to build a railway when the railway company was persuaded by some of the directors of X to award the contract to a new company which they had formed. The directors were held liable to hold the benefit of the contract as constructive trustees for X. There seems no reason why a person other than a director should not be subject to a 'trustee' duty where the facts demand it. As yet there is no judicial decision that information alone can be treated as corporate property and thus subject to the 'trustee' duty imposed on a director (or others). The most important case in point is *Boardman v Phipps* (1967), in which the House of Lords considered the liability of a fiduciary (a solicitor) who had used information properly obtained by virtue of his connection with a trust to make a personal profit in dealings in the shares of a company in which the trust had a substantial minority shareholding. In his dealings, the fiduciary, B, had also benefited the trust. The House of Lords required B to account for his profits to the trust because of his breach of fiduciary duty. Some of their Lordships suggested, *obiter*, that information could be treated as property and if such is the case the obligations of a director in respect of corporate information would not limited to a general fiduciary duty but would be akin to the stricter duty imposed on trustees. Later cases have not yet imposed a stricter duty – see for example, *IDC v Cooley* (1972).

(b) *Fiduciary duties*

What could be called the general fiduciary duty of a director – to act *bona fide* for the benefit of the company – has given rise to specific applications of the duty, particularly the requirement manifestly to put the interests of the company before his own interests. This responsibility has given rise to a number of areas of litigation some of which have been supplemented by statutory provisions. One obvious source of potential conflict between corporate duty and personal interest, in that the director is privy to confidential information by virtue of his office, is corporate contracts. The House of Lords in *Aberdeen Railway Co v Blaikie Bros* (1854) ruled that a director could not benefit directly or indirectly from a contract made by his company. This has been much modified when a director contracts with his company, for example when he enters into a service contract, or a director benefits indirectly from a contract between his company and a third party. Such contracts are now valid if the director adequately discloses his interest in the contract.

The position is less clear when a director benefits by the use of information obtained in his capacity as a director but there is no contract involving the company. Where a director has benefited from his position, liability can be imposed for breach of fiduciary duty but the ambit of this obligation is uncertain. Some cases (see *dicta* in *Regal (Hastings) Ltd v Gulliver* (1942)) suggest that a director must account for any benefit deriving from the use or information gained in a corporate capacity, even if also available elsewhere, but the better view is that a director can benefit from information if there is no real conflict of interest between himself and his company in his use of the information. Where there is a conflict of interest the fact that the company was unlikely to be able to use that information itself does not justify a director using it for his own benefit. For example, in *IDC v Cooley* (1972), C, the managing director of the company was party to negotiations by the company for the design and construction of a gas terminal. It became clear that the company was unlikely to obtain the contract and C feigned illness, resigned his directorship and successfully tendered for the contract on his own account. The judge held C liable to account for the profits he had made on the contract. Even though the company was unlikely to get the contract, C was not entitled to use information concerning it and obtained in corporate service, for his own benefit. In contrast, in *Island Export Finance Ltd v Umunna* (1986), a former director who successfully tendered for a contract with the Cameroon postal authorities was not in breach of his fiduciary duty despite the fact that he had gained useful information and contacts with the authority while negotiating a contract with it on the company's behalf some two years previously. The company had failed to pursue the contacts the director had made or seek further contracts – it had effectively washed its hands of the Cameroons and Hutchinson J saw no reason why the former director should account for his profits to his former company. If a director does use information obtained in a corporate capacity and there is a conflict of interest the profit made by the director can be retained if the company by ordinary resolution so decrees. It is not clear whether a company can absolve a director from liability in advance, rather than relieve him from the consequences of breach thereafter, although *dicta* in *Regal (Hastings) Ltd v Gulliver* (1942), would suggest not. The uncertainty over this issue is widely felt to be unsatisfactory.

(c) *Director-employee duties*

Obligations imposed upon a director as an employee of a company are equally applicable to non-director employees. Employees cannot compete with their employer (*Thomas Marshall (Exporters) Ltd v Guinle* (1978)), even if their is no use of confidential information (*Hivac Ltd v Park Royal Scientific Instruments Ltd* (1946)), nor use or disclose, even after employment has ceased, confidential information obtained in the course of employment. A director who seeks to use confidential information to compete with the company can be restrained by injunction.

Conclusion

While there are many situations where the power of a director to use information obtained in a corporate capacity is subject to legal restraint, it is only when there is someone within the company who is willing and able to pursue the matter that any effective remedy exists. It seems doubtful if directors feel under any great legal restraint and if it is thought appropriate for directors to be limited in their use of corporate information, the current system is of limited efficacy.

Question 25

A friend of yours has been approached by a relative and asked to join the board of the family company. You have no doubts as to your friends honesty and feel he would never act improperly but he lacks any business sense and has no financial expertise. He seeks your advice about such issues as disqualification and the possibility of an action for wrongful trading in the event of the company going into insolvent liquidation. Are there any other risks consequent upon his lack of relevant expertise which you feel you should mention.

Answer plan

This straightforward question divides neatly into three sections:

(a) a discussion of disqualification;
(b) a discussion of wrongful trading;
(c) mention of other actions which can arise if a director fails to display care and skill.

Finally an appraisal of the relative likelihood of all or some of these actions being brought should be made.

Answer

Since your friend is honest any discussion of his liability, if any, in the event of the company going into insolvent liquidation can exclude breach of fiduciary duty which tends to involve a want of probity or fair dealing. He has raised two specific concerns – disqualification and wrongful trading – consider them first.

(a) *Disqualification*

Section 1 Company Directors Disqualification Act 1986 (CDDA), permits a court to disqualify a person from being a director, or being directly or indirectly concerned in the management of a company, in a number of prescribed circumstances. Section 2–6, 8 and 10 CDDA set out the grounds for disqualification; ss 2–5, 8 and 10 give specific grounds – conviction of *indictable* offence in connection with the management of a company, persistent breaches of company legislation, fraud in relation to the running of a company, adverse report by a company inspector etc – but the majority of reported cases involve s 6. Section 6 provides that a person shall be disqualified (for a minimum of two years) from corporate management where he is or has been a director of a company which has become insolvent *and* his conduct as a director of that, or any other company, makes him unfit to be concerned in company management (this second condition also applies to s 8 – adverse report by Inspector). An application for disqualification under any section can be sought by the Secretary of State for Trade and Industry and some sections also confer the ability to disqualify under that section on specified persons. An application under s 6 cannot be heard, unless the court gives leave, more than two years after the company has first become insolvent (as defined in s 6). Acting as a director etc while disqualified is a criminal offence punishable, on indictment, by a fine and/or imprisonment for up to two years.

The crucial question for your friend is whether any incompetence he might display could result in him being disqualified. Judges determining cases on the CDDA, especially s 6, have stressed that the Act, while designed to protect the public and while not a purely penal statute, can result in penal consequences for a disqualified person in that a person may be precluded from trading through a limited company. Indeed even to be the subject of an application for disqualification could have a serious effect on a person's reputation. Consequently, it is not surprising that judges have recognised these possible practical consequences whilst also seeking to give effect to Parliament's intention to limit the activities of unfit directors, in interpreting the Act's provisions. Leaving aside the procedural aspects of the CDDA in what circumstances have the courts exercised their powers of disqualification and the what is the court's view of the appropriate period of disqualification. Guidance is provided by Schedule I of the Act – factors to take into account include breach of fiduciary duty, misuse of assets, responsibility for breaches of mandatory requirements and where the company is insolvent (necessary for s 6), the extent of the director's responsibility for the insolvency.

The leading case on s 6 is *Re Sevenoaks Stationery (Retail) Ltd* (1990). In this case, C, a chartered accountant with an MBA and experience in the City as a merchant banker, had been a director of five companies which had gone into insolvent liquidation between 1983 and 1986 with a total deficit in excess of £650,000. C admitted that he had failed to keep proper books of account, prepare profit and loss accounts or make annual returns; one of the companies had, to his knowledge, traded while insolvent. The Court of Appeal held that the words 'unfit to be concerned in the management of a company' should be treated as ordinary English words which should be simple to apply in most cases. Each case turned on its own facts said the court but a director need not display total incompetence to be unfit. The court approved earlier cases which had held that simple commercial misjudgment should not merit disqualification while a lack of commercial probity and an appropriate degree of incompetence could do so (see, for example, *Re Lo-Line Electric Motors Ltd* (1988)). In *Sevenoaks* five years disqualification ensued. Since each case turns on its own facts your friend cannot be given definite advice about the type of conduct, or lack of action, likely to lead to disqualification but other cases make it clear that leaving everything to others who turn out to have defrauded the company may be enough to render a person 'unfit'. In *Re City Investment Centres Ltd* (1992), the Official Receiver was seeking an order for the disqualification of the three directors, S, D and B, under s 6 based upon the conduct of the directors in connection with City Investment Centres (CIC) and other companies of which they were or had been directors. All the companies were concerned with the 'over-the-counter' market in shares. There was little doubt that S (who was the moving spirit in all these companies) was liable to disqualification and he was duly disqualified for 10 years. D and B sought to escape disqualification by saying that they left all relevant matters to S. D had had 35 years experience as an employee of the Council of the Stock Exchange which included knowledge of disciplinary proceedings – he was called the compliance director. Morritt J had no doubt that D's conduct in allowing CIC to take over the assets and liabilities of other companies controlled by S without proper valuation of the assets (the assets proved illusory, the liabilities were not), allied to the failure of CIC to deliver shares which had been paid for because S had removed funds from the client account without any check by D and his failure to prevent or question CIC lending money to other ailing companies controlled by S compounded by his inadequate supervision of the Unqualified) accounts staff, justified disqualification. The fact that D did not realise that CIC was trading while insolvent and that he relied upon S did not avail him – six years disqualification ordered. B's previous experience had been in connection with marketing and he had no relevant financial experience. He too simply relied upon S's word, when S took money from CIC's accounts he took S's word that it was profit to which S was entitled etc. While it was agreed that B did not know that CIC or other companies in the group were trading while insolvent, he should, said the judge, have known. Morritt J was unimpressed by B's argument that nothing was his fault and that he merely marketed the companies services 'this attitude displays a woeful ignorance of the duties attaching to the office of a director of a company'. B's duty was to question and check where appropriate S's conduct, his failure resulted in considerable loss to the Crown and other creditors – six years disqualification ordered.

The appropriate period for disqualification was discussed in *Sevenoaks* in which Dillon LJ suggested that 10–15 year disqualification should be reserved for particularly serious cases (eg where this was a second disqualification) and two to five years for not very serious cases leaving six to 10 years for serious cases which do not merit the top bracket. Judges have occasionally felt unhappy that two years is the minimum period particularly where incompetence has not been allied to any lack of probity.

(b) *Wrongful trading*

While disqualification would prevent your friend from being a director it would not have direct financial consequences, a finding that a director had engaged in wrongful trading would do so. The concept of wrongful trading was introduced by s 214 Insolvency Act 1986 and it allows a court to declare a director liable to contribute to the assets of the company if the director knew, or ought to have concluded, that there was no reasonable prospect of the company avoiding insolvent liquidation and he did not take every step he ought to have taken to minimise the potential loss to the company's creditors. Thus, on insolvent liquidation the Liquidator can seek a court order for one or more directors of the company to contribute to the assets of the company which will be available to creditors. Section 214 does not authorise an order requiring a director to contribute towards the costs of liquidation or post-liquidation debts. An order is to contribute to the assets of the company and the section does not authorise an order that a particular creditor be paid nor only those creditors whose debts were incurred after the director should have known that the company would go into insolvent liquidation (*Re Purpoint Ltd* (1991)). A director cannot be liable under s 214 unless he both knew or ought to have concluded that insolvency could not be avoided *and* he failed to take every step to minimise loss to creditors which he ought to have taken. The section only envisages the imposition of liability on a director who has not realised what he should have done and has not done what he should have done. In determining whether a director has met the standard expected of him s 214 provides guidance as to the setting of the standard. Sub-section (4) says that a director is to be judged by what a reasonably diligent person with the 'general knowledge, skill and experience that may reasonably be expected of a person carrying out the same functions as are carried out by that director' (ie the director potentially subject to an order) and the 'general knowledge, skill and experience' of the director whom it is sought to make liable. This somewhat obscure provision seems to mean that what a director should have known or done is to be judged by reference to a theoretical director who possesses those skills that may 'reasonably be expected' of a director unless the director is better qualified than this theoretical director when he is to be judged by reference to his own qualifications. The Act is silent as to what qualifications one can reasonably expect from a director. Given that there is no minimum age for a director nor test of competence it could be argued that one cannot reasonably expect a great deal, certainly in *Re Elgindata Ltd* (1991) the judge concluded that poor management was one of the risks which an investor had to bear.

There is only one case which should be drawn to the attention of your friend – *Re Produce Marketing Consortium Ltd* (1989), hereafter *PMC*. In *PMC* the company was engaged in the import of fruit, it traded successfully for some nine to 10 years and remained profitable until 1980. Thereafter, between 1980 and 1984 the company built up an overdraft, and in 1984 had an excess of liabilities over assets and a trading loss. Between 1984 and 1987, when insolvent liquidation ensued, the trading loss continued as did the excess of liabilities over assets but the overdraft approximately halved due to an increase in indebtedness to the company's principal supplier. By February 1987 one of the directors realised that liquidation was inevitable but the company was allowed to trade until October the decision being justified as allowing disposal of the company's supplies of perishable goods which were held in cold-store. The judge found that the directors should have concluded by July 1986 that liquidation was inevitable because, although accounts were not available until January 1987, their knowledge of the business was such that they must have realised that turnover was down and that the gap between assets and liabilities must have increased. Since the Act provides that the directors are to be judged by reference to what they know and what they ought to know Knox J held that they ought to have known the financial results for the year ending 1985 in July 1986 at the latest so that the fact that these results were not known until 1987 was no excuse. Moreover, the directors had failed to take all steps to minimise loss – the directors had not limited their dealings to running down the company's stocks in cold-store even if this was a justified step. Knox J held that both directors must contribute £75,000 to the assets of the company, this being the loss which could have been averted by speedy liquidation. While an action for wrongful trading may be a remote possibility it is potentially extremely disadvantageous. A well-advised friend should check the regularity and accuracy of the management accounts before consenting to be a director. Presumably, non-executive directors are less vulnerable for action under s 214.

(c) *Other risks*

Directors also owe a common law duty of care and skill but it is traditionally very modest. At common law directors are expected to carry out their duties with an appropriate degree of care and skill. The traditional formulation of the nature and extent of this duty is that given by Romer J in *Re City Equitable Fire Insurance Co Ltd* (1925) in which he held that a director:

(a) need display only such skill as may reasonably be expected from a person of his knowledge and experience;
(b) need not give the affairs of the continuous attention; and
(c) is entitled to leave the day-to-day running of the company to the officials of the company and is entitled to assume, in the absence of suspicious circumstances, that such officials are performing their duties honestly.

These propositions remain good law with regard to non-executive directors but executive directors will generally be constrained by their service contracts to devote a set percentage of their time to the affairs of the company. The most important aspect of a director's duty of care relates to the amount of skill he must exercise. Directors are not subject to the Supply of Goods and Services Act 1982 so they need not display reasonable care and skill. It is plain that a director who does his honest best may be held to have exercised sufficient care and skill to evade liability for negligence – the test of liability is subjective and not objective. Certainly your friend can be advised that he need possess no particular skill on appointment (*Re Brazilian Rubber Estates & Plantations Ltd* (1911)) and whether he has been negligent is a question of fact. The courts are beginning to be a little more robust in determining the standard of care which a company can expect (see for example, *Dorchester Finance Co Ltd v Stebbing* (1977)) but the standard still seems rather low. Apart from the modest standard of competence which a director need demonstrate, the ability to sue an errant director is vested in the company and not in individual shareholders so that a director of a solvent company need not fear legal action while he remains on good terms with co-directors.

(d) *Conclusion*

Your friend can be advised that there is little doubt that greater public and Parliamentary scrutiny of the benefits enjoyed by directors can be anticipated. However, given the number of companies (over 1 million) the risk of being a director who is subject to any of the adverse happenings outlined above may seem acceptable.

Question 26

The rules pertaining to the ability of a director to enter into an enforceable contract with the company of which he is a director give shareholders no effective control over such contracts.

Comment on this view.

Answer plan

A relatively straightforward question requiring a summary of the existing rules relating to contracts between a director and his company, the extent to which there is, or is not, effective control and a comment on the desirability of the present situation. The major difficulty in such a question is sticking to the point and not discussing all aspects of the duties imposed on directors and also in gathering together information which may have arisen at different points in a course.

Answer

'Directors, no doubt, are not trustees, but they occupy a fiduciary position towards the company whose board they form' (*Regal (Hastings) Ltd v Gulliver* (1942)). Since a director is not (except when dealing with corporate property) to be treated as a trustee he is not debarred from deriving some benefit from his directorship – most directors are remunerated for their efforts – but, as a fiduciary a director does not have an unfettered right to profit from his position. As a fiduciary each director is individually subject to equitable duties – fiduciary duties – which require him to exercise his powers in a way which has regard to the interests of the person to whom the duties are owed and not to abuse his position of trust and influence within the company. Fiduciary duties are owed to the company, that is current and future shareholders as a body, and not to individual shareholders (*Percival v Wright* (1902)). Consequently, one difficulty faced by a minority shareholder unhappy with contracts between the company and a director is the lack of ability to litigate other than in exceptional circumstances (*Foss v Harbottle* (1843)). The inability to litigate will not matter if there is appropriate control over a director's contracts at an earlier stage, ie when the contract is made. *Foss* does not affect the ability of the company (or a majority shareholder), which has discovered a secret contractual benefit has been made by a director, suing that director.

The general fiduciary duty, which is essentially a duty of fair dealing, has been more precisely formulated in respect of particular aspects of the director-company relationship. Consequently, a director has a duty to put the interests of the company before his own interests. Obviously this impinges upon his ability to contract with his own company. For example, a director who wishes to sell his own property to the company wishes, as vendor, to obtain the highest possible price while his duty, as a director, is to negotiate the lowest possible price on behalf of the company. The potential for conflict between private interest and directorial duty has led to the formulation by the judges of various principles which have been supplemented by statutory provisions.

(a) *Common law*

An early case in point is the House of Lords decision in *Aberdeen Railway Co v Blaikie Bros* (1854). In *Blaikie* the company wished to purchase iron chairs for use on railway stations, the contract was awarded to Blaikie Bros, a partnership in which a director of the company was a partner. The company repudiated the contract and its repudiation was upheld. The Lord Chancellor, Lord Cranworth said '... no-one having [fiduciary] duties to discharge, shall be allowed to enter into engagements in which he has or can have a personal interest conflicting or which possibly may conflict with the interests of those he is bound to protect'. Later cases have modified this view where any possible conflict of interest is 'so small that it can as a practical matter be disregarded' (*Movitex v Bulfield Ltd* (1986)) and have stressed that a potential conflict can arise only where there is 'a real sensible possibility of conflict' (*Boardman v Phipps* (1967)). Where a director enters into a contract in circumstances where there is a conflict of interest or there is a sensible risk of such a conflict, the contract is voidable at the company's option even if the contract is entirely fair and reasonable. Thus, a company can rescind a contract from which a director benefits, directly or indirectly, if he has entered into it in breach of fiduciary duty even if the contract terms are fair and are no less favourable to the company than those obtainable from non-directors. This would not appear to be fair to directors. However, a company while a company can rescind a contract entered into by a director when he is in breach of his fiduciary duty, the law does not say that a director can never benefit from a contract with a company with which he is a director.

A director can benefit from a contract between himself and his company provided that he makes adequate disclosure of his own interest before the contract is entered into. Originally disclosure to the shareholders was required to remove any issue of conflict but companies soon began to adopt articles which provided that disclosure to the directors would suffice. It remains the law that disclosure must be to the shareholders unless the articles provide otherwise: Table A, art 85, permits disclosure to the board. Since disclosure to the board is not as onerous as disclosure to the shareholders, s 317 provides rules for the nature and degree of disclosure where the articles of a company allow disclosure to the board. The requirement of disclosure is strict. In *Neptune (Vehicle Washing Equipment) Ltd v Fitzgerald* (1995), a sole director who failed to disclose his interest in a contract between himself and the company to the board, ie to himself, was in breach of the section. The judge rules that he should have revealed his interest in the minutes of board meetings and that his knowledge of his interest did not exempt him from the provisions of the Act. In addition to the requirements of s 317, companies may adopt their own disclosure rules; Table A, arts 84–94, provide guidelines as to the type of disclosure requirements companies might adopt. The Table A provisions limit the ability of an interested director to vote on his own contracts but a company may, of course, choose to adopt a different set of disclosure requirements than Table A envisages which allow an interested director to vote. As with failure to make adequate disclosure to the shareholders, failure to make disclosure in accordance with the requirements of the articles allows the company to rescind any contract. On a vote to adopt or reject a contract entered into without adequate disclosure an errant director who is also a shareholder is permitted to vote unless the articles provide otherwise (*NW Transportation Co Ltd v Beatty* (1887)). Failure to comply with s 317 is a criminal offence but it is less clear if a company can set aside a contract with a director who has complied with the articles of the company but not with s 317. In *Guinness plc v Saunders* (1990) members of the House of Lords were split upon whether simple breach of s 317 would render a contract voidable. In *Hely-Hutchinson v Brayhead Ltd* (1968), the majority of the Court of Appeal took the view that breach of s 317 would render the contract voidable. The views on s 317 were *obiter* in both cases.

Since most companies treat disclosure to the board as compliance with a director's fiduciary duty, the shareholders have little control over directors contracts. Shareholders must be informed of contracts which benefit a director in the annual accounts (s 232). Perhaps because disclosure to the board might allow a cosy cartel among directors, a number of statutory provisions affect the ability of a director to contract with his company.

(b) *Statutory intervention*

There are a number of statutory provisions which could be described as designed to ensure fair dealing by directors. Section 319 places restrictions upon the service contract which a director can make, s 320 affects 'substantial property transactions' and s 330 prohibits a company from making loans to directors. The general thrust of these provisions is not to prohibit contracts between directors and their companies but rather to ensure that such contracts are valid only if affirmed by the shareholders in general meeting. Sections 320 and 330 extend to shadow directors, ie those 'in accordance with whose directions or instructions the directors of the company are accustomed to act' other than only because 'the directors act on advice given ... in a professional capacity' (s 741).

Section 319 prohibits any term in a contract with a director whereby he is to be employed as an executive or non-executive director for a period of more than five years without provision for termination (or where termination is possible only in specified circumstances) unless the term is first approved by the company in general meeting. One consequence of s 319 is that directors now tend to have contracts for less than five years, thus removing the necessity of exposing the contract to the shareholders for their approval, but which contain a provision for re-appointment for a similar period on the same terms, ie including a re-appointment term. Certain large investors (notably POSTEL) have expressed disapproval of rolling contracts or contracts whereby the directors are appointed for too lengthy a period.

Sections 320–322 provide that if a transaction between a director and a company is a 'substantial property transaction' it is voidable unless approved in advance by the shareholders in general meeting (a director-shareholder could vote on a resolution to ratify).

Approval of such a transaction can be informal, see *Niltan Carson Ltd v Hawthorne* (1988), where knowledge and acquiescence by the majority shareholders was held to constitute approval of the activities of the director. A transaction is a substantial property transaction if a director acquires an interest in a non-cash asset from the company, or the company acquires an interest in a non-cash asset from a director, where the value of the asset is over £100,000 or 10% of the asset value of the company (subject to its value exceeding £2,000). However, the section provides that an unapproved substantial property transaction is voidable at the instance of the *company*. Thus it seems that a shareholder has no locus to challenge an unapproved transaction. A transaction entered into in breach of these sections ceases to be voidable even by the company if it is too late to avoid it or the company in general meeting has affirmed it. It should be noted that where a board lacks the authority to enter into a transaction (eg a substantial property transactions) the provisions of s 35A, which would normally confer authority on the directors and thus validate the contract, do not apply and the transaction remains voidable (s 322A).

Sections 330–346 provide a highly elaborate set of provisions affecting the ability of a company to make loans, or enter into related transactions with, to directors. These provisions provide both civil remedies and, where the company is a relevant company, criminal penalties. These sections restrict the ability of a company to make loans (or guarantee a loan) to a director of the company, or a director of a holding company, or to a shadow director (s 330(1)). Further, where the company is a relevant company the prohibition is extended to quasi-loans and credit transactions (or guarantees thereof) to the same people or to a person 'connected' to such a person (s 330(2)). A company is a relevant company is either a public company or is a member of a group one of whose members is a public company (s 331). A connected person includes a spouse and children under the age of 18 (s 346) of a director of a company. Sections 332–338 provide a number of exceptions to the basic prohibition some of which operate only with the approval of the shareholders in general meeting. For example, s 337, which allows a company to provide a director with funds (limited to £20,000 maximum for a relevant company) to carry out his duties on behalf of the company provided that the provision of funds is disclosed to and approved by the shareholders in advance or at or before the next AGM of the company (s 330(4) specifies what is to be disclosed to the shareholders). Failure to obtain the necessary approval or inadequate disclosure will result in the director having to repay the sums provided within six months of the AGM. Loans etc to directors must be disclosed in a company's accounts.

(c) *Conclusion*

The position at common law was such that the shareholders had little or no control over contracts entered into by directors. The position has been modified by statute but not to any significant degree. Disclosure and approval in advance may now be required but breach of these provisions is likely to render the contract voidable at the option of the company and not the shareholders and there is but a limited ability for shareholders to object to contracts in advance. Perhaps contracts between a company and a director should be void unless approved in advance by the shareholders in general meeting and this should include all service contracts, including terms as to salary.

Chapter 5

The Shareholders and their Rights

Introduction

In considering the shareholders and their rights three issues arise – who is a shareholder, what rights do shareholders have and against whom are these rights exercisable. The first issue, who is a shareholder, concerns the validity of the allotment, or transfer of shares, and is addressed primarily in Chapter 6 (Share Capital) although it has been touched on in the previous chapter (validity of allotment made by directors for improper purpose). Thus, in this chapter the question of whether a person *is* a shareholder will not be central to any question.

The other issues, the nature of rights of shareholders and their enforcement can arise in many contexts. Such matters have already formed part of questions in previous chapters, for example when considering *ultra vires* and division of power within a company, and will arise in later chapters, for example when appraising rights to dividends and the variation of class rights. In this chapter it is the ability of shareholders (generally a minority shareholder) to do something either when dissatisfied with corporate management, or generally unhappy with the way the company is operating, which may involve the board and/or the majority shareholder, or when unable to co-exist happily with his fellow shareholders. A majority shareholder is able to dismiss the board (s 303) and may be able to give the board instructions on how the company is to be run (Table A, art 70) or even change the articles (s 9) so has less need, but may still wish, to use the remedies discussed in this chapter. Since it is the company who generally has the sole right to challenge the actions of the board, any question which demands advice for a shareholder is necessarily asking you to consider not merely the cause of action open to a shareholder but also how, if at all, the shareholder can enforce his rights (a *locus* question which issue also played a prominent role in the previous chapter). Where, as is common, the company is the only potential plaintiff, the student should necessarily appraise alternative remedies. Possible general alternative remedies being just and equitable winding up (s 122(1)(g) Insolvency Act 1986) and an 'unfair prejudice' action (s 459). Both statutory provisions have generated considerable case law much of it recent. In rare cases a shareholder may also be able to persuade the DTI to initiate an investigation into a company. These remedies can also apply to situations where a shareholder wishes to challenge the actions of fellow shareholders in the limited cases where shareholders owe duties to fellow shareholders.

As with questions on the directors, it is possible to combine questions on shareholder remedies with almost any other part of a company law syllabus.

Question 27

Despite the wide interpretation given by judges to s 459 Companies Act 1985, it is unlikely to be applied to a complaint about the mismanagement of a company. In such cases the rule in *Foss v Harbottle* still represents a substantial, unjustifiable barrier to litigation by minority shareholders.

Comment on this view.

Answer plan

General introduction to problem of *locus* then discussion of the two main issues:

(a) what is *Foss v Harbottle* and does it have the effect claimed? and
(b) width of interpretation of s 459 and likelihood of it being applied to private and public companies,

ending with a conclusion as to the validity of the view expressed in the question.

The crucial thing to beware is writing an answer which is simply a discussion of s 459 followed by a discussion of *Foss*. It is important to use material selectively so that it is tailored to the question.

Answer

What courses of action are open to a minority shareholder who is unhappy with the way a company is being operated? The simplest remedy available to a shareholder in a public company is to sell his shares and seek a better investment, although if others are equally unhappy the sale price may represent a loss. It is unlikely that a shareholder will find a ready market for a minority shareholding in a private company unless the directors or other shareholders wish to buy the shares (or its a football club where people buy in for non-investment reasons). Further, the price of shares in a private company may well not represent the asset value or earnings potential of the company making sale, even where possible, an unattractive option. If the shareholder wishes to stay with the company but improve its operation he could seek to change the management (s 303, ordinary resolution required) or to instruct the board how to operate (Table A, art 70 or s 9, both special resolution) but both require the support of others. Assuming the unhappy shareholder cannot persuade others to join him he can consider two approaches. First, he could seek to initiate litigation on his own account or second he could attempt to sue on behalf of the company. In respect of both approaches, the courts have been greatly influenced by the view that a company is a democracy and that a shareholder who is out-voted should abide by the result of a vote and a court should intervene only when the interests of justice clearly demand it. As Lord Wilberforce put it, 'Those who take interests in companies limited by shares have to accept majority rule'.

A person can sue on his own account when a wrong has been done to him. Such a wrong would arise in respect of mismanagement if such was a breach of a common law or statutory duty owed to the shareholder. Unfortunately, at common law a shareholder is unlikely to be able to establish such a wrong if his complaint relates to simple mismanagement. The reason is two-fold. First, mismanagement may not be a breach of director's duty since the standard of care and skill required of honest directors is traditionally very modest. Second, the duty of care and skill is owed to the company and *not* to an individual shareholder (*Percival v Wright* (1902)). Section 214 Insolvency Act 1986 may impose a higher standard of care on directors but this but the section does not give shareholders a right to sue to restrain incompetence, rather it imposes personal liability to creditors on directors when the company has gone into insolvent liquidation and there has been 'wrongful trading'. Even where the alleged mismanagement consists of irregularity in conducting the affairs of the company, a shareholder may find that a wrong has not been done to him but only to the company. For example, an internal irregularity which is capable of ratification by ordinary resolution, is not regarded as a wrong done to a member and hence an individual shareholder cannot sue those responsible for the irregularity (*MacDougall v Gardiner* (1875)). In contrast, where the wrong complained of consists of breach of a personal right vested in a member, the member can sue. There is no clear test of what is a personal right (breach cannot be ratified so individual member can sue) as opposed to a right to have the business of the company carried out properly breach of which may be ratifiable (where wrong is ratifiable a member cannot sue). A right conferred on an individual by a contract or by a statute would be a personal right and some provisions in the articles are also deemed to be personal rights (by virtue of s 14) while others are not (see *Hickman v Kent or Romney Marsh Sheepbreeders' Association* (1915)). Consequently, if the alleged mismanagement consists of ignoring provisions in the articles it may or may not allow a member to sue (but note that some commentators treat the right to have the business of the company conducted in accordance with the articles as a personal right). Certainly, where the alleged mismanagement consists of breaches of procedures laid down in the articles, an individual shareholder is unlikely to be able to claim a wrong has been done to him (*MacDougall v Gardiner* (1875)). For example, if a meeting is called with short notice or by an inquorate board the decisions taken at that meeting would not be set aside at the instance of a minority shareholder if the decisions were passed by a substantial majority so that the irregularity was irrelevant to the result of the meeting (*Bentley-Stevens v Jones* (1974)). The justification given for denying a shareholder the right to sue, other than when a personal right is breached, is two-fold. First, that where there is a mere irregularity there is little point in allowing litigation where the majority can ratify and second, that to allow litigation on every procedural irregularity would open the famous floodgates of litigation. Where there is no common law right to initiate litigation about mismanagement a shareholder may find a remedy by using s 459 (see below).

The circumstances in which a member can sue to enforce the rights of the company are even more limited. In *Foss v Harbottle* (1843), Wigram VC laid down the basic principle that a shareholder could not sue in respect of wrongs done to a company (by insiders or outsiders); this remains the basis of the modern law – the wrong has been done to the company, the proper plaintiff is the company. This decision has been approved by the Court of Appeal and the Privy Council in *Burland v Earle* (1902). *Foss* itself, and later cases, have confirmed that there are limited exceptions to its basic principle. Most of the so-called exceptions are cases where *Foss* does not apply, for example where the company acts *ultra vires*, or where a shareholder's personal rights are breached. The principal exception to *Foss*, whereby a shareholder can bring a derivative action to enforce the company's rights, arises where there is fraud on the minority by those in control of the company; if mismanagement falls into this category, a minority shareholder could sue on behalf of the company. One difficulty with this exception is that 'fraud' must be proved. Moreover, in *Prudential Assurance Co Ltd v Newman Industries* (1982), the Court of Appeal, *obiter*, stressed that a court should not allow a derivative action by a shareholder to commence unless the shareholder could establish a *prima* case that the company was entitled to the remedy claimed *and* that it was an appropriate case for a person to litigate on behalf of the company when the company has chosen not to litigate. In *Prudential*, the company had not sued two directors whom, it was alleged, had misled the company. Vinelott J had allowed a derivative action, at the behest of the plaintiff, to proceed without investigating closely the question of whether Prudential, a minority shareholder, had locus. He took the view that the merits of the case and the question of locus could be heard together and both issues would be determined at the conclusion of the case. The Court of Appeal rejected this approach and said that the law should not permit a thirty-day hearing to see if there should be a thirty-day hearing. The costs in this case were enormous and the Court of Appeal clearly felt that if a shareholder was allowed to drag a company into expensive litigation (which the company might have to fund and which in this case it had reluctantly chosen to fund) the courts should save companies from their 'friends'. Even where a shareholder crosses the *prima facie* barrier on the issue of fraud, he may still be denied locus if he is an inappropriate plaintiff, for example where he participated in the fraud or had benefited from it (*Nurcombe v Nurcombe* (1985)), or was seeking to sue for an ulterior motive (*Barrett v Duckett* (1995)), or where he has failed to establish that it is the fraudsters who are blocking litigation by the company (the control issue). Thus, in *Smith v Croft (No 2)* (1988), Knox J held that where the decision by the company not to litigate had been made 'by an appropriate independent organ' the shareholder was not allowed to bring a derivative action – for in such a case it was not the fraudsters who were blocking litigation but others unconnected with the fraud. He pointed out that the appropriate independent organ might have good reason to refuse to litigate, for example unnecessary expense or the unlikelihood of any judgment being satisfied. What constituted an independent organ would depend on the facts of the case but where a majority of shareholders had indicated no desire for litigation their '... votes would be disregarded if, but only if, the court is satisfied either that the vote or its equivalent is actually cast with a view to supporting the defendants rather than securing a benefit to the company, or that the situation of the person whose vote is considered is such that there is a substantial risk of that happening'. While a difficult test to apply, it clearly militates against action by a minority shareholder in a case of mismanagement. Assuming the votes of the directors are disregarded it would be a bold decision for a court to rule that the remainder of the shareholders had rejected litigation for an improper purpose particularly in a public company where shareholding is widely spread. Even where a shareholder has locus and sues successfully on behalf of his company, the benefits accrue to the company and not the shareholder.

Does s 459 provide the answer for a shareholder who regards the management as incompetent? There is no locus problem with the section since 'A member of a company may apply to the court' and the definition of a member includes 'a person who is not a member of a company but to whom shares in the company have been transferred or transmitted by operation of law'. Consequently, for example, a person who had inherited shares, and whom the directors were refusing to register as a member, would have locus. In common with an action for breach of personal rights, any relief can benefit the petitioner although the benefit may be indirect, for example where the court orders the articles of the company to be changed. A shareholder must bear the cost of a s 459 action himself. However, merely because that court will hear an application does not mean that a member has been unfairly prejudiced. Two cases are pertinent. In *Re Elgindata Ltd* (1991), the petitioner had joined the company on the basis of detailed written agreements which were reflected in the articles, the court accepted it could find, but refused so to do on the facts, that the petitioner had interests other than those set out in the agreements. Hence, a shareholder unhappy with the management of the company may simply find that, provided the incompetent directors are complying with the memorandum and articles, he can expect no more. While it is unlikely to be a specific provision in the articles, a member of a company could claim that he, in common with all shareholders, legitimately expects the company to be properly managed and that mismanagement is unfairly prejudicial. Certainly, mismanagement allied to attempts to do down a shareholder has been held to be unfairly prejudicial (*Scottish CWS Ltd v Meyer* (1959)) as has mismanagement linked to breaches of company law (*ex p Shooter* (1990)) but simple incompetence is unlikely to be within the section. In *Re Elgindata Ltd* (1991), the petitioner alleged, *inter alia*, that incompetence by management was unfairly prejudicial. In a lengthy judgment Warner J held that in an appropriate case a court could find that serious mismanagement might be unfairly prejudicial but that courts would be extremely reluctant to accept that managerial decisions could be so. A more recent case in point is that of *Re Saul Harrison & Sons plc* (1995), in which the holder of non-voting shares claimed that the directors of the company were keeping the company running purely to earn substantial salaries when a reasonable board would, given the company's prospects, have liquidated the company and distributed its assets. The action was based partly on an allegation of fraud and partly on an allegation of incompetence. The company was a long-established, family-owned and run company dealing mainly in paper and textile wiping cloths which had in recent years suffered declining profitability. In support of her claim for unfair prejudice the petitioner claimed that when in 1990 the company negotiated a sale of its premises prior to the passage of a bill which would have authorised compulsory acquisition, it was the ideal time to wind up the company and distribute its assets rather than, as had happened, to acquire new premises and that the directors had failed to wind up the company simply to continue to receive large salaries as directors. The Court of Appeal upheld the judge's decision to strike out the petition. In deciding what is fair or unfair for the purposes of s 459, one judge held that 'it is important to bear in mind that fairness is being used in the context of a commercial relationship'. The relationship of shareholders is primarily governed by the memorandum and articles of the company and commercial fairness can be seen as predominately a question of complying with them. Even if conduct is not in accordance with the memorandum or articles and the powers thereby conferred it is not necessarily unfair. For example, trivial and technical infringements of the articles will not attract the statutory remedy. Where, however, the memorandum and articles do not represent the understandings upon which the shareholders are associated (a principle recognised in the leading case of *Ebrahimi v Westbourne Galleries Ltd* (1973)) it may be unfair to a shareholder for those who control a company to exercise the powers set out in the memorandum and articles if to do so denies the legitimate expectations of the shareholder. Such expectations may derive from a contract independent of the memorandum and articles but is not restricted to such cases, as in *Ebrahimi* it is a question of whether equitable considerations require express or implied promises not contained in the memorandum and articles to be honoured. One judge concluded that where there is no reason to look beyond the memorandum and articles to determine the relationship of the shareholders, compliance with them can not be unfair. In this case the petitioner had no legitimate expectations beyond the general expectation that the memorandum and articles would be complied with and its powers exercised properly. Lord Justice Neill agreed on the question of legitimate interests and the primacy of the company's constitution but added an important rider. He accepted that serious mismanagement could constitute unfair prejudice albeit in exceptional circumstances since in most cases a shareholder must accept that managerial decisions in the best interests of the company as a whole may dictate conduct which is prejudicial to some individuals. On the facts of this case the accusation of mismanagement was not made out.

In conclusion, a shareholder who regards a company as incompetently managed is unlikely to have a remedy under s 459, nor is an action for breach of personal rights likely to be attended by success, and will continue to find *Foss* a barrier to litigation on behalf of the company.

Question 28

Whatever the difficulties of enforcement, shareholders have means at their disposal to control the conduct of directors. What is needed by minority shareholders is a system whereby the actions of the majority shareholders can be controlled. To what extent do shareholders currently have control over the conduct of their fellow shareholders? Should the current position be changed?

Answer plan

What is needed is a brief consideration of the problems majority shareholders can cause to minority shareholders followed by an evaluation of the degree of control currently exercisable and an appraisal of any necessity for change.

Answer

Directors of a company, even when acting within the powers conferred upon them, are required to comply with fiduciary, common law and statutory obligations in exercising those powers. A shareholder may encounter difficulties in enforcing his rights (due to *Foss v Harbottle* (1843)) but the existence of the obligations is certain. However, a minority shareholder may not be unhappy with the conduct of the directors but feel that the conduct of other shareholders in the company (generally a majority or another class) is prejudicial to his interests. For example, the majority shareholder may vote to change the articles, or block a decision to sue an errant director, or ratify the actions of that director, or voting shareholders may change the rights attaching to non-voting shares, contrary to the wishes of the minority or the non-voting shareholders. What, if anything can the disgruntled shareholders do? Of course the majority shareholder must comply with the provisions of the Companies Acts the provisions of which may set out particular majorities which are required for certain ends to be approved. For example, s 9 (changing the articles) requires a special resolution, a vote to relieve a director from the consequences of entering an *ultra vires* contract requires a special resolution (s 35) and some variations of class rights require the class to be varied to approve the variation (s 125(3)). But is there a general fiduciary duty akin to that imposed on directors, imposed on shareholders?

A shareholder may be liable to a fellow shareholder by virtue of a function he exercises within the company. For example, a shareholder may be treated as a director if he 'occupies the position of director, by whatever name called' or as a shadow director if he is 'a person in accordance with whose directions or instructions the directors of the company are accustomed to act' unless the directors only 'act on advice given by him in a professional capacity' (s 741). A shareholder who is a shadow director may either be subject to all the usual obligations imposed on directors or merely be subject to those statutory provisions that are specifically stated to be applicable to shadow directors. For example, shadow directors are subject to the rules on loans to directors and can be liable for wrongful trading. However, these statutory duties arise from the directorial functions exercised by the shareholder not from his position as a shareholder. Further, a shareholder may incur liability as a constructive trustee if he receives property misapplied by a fiduciary or assists in such misapplication without receiving anything himself provided that, in either case, the appropriate degree of knowledge of the wrongdoing was possessed. Again this liability is not imposed because the shareholder is a shareholder but because of his knowledge of the breach of fiduciary duty.

There are a number of cases which suggest that shareholders have a duty as shareholders to vote *bona fide* for the benefit of the company as a whole' (see *Allen v Gold Reefs of West Africa* (1900) for the first use of the phrase) but closer analysis of these cases does not, in my view, support the idea that a fiduciary duty is imposed on majority shareholders in all cases. Shareholders are generally free to vote how they wish, even to ratify wrongful acts committed by themselves while acting as directors if need be (*North West Transportation Ltd v Beatty* (1887)) and they can sell their votes to another thereby pledging themselves to vote to the order of another. No distinction appears to be drawn between shareholders who have only residual powers in respect of corporate management (the norm where a company has adopted Table A) and those who effectively run the company, for example where the board is in deadlock and unable to act. While it is difficult to discern a general duty cast upon shareholders there are circumstances where the court will require shareholders to vote 'bona fide for the benefit of the company' and not just consider their own interests. There is no definitive list (or definition) of such circumstances but some cases suggest that wherever the majority has acted in a manner which constitutes fraud on the minority it will be deemed to be in breach of fiduciary duty. This is a difficult test to apply without a clearer indication of what constitutes fraud but there are certain areas where 'fraud on the minority' is likely to exist, ie shareholders can expect to be treated as subject to a fiduciary duty.

Firstly, shareholders voting to absolve from liability a fiduciary who has misappropriated corporate property (or to appropriate corporate property to their own use) are subject to the duty to vote *bona fide* for the benefit of the company. Since misappropriation can hardly be beneficial to the company a vote to absolve is, traditionally, ineffective (*Cook v Deeks* (1916)). However, the inefficacy of such a vote must be looked at in the light of *Smith v Croft (No 2)* (1988). In *Smith v Croft (No 2)*, Knox J held that where the decision by a company not to litigate, eg not to sue a director who had misappropriated corporate property, had been made 'by an appropriate independent organ' no action could ensue and a minority shareholder would not be allowed to bring a derivative action on behalf of the company because the majority of shareholders, assuming them to be the independent organ, did not wish to pursue the errant director. The judge pointed out that the appropriate independent organ might have good reason to refuse to litigate, for example unnecessary expense or the unlikelihood of any judgment being satisfied. However, in determining what constituted an independent organ he said that where a majority of shareholders had indicated no desire for litigation their '... votes would be disregarded if, but only if, the court is satisfied either that the vote or its equivalent is actually cast with a view to supporting the defendants rather than securing a benefit to the company ...' 'which seems to retain the possibility of ignoring the vote to discontinue action against a director if the vote was not designed to secure a benefit to the company. Consider also s 322A which provides that a transaction entered into by a company with a director, which the directors do not have the power to negotiate (or the company lacks the capacity to enter into), are valid if approved by the company. Suppose the directors misappropriate corporate property (clearly beyond their powers), s 322A suggests this is ratifiable by the company and the section does not suggest that shareholders or director-shareholders in voting to ratify are subject to any fiduciary duty at all.

Secondly, when shareholders vote to expropriate the shares of another member they are subject to a fiduciary duty and must vote 'bona fide for the benefit of the company' (Brown v British Abrasive Wheel Co (1919)). This does not mean that a majority cannot approve an expropriation but that they must have a reason for so doing which is good for the company. For example in Sidebottom v Kershaw Leese & Co (1920), a change of articles allowing the board to require a shareholder in competition with the company to sell their shares, at a fair price, to nominees of the directors, was upheld as beneficial to the company.

It cannot be denied that there are dicta which would support the imposition of a fiduciary duty on shareholders in cases other than those where fraud on the minority (in the sense outlined above) is present. However, even those cases where the dicta are widest do not always find a fiduciary duty was owed by the majority. For example, decisions do not seem to support the view that a want of fair dealing by itself will impose a fiduciary duty on shareholders. In Greenhalgh v Arderne Cinemas Ltd (1946), the directors of the company were desperate for new capital and persuaded G to invest in the company by purchasing ordinary shares. To protect G's position, his shares were sub-divided into five shares thereby quintupling his votes and giving him the power to block a special resolution. The company then proposed similarly to sub-divide the rest of the ordinary shares thereby affecting the efficacy of G's votes and depriving him of negative voting control. This proposal was approved by ordinary resolution (under what is now s 121) and G unsuccessfully challenged the sub-division. The Court of Appeal upheld the proposal despite the apparent unfairness to G. The result was to alter the voting equilibrium of the shareholders and deprive G of the negative voting control which had been a condition of his investment. In a later case between the same parties (Greenhalgh v Arderne Cinemas Ltd (1951)) the new majority sought to change the articles to remove the right of pre-emption conferred on G. He challenged this change again alleging that in voting in favour of the resolution the majority had failed to vote 'bona fide in the interests of the company'. Again G failed, the Court of Appeal was critical of the conduct of the majority but refused to strike down the alteration. *Dicta* suggest that the shareholders were subject to a fiduciary duty which they satisfied. If such is the case the fiduciary might be thought to be so ephemeral as to be effectively non-existent. It could equally be argued that there was no fiduciary duty in that case. However, *Greenhalgh* can be contrasted with the case of *Clemens v Clemens Bros Ltd* (1976) where Foster J felt able to distinguish the earlier decision and find a breach of fiduciary duty by the majority. In *Clemens*, the majority shareholder (55%), who was also the dominant director, authorised the allotment of shares to other directors thereby depriving the minority shareholder (45%) of her negative voting control. The judge set the allotment aside; he felt able to classify the allotment as a breach of the fiduciary duty imposed on a majority shareholder although he, wisely, did not attempt to explain why *Greenhalgh* did not apply. In two other cases, *Re Holders Investment Trust* (1971) and *Estmanco (Kilner House) Ltd v GLC* (1982), the judges struck down votes by shareholders on the basis that they were not taken *bona fide* for the benefit of the company as a whole although both could have been decided on other grounds. In *Estmanco*, Megarry VC took the view that no shareholder could vote in his own selfish interests or ignore the interests of the company but these *dicta* are wider than anything contemplated by the Court of Appeal in *Greenhalgh* and should be confined to the, unusual, facts of the case.

A further problem encountered if the majority shareholder is under a general fiduciary duty to subjugate his own interests to those of the company, is what is meant by the company in this context (a hypothetical member according to *Greenhalgh*). The court in *Greenhalgh* acknowledged another difficulty in imposing a general fiduciary duty on all shareholders whenever a vote is taken – should liability be imposed only on those who consciously fail to put the company's interests first or should those who voted without giving the matter any thought also be liable?

Arguably, the existence or non-existence of a fiduciary duty cast upon members is irrelevant given s 459. This section allows any shareholder to petition the court where the affairs of the company are being, have been, or will be, conducted in a manner unfairly prejudiced to him. The section does not differentiate between acts etc which are initiated by the board and those initiated by the majority shareholder, the crucial issue is whether their is unfair prejudice to the interests of a member. An advantage of bringing an action against the majority at common law seems to be that it is treated as a derivative action thereby allowing the petitioner to seek an immediate indemnity from the company rather than waiting for an order for costs if successful. Another advantage could be that the burden of proof in cases at common law *may* fall on those seeking to support a vote (see *Re Holders*) rather than on the petitioner as with s 459. It is my view that any general common law fiduciary duty should be abolished and that shareholders actions should be judged by reference to unfair prejudice alone. It is also arguable that even where a vote is authorised by statute the resulting decision should be reviewable if it is unfairly prejudicial (note the case in evidence where judges have a discretion to exclude evidence where its admission would be unfair to the accused even if it is rendered admissible by statute).

Question 29

In 1988 Albert began a book-selling business with two of his children, Ben and Connie. In 1991 a company, Bookit Ltd, was formed and the business was sold to the company in exchange for shares in the company. Albert, Ben and Connie had equal shareholdings and were directors of the company; most of the profits of the company were paid to the directors in salaries. In 1993 Albert died leaving his shares to his wife, Anna, who was appointed to the board and draws a salary as a director although she takes no part in running the business and rarely attends meetings. On Albert's death, Ben took over as managing director and his wife, Diana, was appointed as a director.

In 1994 Ben proposed that the company specialise in books relating to sport and begin selling sporting memorabilia. Connie disagreed with this change of policy but Anna and Diana supported Ben and the plan went ahead. During the next financial year the company made a loss. Consequently, Ben, proposed to sell the company's premises to raise working capital, Connie objected to the sale but was voted off the board and the sale went ahead. The company is now beginning to prosper and Ben has suggested that the company should lend money to a company controlled by Diana which manufactures china models of sporting figures to enable it to expand. Anna wishes to sell her shares to the company and emigrate to Spain but the company has refused to purchase them.

Advise Anna and Connie.

Answer plan

The main issues are:

- Anna – refusal to buy shares and consequent inability to realise value of shares;
- Connie as a director – removal from the board;
- Connie as shareholder – lack of dividends, change of policy, sale of premises, loan to Diana's company.

Answer

Bookit is a company which is beginning to prosper financially but is facing boardroom turmoil. Assuming the parties cannot be reconciled with each other what does the law provide. A, B and C have equal shareholdings so that any one of them can block a special resolution and any two in combination can pass an ordinary resolution. The shares were allocated in exchange for non-cash consideration, the business, and as such can be treated as fully paid up (s 99). There is no requirement that non-cash consideration be valued when it is used to purchase shares in a private company (s 103 imposes such a requirement in respect of public companies) and a court will treat shares paid for other than in cash as fully paid up unless the consideration is illusory or it is manifest that they are issued at a discount (*Re Wragg* (1897)). For example, shares allotted in return for the assignment of a statute-barred debt would be issued at a discount. Anna and Connie, two of the three shareholders, are unhappy with aspects of the company's operation but unless they combine to form a majority they have a limited ability to influence the affairs of the company. Turning to their specific complaints.

Anna, who plays little part in operating the company, would like to realise the value of the shares and emigrate. Since Bookit is a private company there is no ready market in the shares and an outsider is unlikely to be interested in purchasing a minority shareholding in a family company. This is a common problem for those holding shares in private companies and wishing to retire and is indeed one of the reasons that the law was changed to allow a company to purchase its own shares (s 162). However, while a company may be empowered to purchase its own shares (the articles must allow it and there must be strict compliance with the statutory provisions) that does not mean that it is required so to do at the behest of a shareholder and the board can legitimately decline to purchase Anna's shares. On her own Anna cannot change the board nor can she issue instructions to the board as to how they are to operate the company nor can she change the articles and take the power to run the company away from the board. However, in combination with Connie she could pass a special resolution sacking Ben and Diana (s 303) and then run the company herself. Assuming Anna does not have Connie's support she could consider an action for unfair prejudice under s 459 or seek a just and equitable winding up under s 122(1)(g) Insolvency Act 1986. A successful application under s 122(1)(g) would result in an order to wind up the company thus releasing its asset value to the shareholders. It is of little use to Anna if the company has no assets and it destroys what appears to be a viable business. There is an important statutory restriction on a court's ability to wind up a company on the basis that it is just and equitable so to do – s 125(2) Insolvency Act 1986. This provides that where the petitioner is a contributory (s 79), which Anna is, and it would be just and equitable to wind the company up the court will *not* order winding up if there is some other remedy open to the petitioner *and* they are acting unreasonably in seeking winding up rather than pursuing that other remedy.

First, would it be just and equitable to wind this company up? The courts have used this provision where there is deadlock within a company so that it cannot operate (*Re Yenidje Tobacco* (1916)), or where the shareholders have justifiably lost confidence in the management who appear to be lacking in probity (*Loch v John Blackwood Ltd* (1924)), neither of which appear to be applicable. The courts also use s 122(1)(g) when the company is of the appropriate type (traditionally called quasi-partnership companies) and relations within the company are such that, had the company been a partnership it would have justified dissolution, ie where there is a mutual justifiable loss of confidence in ones fellow shareholders. It is probable that Bookit would be a quasi-partnership company since it bears many of the hallmarks listed by Lord Wilberforce in the leading case of *Ebrahimi v Westbourne Galleries* (1973) – the fact that the company is small or private is not enough – in addition the company should display all or some of the following factors. First, it will be an association formed or continued on the basis of a personal relationship involving mutual confidence – this may not apply since Anna is not one of the founders of the company and has taken little part in its operation. Second, the company is one in which it has been agreed that all, or some, of the shareholders would participate in management – this seems to apply. Third, the shares of the company will not be freely marketable thus locking a disappointed shareholder into the company – clearly applicable. If Bookit is within the ambit of the section it is unlikely that simple failure to buy Anna's shares would be sufficient to justify winding up. Moreover, the change of direction and sale of the premises were supported by Anna and cannot form the basis of her complaint. The possible loan to Diana's company might be regarded as a breach of director's duty by Ben (and Diana) but again seems unlikely by itself to justify just and equitable winding up. Arguably, Connie has a better case for winding up that Anna in that she has been excluded from management. Even if winding up is possible the court would not order it if Anna (or Connie) has an alternative remedy which she is rejecting unreasonably. Is there such a remedy?

Section 459 allows any member of a company to petition the court for an order that the affairs of the company are being, have been or will be conducted in a manner which is unfairly prejudicial to her interests. Extensive case law since 1980, when the section was introduced, has led to the formulation of several principles in determining applications under this section. First, a shareholder can be unfairly prejudiced whether that was the intention of the company or not, ie *mala fides* is not required although lack of *mala fides* may render prejudicial conduct 'fair'(*Re a Company (No 007623 of 1984)* (1986)). Second, misconduct on the part of the petitioner does not preclude a remedy (*Re RA Noble Ltd* (1983)). Third, a member must be unfairly prejudiced in her capacity as a member, eg failure to buy goods from a shareholder would not affect a member in a shareholder capacity, (*Re a Company* (1983)). Fourth, what constitutes unfair prejudice depends on the facts, but inability to work together leading to the exclusion of a director is not necessarily unfair (*Re a Company (No 007623 of 1984)* (1986)), what is needed is a lack of fairness in the circumstances. Examples include, dilution of a member's shareholding (*ex p Harries* (1989)), denial of benefits legitimately anticipated by the member, including a right to participate in management, (*Re Kenyon Swansea Ltd* (1987)) and failure to increase dividends to shareholders while increasing payments to directors (*Re Sam Weller Ltd* (1990)). Failure by the management to pursue the course desired by the petitioner is unlikely by itself to be sufficient (*Re a Company* (1983)) and this seems likely to apply to Anna. In *Re a Company* (1983), a shareholder alleged unfair prejudice on the basis that the company had failed to purchase the member's shares at the price he wanted and the company was expanding into new fields (a wine-bar) which might prove unsuccessful. The court rejected both arguments, failure to buy the shares did not prejudice the petitioner as a member and the court was reluctant to intervene in a commercial decision by the board to expand the company's business even if there was so risk of loss to the company. Her final complaint, the proposed loan, might be sufficient in that it may be breach of director's duty, for an action to proceed but an appropriate remedy is unlikely to include an order to buy her shares. Anna is unlikely to have any legal remedy for her complaint.

Connie could seek just and equitable winding up as well with a greater chance of success. She was a founder member of the company and had been part of the business from its foundation so that she might well argue that her exclusion from management, with its consequent loss of income, justified winding up the company. The facts of the case are similar to those in *Ebrahimi* where a founder-member who was legally excluded from the company which had taken over his business was able to obtain a winding up order. However, unlike Anna, Connie may be more concerned with regaining a place in the company and the court might regard such a remedy as a better alternative than winding up a profitable company. Has Connie a s 459 case?

There is no doubt that exclusion from management has been accepted as unfairly prejudicial to the interests of a *member* where the member's interests included a legitimate expectation that she would be entitled to participate in management. In such cases to dismiss a director could found a successful petition (*ex p Holden* (1991) is an example). However, to dismiss a director, even a founder-director, is not necessarily unfair prejudicial, each case turns on its facts. The lack of attention paid to the business by Anna might form part of an unfair prejudice claim (even if unlikely to be a breach of director's duty given the modest level of attendance required of non-executive directors) and could any gross over-payments to the directors (*Re Cumana* (1986)) especially where the company pays only small, or no, dividends (*Re Sam Weller Ltd* (1990)). Allied to the exclusion from management, the lacklustre attendance record of Anna and the lack of dividends, Connie could also raise the proposed loan. Loans to directors, or persons connected to directors (Diana's company) are prohibited (s 330) and are voidable at the company's option (s 341). While the company is *prima facie* the proper plaintiff to pursue recovery of such a loan (unlikely here) so that Connie might not be able to succeed in an action for breach of director's duty, the loan could form part of the s 459 claim. There are exceptions to s 330 (eg s 335, small loans in the course of business) but it is not obvious that any of these exceptions would apply to Diana. In addition, any loan authorised by the directors must be for a 'proper purpose' (breach is ratifiable) and if such is not the case with this loan, the directors conduct would strengthen Connie's unfair prejudice claim. The change in the business and sale of the premises are not likely to be regarded as matters for the courts (as with the wine-bar case) unless the directors have acted improperly, for example in the sale was to a director who failed to declare an interest. If Connie succeeds in claiming unfair prejudice on the part of the company, the court has an unfettered discretion as to the remedy (s 461). The court could order her to be bought out at a fair price, or that she be restored to the board or even require the other shareholders to sell their shares to her (as in *ex p Shooter* (1991)), or any other remedy it can think up. It is likely that the proposed loan would be declared invalid at the very least and if she remained a shareholder but was not re-instated as a director the court might order the payment of dividends to protect her income.

Perhaps Annie and Connie should combine their votes to become majority shareholders and achieve their aims without going to court.

Question 30

In 1990 Margaret, Neil and Paddy formed Parliament Ltd, a company providing advice to people lobbying Members of Parliament. Each of them became a director and was allotted one-third of the issued share capital. The articles of the company provide that any shareholder who wishes to sell his or her shares must first offer them to the other shareholders at a price calculated by the company's auditors in accordance with a stated formula. The articles also provide that if any person ceases, for any reason, to be a director he or she must, if asked to do so, transfer his or her shares to a remaining director or directors at a price calculated in accordance with the same formula.

The company has generated a large income but in order to develop the business all profits, except for directors' remuneration, have been re-invested in the company. In 1990 Margaret died and her husband John inherited her shares; he now needs funds to develop his own business and wishes either to sell his shares to Jacques, who runs a similar business in Brussels, or persuade the company to pay dividends. Paddy, who is extremely short-tempered, has fallen out with Neil and would like to remove him from the board, purchase his shares and replace him with his (Paddy's) wife, Glenys. Neil is refusing to resign from the board and has said that he will not sell his shares if asked to do so because, he claims, the price-fixing formula for the shares is unfair.

Advise John and Neil.

Answer plan

Careful consideration must be given to the particular needs of the parties whom you are asked to advise:

(a) John wants to sell his shares to an outsider, can he do so, alternatively can he force the company to pay dividends;

(b) Neil does not wish to be forced out of the company or to sell his shares.

Answer

The relations between the shareholders seem so unhappy that they might be best advised to wind the company up and if the shareholders cannot agree to a voluntary winding up perhaps Neil should petition for a just and equitable winding up under s 122(1)(g), Insolvency Act 1986 since it seems plain that there is a mutual loss of confidence between the three shareholders. However, the difficulty with a business of this type (people and skills based) is that its break up value is not likely to be large. A company may be capable of generating large profits but have little in the way of assets so that winding up is killing the (potential) golden goose, but there may be no other solution to the shareholder-antipathy. Assuming the shareholders do not seek voluntary winding up what course of action is open to John and Neil?

(a) *John*

John wishes to sell his shares to an outsider so it can be assumed that Jacques is willing to pay a higher price than that generated by the price-fixing formula in the articles, perhaps because being in the same line of business he intends to try and merge the companies. However, John is not totally unhappy with Parliament since he would be willing to remain a shareholder if the company paid dividends. Obviously, John sees his shares as a means of generating revenue so that he is neutral as to how this arises but selling to Jacques would produce a capital sum and would, it is assumed, be preferred by John. A shareholder, however, he acquired his shares, is bound by the articles of the company and s 14 provides that the articles constitute a contract between the shareholder and the company (and by implication vice versa) and also between each and every shareholder *inter se*. It is not clear how a shareholder enforces this contractual right, *dicta* in the House of Lords suggested that it could only be enforced through the company (*Welton v Saffery* (1897)) but in *Rayfield v Hands* (1960), Vaisey J held that a shareholder could enforce relevant articles directly without joining the company. Thus in *Rayfield* the directors were able, as members, to enforce a provision which required a shareholder wishing to sell shares to offer them first to the directors – similar to the provision in this case. While criticism has been levelled at *Rayfield*, particularly in allowing *directors* to enforce the articles, it seems likely to be applicable here. Consequently, any attempt to sell shares without giving first refusal to the existing shareholders could be restrained by injunction and John should be so advised. However, John cannot force the existing shareholders to buy the shares, the articles require him to offer it does not required them to purchase. Should the other shareholders decide to purchase John's shares, s 14 would render the price-fixing formula enforceable against him. For a consideration of whether the price-fixing formula could be ignored see Neil below.

John cannot require the company to pay dividends, the dividend policy is for the directors to determine so he cannot guarantee an income from his share-holding. There are, however, a limited number of cases in which the courts have rules that failure to pay an adequate dividend could constitute unfair prejudice to the interests of a member, ie s 459, and have used their power under s 461 to instruct the directors to reconsider their dividend policy. A degree of caution should be exercised in advising John of these cases since any application under s 459 necessarily turns on its own facts and simple non-payment of dividend may not be sufficient to constitute unfair prejudice. In *Re Sam Weller Ltd* (1990), the company had substantial net assets (including cash) and in 1985 made net profits of £36,330. The sole director, W, who was a minority shareholder, proposed a dividend of 14p per share absorbing £2,520, the same dividend as had been paid for the previous 37 years and the petitioner alleged that the director was running the company for the exclusive benefit of himself and his two sons, who were employees of the company. In a preliminary action to strike out the petition, Peter Gibson J, in refusing so to do, held that it was arguable that failure to pay dividends at anything other than a very modest level, where profits were substantial, which decision was made by those who derived their income from the company, was unfairly prejudicial. He firmly rejected the idea that low dividends would be unfairly prejudicial in all cases and was influenced by the apparent use of company money by W to buy a holiday home for his sons and W's refusal to register the petitioners as holders of shares which they had inherited. While the directors of this company are not paying dividends and are taking directors fees the situation is different from *Weller*, the company is relatively new and unlikely to have substantial reserves, retaining funds to develop the business seems only prudent and there is no allegation that the directors are effectively preferring themselves at the expense of shareholders in their use of profits. John's action for unfair prejudice is unlikely to succeed.

(b) *Neil*

Paddy and John between them could vote Neil off the board (s 303, ordinary resolution) although if this also has the effect of terminating a service contract substantial damages might be payable to Neil. If Paddy is determined to sack Neil, John could use this as a bargaining counter to get what he wants in return for his votes. If Neil ceases to be a director, the articles provide that he may be required to transfer his shares to Paddy (the only director left) and he is bound by this provision (see argument above re John and the article on share-transfer). If Neil is dismissed can he complain and is there any way he can evade either the requirement to sell shares or the price-fixing formula?

Section 459 permits a shareholder to petition the court alleging that the affairs of the company are being, have been or will be conducted in such a way as to be unfairly prejudicial to his interests. Interests in this context have been held to be interests as a member only (see *Re JE Cade Ltd* (1991) for a re-affirmation) but interests extend beyond rights. Consequently, even where rights under the articles have not been infringed an action for unfair prejudice may lie. Interests of a member can include a legitimate expectation that, where he has ventured capital on the understanding that he would participate in management, he would continue as a director (*Re a Company (No 00477 of 1986)* (1987)). The wider equitable considerations that the wording of the section has been held to permit would allow a court to rule that reliance by the company on its legal rights, eg use of s 303, would be unfairly prejudicial. However, where the articles accurately reflect the intentions of the members a court would be unlikely to treat reliance on the articles as unfairly prejudicial although there are *dicta* that suggest that the court could rule the articles to be unfair. Neil could well argue that attempts to dismiss him, particularly where his conduct does not seem to justify it, would be unfairly prejudicial. If such is the case, a court could order any dismissal to be invalid but the powers of the court under s 461 are not limited to any particular remedy. Since it seems unlikely that Neil and Paddy can continue working together a court might think it apt that one or other of them should be ordered to purchase the shares of the other (or perhaps s 122(1)(g) Insolvency Act 1986 should be used). If such an order is made the question arises as to how the shares should be valued. If Paddy is allowed to exercise his right to purchase contained in the articles will the court simply adopt the formula in the articles? Early cases on s 459 held that where the articles contained, as here, a price-fixing formula which the majority proposed to use, the court would not intervene but this has been modified in more recent decisions. In *Re a Company (No 00330 of 1991, ex p Holden* (1991), the majority shareholders (who were also the directors) argued that since the articles provided for expert valuation by the auditor Holden was assured of a fair price and consequently, the court had no need to usurp the function of the articles in substituting its own price-fixing formula. Harman J accepted that where the articles provided an adequate price-fixing formula for the compulsory purchase of the shares of the minority, the court would not usually intervene (see *Re a Company (No 006834 of 1988), ex p Kremer* (1989)) but that this issue must be adjudged in the light of the Court of Appeal decision in *Virdi v Abbey Leisure Ltd* (1990). In *Virdi* the Court of Appeal accepted that a petitioner could reasonably refuse to accept a valuation conducted in accordance with the articles, and the court should not follow it, if there was a risk that that method of valuation would depreciate the value of the interest. For example in *Holden* the judge found that such a risk arose in that the auditor/valuer was not required to explain how he reached his valuation, leaving H no basis to attack it, and also in that there was no machinery for H to put relevant matters to the valuer, particularly those relating to any other legal claims against the company (the effect of which might considerably affect the value of shares), and the potential capital gains tax liability the company's valuation procedure would impose on H. Neil could argue that any attempt to use the formula was itself unfairly prejudicial, and the court should not use it, if the price-fixing formula did not accurately reflect the value of his interest. Situations where a court has rejected the valuation machinery in the articles (apart from *Holden*) have included – where the conduct of those prejudicing the petitioner has depressed the value of the shares (*Re a Company (No 006834 of 1988)* (1989)) or where the valuation machinery is arbitrary and unfair on its face (*Re a*

Company (No 00477 of 1986) (1987)). Where a court substitutes its own valuation machinery for shares, it can also fix its own valuation date, for example, the date of the judgment or petition or a date preceding the unfairly prejudicial conduct whichever it thinks most appropriate.

Since Neil has not yet been dismissed or requested to sell his shares, he should present an interim petition to the court asking that the affairs of the company be frozen until a full hearing. It must be said in this case, that Neil might be well advised to try and buy John's shares (although John might challenge the price-fixing formula and he is not compelled to sell) and put himself in a majority, or sell his shares and go (if the price is right), or seek a just and equitable winding up since it is plain that there is a loss of confidence between the remaining directors of what is plainly a quasi-partnership (noting as with John the probable lack of break up value).

Question 31

'A limited company is more than a mere legal entity, with a personality in law of its own: ... there is room in company law for recognition of the fact that behind it there are individuals, with rights, expectations and obligations *inter se* which are not necessarily submerged in the corporate structure' (Lord Wilberforce in *Ebrahimi v Westbourne Galleries Ltd*).

How does the interpretation placed upon the now s 122(1)(g) Insolvency Act 1986 'recognise the rights of individuals'? Is such an interpretation consistent with the traditional reluctance to 'lift the veil' of incorporation?

Answer plan

Another question where selectivity is important, the question is not an invitation to write two essays but requires an outline of s 122(1)(g) with particular reference to the point raised in the quote from *Ebrahimi* followed by a comparison with comparable cases on lifting the veil. There is no need to provide a lengthy exposition of the law on lifting the veil.

Answer

Section 122(1)(g) Insolvency Act 1986 re-enacts a provision which has existed since the 19th century, it provides that a court has the power to wind up a company when it 'is of the opinion that it is just and equitable that the company should be wound up'. The courts have always held that this provision gives them an unfettered discretion and that its operation should not be restricted to particular circumstances. However, there are certain factual situations where a case for just and equitable winding up is likely to be in issue. The principal areas when, traditionally, just and equitable winding up was sought were when members of a company could not agree on how the company should be run so that the company was effectively inoperable or, while the company was operable and indeed operating, a minority shareholder or shareholders felt that the company was not being run in a manner which reflected the intentions of the shareholders agreed when the company was formed. These areas overlap. It should be noted that the efficacy of s 349 as a remedy for disgruntled shareholders, particularly when their legitimate expectations as to how the company will operate have been dashed, has led to a marked reduction in the number of cases where just and equitable winding up is awarded.

One of the early cases on s 122(1)(g) was a situation where there was deadlock and the intentions of the parties were not being reflected in the way the company was operating. In *Re Yenidje Tobacco Co Ltd* (1916), in which two tobacco traders, W and R, agreed to merge their businesses into a company in which they were the sole shareholders and directors with had equal voting rights. The articles provided that a quorum for the board was one and for arbitration in the event of disagreement between the shareholder/directors. Within a year the parties fell out and were not on speaking terms, R refused to accept the rulings of the arbitrator and sued W for fraud but the company continued to operate profitably. W sought just and equitable winding up. Legally the company could operate and was operating (at least in the short term) but equally clearly the parties had embarked formed a company as a type of joint venture. The Court of Appeal held that where a business was in corporate form but was in essence a partnership, the court would wind the company up if the disputes between the shareholders would have led to the dissolution of a partnership. The words 'just and equitable' are taken from the Partnership Act 1890 and the court felt able to apply the analogy of partnership to this company. The feeling was that if it was a partnership in all but name, the court should reflect the intentions of the 'partners' and not be restricted by the technicality that they had chosen to trade in corporate form. There was no doubt that in this case the relationship of W and R had irretrievably broken down and a winding up order was made. One judge stressed that the partnership analogy should not be pushed too far – in this case there were only two shareholders and the default powers of the general meeting could not operate but he was reluctant to treat a company as a partnership when it could operate despite disagreements between shareholders. In the 1930s, the courts took a restricted view of their power to wind up where just and equitable so to do and were inclined to find that if company law had not been broken and the company could operate despite disputes between shareholders, winding up was not appropriate (see *Re Cuthbert Cooper & Sons Ltd* (1937) for an example). Where people had chosen to trade in corporate form they were bound by the rules of company law and shareholders could not expect the benefits of incorporation without recognising, and being bound by, any concomitant disadvantages. A change was detectable in the 1950s and 60s and the definitive view of the operation of the relevant section was provided by the House of Lords in *Ebrahimi v Westbourne Galleries Ltd* (1973).

In *Ebrahimi*, E and N traded in partnership as sellers of fine carpets from about 1945. In 1958 they incorporated the business becoming the sole directors and shareholders. Shortly afterwards, N persuaded E to admit his son, G, into the business and G became a director and was given shares by both N and E; N and G held the majority of the shares. The company traded profitably and all profits were paid out as directors fees. In 1969 disputes arose and N and G combined to vote E off the board (using what is now s 303). E sought as his primary remedy an order under s 210 Companies Act 1948 (the somewhat feeble precursor of s 459) but abandoned this claim before the House of Lords (it having been rejected by the Court of Appeal), and in default of this remedy, just and equitable winding up. In ordering the winding up of the company, Lord Wilberforce reviewed the existing case law and laid down general principles for the operation of the law. He stated that the words 'just and equitable' (as in the quote in the question) allowed the court to look behind the strict legalities and consider the rights and expectations of the shareholders. Justice and equity will not allow a one party to disregard the obligations he undertake on entering a company and the section allows a court to subject the exercise of legal rights to equitable considerations – considerations of a personal nature arising between the parties which might make it unjust or inequitable for one party to be able to rely on his strict legal rights. In other words he accepted that where people had combined to form a company consideration must be given to their legal rights tempered by reference to the agreements and expectations of the parties in entering into the company. He accepted that this equitable overlay could not apply to all companies but only those which displayed specified characteristics (traditionally such companies are called quasi-partnerships but Lord Wilberforce rejected the name). When, he said, the circumstances which permit the ingress of equitable considerations arise cannot be laid down conclusively – the fact that the company is small or private is not enough but, typically, a company will display all or some of the following:

- it will be an association formed or continued on the basis of a personal relationship involving mutual confidence;
- in which it was agreed that all, or some, of the shareholders would participate in management;
- and the shares of the company will not be freely marketable thus locking a disappointed shareholder into the company.

When, as here, the company is of the appropriate type the conduct of the majority should not be judged purely by reference to their legal rights but by reference to the hopes and expectations of the parties. Plainly E had anticipated remaining part of the company he had founded and since his hopes had been dashed it was just and equitable to wind the company up.

A major drawback of s 122(1)(g) is that it destroys the company which is why s 459 is likely to prove a more popular remedy both for those shareholders who are unhappy (they are likely to be bought out) and for those causing the unhappiness, they still have a viable company. However, s 459 was created in 1980 and until that date courts which wished to aid legitimately unhappy shareholders were, effectively, limited to s 122(1)(g). Can it be said that the desire to aid those who had been treated unjustly led the courts too readily to ignore the corporate veil? In most areas of company law the courts rarely depart from the famous case of *Salomon v Salomon Ltd* (1897). In *Salomon*, S converted his existing, successful, business into a limited company of which he was the managing director. S valued his business at £39,000 (an honest but optimistic valuation) and received from the company in discharge of this sum, cash, a debenture and 20,001 £1 shares out of the issued share capital of £20,007. S's wife and five children each held one of the remaining issued shares (seven being the minimum number of shareholders at that date), probably as his nominee. The company went into insolvent liquidation within a year with no assets to pay off the unsecured creditors. The issue for the courts was whether S was liable for the company's unpaid debts. The House of Lords, reversing the Court of Appeal, held that the company had been properly formed and was a legal person in its own right notwithstanding the dominant position of S within the company. The company was not S's agent and consequently, S's liability was to be determined solely by reference to the Companies Act. Since S had paid for his shares in full (by transferring the business to the company) his liability to creditors was exhausted in that the full nominal value had been paid. Thus, Salomon's case established that legal personality would be recognised even when one shareholder effectively controlled the company and had fixed the value of the assets used to pay for his shares.

Even, where a company abandons its insolvent subsidiary the courts will not ignore the separate legal form of the subsidiary (see the somewhat caustic comment on this by Templeman LJ in *Re Southard & Co Ltd* (1979)).

There are many other cases where the courts fail to recognise the expectations of shareholders and insist that where shareholders have taken the benefits of incorporation they must accept any disadvantages incorporation might bring. A good example is *Woolfson v Strathclyde Regional Council* (1978), in which a single business (a shop) had gradually taken over a number of adjacent retail units and incorporated them into the original shop by knocking doorways through walls. The original shops, having been acquired at different times, were leased to different companies all of which were, effectively controlled by W. However, the structures and shareholdings of the various companies were not identical. The business was looked upon by the shareholders as one economic unit but the House of Lords held, on the facts, that there was no justification for ignoring the separate legal identities of the various companies.

Perhaps some link can be seen between those cases where the veil is lifted and the s 122(1)(g) cases in that lifting the veil of incorporation is most likely to occur when corporate form has been used to commit fraud. In *Jones v Lipman* (1962), for example, the defendant sought to evade the effect of a binding contract for the sale of a house by transferring it to a company which he controlled. The court ordered the lifting of the veil and the defendant and the company were treated as one and the same. In *Gilford Motor Company Ltd v Horne* (1933), H was subject to a lawful covenant not to compete with the company. He attempted to evade the covenant by getting his wife to set up a competing company, the Court of Appeal characterised the new company as a 'cloak or sham' designed to enable H to ignore the legitimate covenant to which he was subject. While the cases on just and equitable winding up do not, generally, involve fraud in the legal sense they might be seen as cases where there was a want of probity and fair dealing, a lack of *bona fides* on the part of the majority shareholder. If such is the case, it may be possible to reconcile the traditional reluctance of the courts to lift the veil with their apparent willingness so to do in determining the effect of s 122(1)(g). This attempt to reconcile the two strands of cases is not wholly successful, however, and it may be that the cases on s 122(1)(g) will come to be seen as an anomalous group which, given the alternative remedy provided by s 459, need not be followed (and see s 125 Insolvency Act 1986).

Question 32

In 1975, Wisley, who had taken early retirement from his job as a teacher, began to develop his hobby of rose growing as a business. Five years later he incorporated what was by then a thriving nursery as Rosejoy Ltd and he became 'director for life'. The articles of the company create two classes of ordinary share the 'A' shares and the 'B' shares, each share carries one vote. The articles further provide that the holder of the 'A' shares has a right to veto a takeover and that on a vote to dismiss a director the 'A' shares carry 10 votes. On incorporation, Wisley was allotted all 100 of the 'A' shares and 200 of the 'B' shares; he gave 300 'B' shares to his son, Inverewe, who is also a director of the company, and the remaining 500 of the 'B' shares to his wife who acted as company secretary. Wisley and his wife have always drawn a reasonable salary from the company which has never paid dividends.

Wisley has continued to run the company as if it was still his own private business and as he becomes older enters into increasingly hazardous business ventures. Inverewe would like to be more involved in the business but his father refuses to allow him to take any significant part in management. Wisley's wife has recently died and has left her shares equally to her daughter, Malmaison, and Arnega, Inverewe's son, who would like to sell the company to a property developer who would use the land for building.

Malmaison, who is a highly successful accountant, is unhappy with the level of competence displayed by both Wisley and has no great faith in her brother's business acumen and she has suggested she should join the board. All her complaints, and Arnega's proposals, have been brushed aside by Wisley and Inverewe who habitually refuse to have company meetings.

Advise Malmaison and Arnega.

Answer plan

Another question with lots of issues. It is important to note that it is which shareholders seek your advice, between them they hold 500 of the 1,100 shares which is sufficient to block a special resolution but insufficient to pass any type of resolution without the support of Inverewe (Inverewe's position is the same). They do not want the same thing but may form a tactical alliance. Issues which could arise include:

(a) retirement of W – problem of weighted voting etc;
(b) dismissal of I;
(c) effectiveness of the anti-takeover provision;
(d) level of management competence – no dividends, absence of meetings etc;
(e) s 122(1)(g), s 459.

Answer

The shareholdings in this company give rise to several possible voting blocks. M and A hold between them 500/1,100 shares in the company so that without the support of another shareholder they cannot pass an ordinary resolution but they have (together) the power to block a special resolution. W and I each hold 300/1,100 so on their own they cannot pass an ordinary resolution (they can acting in concert) but can, individually, block a special resolution. M or A acting with W or I would have 550/1,100 shares and could block a special resolution but could not pass an ordinary resolution (the votes are evenly split and no-one has a majority). In addition the 'A' shares have a weighted voting provision in respect of a vote to dismiss a director (not merely W but any director) which, if valid, gives the holder of the 'A' shares the ability to dismiss (or block the dismissal) a director on his own if he also holds any 'B' shares (W has 1,200 votes on this basis and the remaining shareholders have 800). Can a combination of shareholders dismiss either W or I from the board?

(a) *Dismissal of W*

W is named in the articles of the company as 'director for life' and to make extra sure a provision has been included that on a vote to dismiss a director W's 'A' shares carry 10 votes. This entrenches W but not I since he only holds 'B' shares. There is no age restriction on directors of private companies so that W cannot be forced to step down because of increasing age or infirmity. The provision that W is to be a director for life is valid insofar as it applies to a non-executive role but is ineffective as a basis for claiming that a lifetime service contract (s 319). Section 319 provides that a contract providing for the employment of a director by a company cannot, without the prior approval of the general meeting, exceed five years. A contract which purports to exceed five years is invalid and the contract is terminable by reasonable notice. W alone could not approve his own service contract so that any service contract exceeding five years would be terminable by reasonable notice. One difficulty would be who gives the notice? Presumably the board would be split on the issue so that whoever has a casting vote (likely to be W) would prevail. If the power of dismissal was vested in the general meeting either by the articles or because of deadlock on the board (as, for example, in *Barron v Potter* (1914)) the question of dismissal, if put to the vote, would allow W to exercise his weighted voting power assuming it to be valid (see below). Any attempt to terminate W's directorship (executive or non-executive) using s 303 would again fail because W could muster 1,200 votes (opposition 800) if the weighted voting clause is valid. In *Bushell v Faith* (1970), the House of Lords upheld the validity of a weighted voting clause similar to this one. The clause conferred extra votes on a director threatened with dismissal even though the effect was to make him unsackable and thus, it was argued, to render s 303 useless. The House of Lords did suggest that a weighted voting clause might not have been upheld had the company not been a small, private family-run company but this would not help I since Rosejoy seems to fit this description. With the current voting structure there seems no chance of removing W even with the support of all other shareholders. Indeed, since W can, on his own, block a special resolution M, I and A cannot band together to delete the clause. Further, any attempt to sack W might be unfairly prejudicial to his interests allowing him to petition the courts using s 459.

(b) *Dismissal of I*

I is in a weaker position than W in that the shareholders acting in concert can dismiss him but M and A cannot dismiss him on their own. Indeed if I retains the confidence of W he is probably secure in that W has a weighted voting clause which is applicable in respect of a vote to dismiss *any* director (not merely W). I should be cautious in trying to take more part in management if this is likely to prejudice W against him.

(c) *The take-over bid*

Merely because a shareholder wishes to sell the company to a take-over bidder does not mean the company must be sold. However, if M and I were to act with A they would command a majority of the votes and might seek to instruct the directors to sell. However, since this company has Table A, art 70 the directors need not comply with instructions given by ordinary resolution but only those given by a special resolution which they cannot muster. Nor can this majority be changed other than by altering the articles – again a special resolution is required. A company can create further shares (s 121 ordinary resolution required) and if the share structure was altered A (with M and I) might be able to out-vote W. However, W seems to have a right to veto a take-over bid and attempts to ignore such a clause have been rejected by the courts (*Quin & Axtens v Salmon* (1909)). Attempts to delete such a clause would require a change of articles (special resolution required) and might be challenged by W as a variation of class rights, ie he would have to approve the deletion of his right of veto at a separate class meeting. Ignoring a possibly lucrative take-over bid might be a factor which could be taken into account in determining if s 459 applied but disagreement about company policy is not usually regarded as unfairly prejudicial.

(d) *Level of management competence*

M and A are unhappy (as is I on different grounds) about the way the company is being run. They might well be successful in obtaining a remedy if they petitioned the court under s 459 (unfair prejudice) or s 122(1)(g) Insolvency Act 1986. It is unlikely that the shareholders would be able to sue for breach of duty by the directors because the obligations of the directors are owed to the company and not the shareholders (*Percival v Wright* (1902)) so that the company is the proper plaintiff to complain about any incompetence on their part (*Foss v Harbottle* (1843)). The company in this context means those running the company, ie the board, and while there are exceptional cases where the shareholders can sue to enforce the company's rights it is not certain that any exception operates in this case. Even if the shareholders could sue their main complaint, the incompetence of management and low level of dividends, would almost certainly not be regarded as a breach of duty by W and I. The directors have the power to fix the dividends and the degree of competence required of directors is traditionally modest. At common law directors are expected to carry out their duties with an appropriate degree of care and skill. The traditional formulation of the nature and extent of this duty is that given by Romer J in *Re City Equitable Fire Insurance Co Ltd* (1925) in which he held that a director:

- need display only such skill as may reasonably be expected from a person of his knowledge and experience;
- need not give the affairs of the continuous attention; and
- is entitled to leave the day-to-day running of the company to the officials of the company and is entitled to assume, in the absence of suspicious circumstances, that such officials are performing their duties honestly.

These propositions remain good law with regard to non-executive directors but W (and I perhaps) as an executive director would be constrained by his service contract and would have to comply with any greater obligation it imposed. The most important aspect of a director's duty of care relates to the amount of skill he must exercise. Directors are not subject to the Supply of Goods and Services Act 1982 so they need not display reasonable care and skill so that W and I need only display such skill as may reasonably be expected of them and perhaps little can be expected. If either of them holds professional qualifications the degree of skill which can be expected is, of course, higher. It is plain that if W and I are doing their honest best they may be held to have exercised sufficient care and skill to evade liability for negligence – the test of liability is subjective and not objective. However, conduct which is not capable of litigation by the shareholders can be taken into account in determining applications under s 459 or s 122(1)(g). Failure to hold meetings might also be evidence in any application under these sections. In addition failure to hold certain meetings is a breach of the Companies Act; a company must hold an annual general meeting (unless dispensed with by elective resolution, s 366A) and failure to do so allows a shareholder to petition the DTI to order the calling of a meeting. In addition, shareholders holding at least 10% of the paid up share capital can requisition an extraordinary general meeting (s 368). However, breaches of the Act which are trivial or technical (failure to hold meetings would not be characterised as trivial) would not attract a statutory remedy (*Re Saul Harrison and Sons plc* (1995)).

If the shareholders simply wish to liquidate their investment in the company they could apply for the company to be wound up on the basis that it is just and equitable so to do (s 122(1)(g)). However, a court has to determine whether winding up would be just and equitable in this case. The company appears to be a quasi-

partnership albeit W did give the shareholders their shares so that
their investment may be locked in but it is not their money which
was hazarded. There may be a justifiable loss of confidence in the
management which could warrant winding up but perhaps only if
allied to a want of probity on the part of the board (there are
parallels with *Loch v John Blackwood Ltd* (1925) where winding up
was ordered). Even if just and equitable winding up would be
permissible, s 125 Insolvency Act 1986 provides that it should not
be ordered if the petitioners have an alternative remedy which they
are unreasonably failing to pursue. The possible alternative, and
one which the shareholders might well prefer, is an action alleging
unfair prejudice.

Section 459 allows any member of a company to petition the
court for an order that the affairs of the company are being, have
been or will be conducted in a manner which is unfairly prejudicial
to her interests. Extensive case law since 1980, when the section
was introduced, has led to the formulation of several principles in
determining applications under this section. First, a shareholder
can be unfairly prejudiced whether that was the intention of the
company or not, ie *mala fides* is not required although lack of *mala
fides* may render prejudicial conduct 'fair'(*Re a Company (No 007623
of 1984)* (1986)). Second, misconduct on the part of the petitioner
does not preclude a remedy (*Re RA Noble Ltd* (1983)) – thus W
might be able to petition despite any shortcomings in his own
conduct if he was dismissed as a director. Third, a member must be
unfairly prejudiced in his capacity as a member, eg failure to buy
goods from a shareholder would not affect a member in a
shareholder capacity, (*Re a Company* (1983)). Fourth, what
constitutes unfair prejudice depends on the facts of each case and
conduct which is fair in one context might not be so in another.
Examples of unfair prejudice include, dilution of a member's
shareholding (*ex p Harries* (1989)), denial of benefits legitimately
anticipated by the member even if not set out in the constitution of
the company, including a right to participate in management, (*Re
Kenyon Swansea Ltd* (1987)) – relevant for W if sacked and perhaps
for I, and failure to increase dividends to shareholders while
increasing payments to directors (*Re Sam Weller Ltd* (1990)).
However, the Court of Appeal has stressed that where the conduct
complained of by the petitioner is in compliance with company law
and the constitution of the company there must be a good reason

why the court should consider other expectations without some good reason so to do. Hence, the mere fact that A would prefer the land to be sold for building gives him no reasonable expectation that it would be sold (even if financially beneficial to the company) and would not found a s 459 action (see *Re Saul Harrison and Sons plc* (1995)). M and A could also point to W's eccentric conduct and failure to recognise the fact that he is no longer a sole trader (this might preclude a successful s 459 action by W) drawing comparison with *Re HR Harmer Ltd* (1958) where conduct similar to that of W was held to justify an action under the precursor of s 459.

If, as seems possible, M and A are successful in their application under s 459 (I's case looks less strong), the court can award any remedy it sees fit (s 461). For example, in *Harmer*, the Court of Appeal allowed an elderly director who snooped on staff, ignored board decisions and insulted customers to remain as Chairman with no executive role and this might be applicable in the case of W. I could be brought more into management (or eased off the board) and the weighted voting clause could be deleted. Alternatively, the court might favour an order for W or I or the company to buy out M and A at a fair price or indeed for them to buy out W and/or I. The court cannot make I competent if he is not nor can it order everyone to get on with each other and if relations have broken down irretrievably the court might have no option but to order winding up.

Chapter 6

Share Capital

Introduction

Questions about shares and share capital can cover a wide variety of issues many of them dependent upon statutory provisions of immense complexity. Few questions are likely to be in the form of essays on the power to allot shares or reduce share capital etc but such issues could arise in the context of other questions particularly ones involving directors, variation of class rights and shareholder remedies. This is one area where diagrams and/or sums may make an answer more comprehensible. The ability, where relevant, to explain the facts of *Brady v Brady* cannot fail to impress!

General questions arising in this area are such matters as the power of the company and/or the board to issue or re-arrange share capital (including schemes of arrangement under ss 425–427 Companies Act 1985) and the capital maintenance doctrine. The capital maintenance doctrine covers the issue of shares (including the nature of the consideration and valuation procedures) and also dealings in respect of shares such as the payment of dividends out of capital and the ability of the company to buy (or assist others to buy) its shares. In addition to questions on the issue of shares, this chapter includes questions on doing things with shares, for example the transfer of shares, variation of class rights and issues relating to take-overs may also arise in this context – when, for example, must a bid be made and when can a take-over bidder acquire shares compulsorily (ss 428–430F Companies Act 1985).

Some courses consider the Stock Exchange listing requirements but this is more a matter for a course on financial services.

Question 33

Sandy, Laura and Mark are the directors of Bombay Ltd; each of them holds 15% of the company's shares. Of the remaining shares, 50% are split between a number of smaller shareholders, none of whom has more than 10%, and 5% remain unissued. The articles of the company deviate from Table A in that they include a provision which requires any shareholder who wishes to dispose of his shares to offer them first to existing shareholders who will buy them at a fair price. One shareholder has recently died and his widow is anxious to sell his shares. The directors would like to increase their total shareholding so that between them they hold at least 51% of the shares. A significant minority of shareholders are reluctant to allow the directors voting control of the company.

Advise the directors how they might achieve their aim including, if relevant, how a scheme might be funded.

Answer plan

An open-ended question which does not point a student in any particular direction. There are two obvious ways of increasing a shareholding – buying issued shares from existing shareholders (or their representatives) and obtaining the allotment of unissued shares. Where this does not achieve the necessary majority, the creation and allotment of further share capital is a possibility. If the directors are seeking to obtain a voting majority they could also seek to insert a weighted voting clause in the articles or to sub-divide their shareholding while keeping one vote per share. Consider these possibilities, and any other schemes, bearing in mind potential opposition.

Answer

The directors of Bombay wish to acquire at least 51% of the shares in the company. This may mean that they wish to obtain voting control rather than being concerned about the number of shares they own. If this is so, they could attempt to achieve their objective without altering the size of their shareholding or re-organising the company's share structure. For example, it is possible to alter voting rights of existing shares by the insertion in the articles of a weighted voting clause. Unfortunately for the directors, alteration of the articles requires a special resolution (s 9) and obtaining a majority of three-quarters of those present and voting, given the likely opposition of existing shareholders, seems doubtful. Alternatively, the directors could seek to sub-divide their shares into two or more shares each of which carries a vote. Section 121 permits a company, whose articles so authorise (Table A, art 32 provides authority), to sub-divide shares into shares of smaller nominal value than that fixed in the memorandum. The decision to sub-divide must be made by the company in general meeting, ie an ordinary resolution is required. An ordinary resolution cannot be passed by the votes of the directors alone (unless some shareholders fail to vote) but they may be able to persuade holders of some shares to their side and allow the sub-division. A sub-division will decrease the voting strength of the non-director shareholders but since their rights (one vote per share) remain unaltered a sub-division is not treated as a variation of their class rights (*Greenhalgh v Arderne Cinemas Ltd* (1950)) and the requirements for the variation of class rights are not relevant. The literal approach to class rights taken by the Court of Appeal in *Arderne*, where no regard was paid to the fact that A's shares, each carrying one vote per share, were rendered less valuable in voting terms when the shares of others were divided into five (thus quintupling their voting efficacy), was rejected by Foster J in *Clemens v Clemens Bros* (1976). In *Clemens*, the shares of the minority shareholder were reduced in voting value from 45% to less than 25%, the judge, for no very clear reason, struck down the scheme which achieved the effect of diluting the voting strength of the minority shareholder. While the directors could be advised that *Clemens* may not be followed they should note that an attempt to dilute the voting strength of the majority has been held to be unfairly prejudicial and subject to s 459 (see *Re OC Transport Ltd* (1984) for an example). If attempts to alter the weight of the two voting blocks are unlikely to succeed the directors might wish to consider the acquisition of further shares.

The simplest solution open to the directors is to purchase shares from existing shareholders. In seeking to purchase shares, the directors do not owe a fiduciary duty to shareholders (*Percival v Wright* (1902)) nor are they at risk from the rules on insider dealing which apply only to public companies. However, purchase of shares depends upon the existence of a willing seller and fortunately there is one available. However, the articles of the company provide that shares must be offered to existing shareholders. Section 14 determines that the articles of the company create contractual rights between members and members and while there is doubt about the precise effect of s 14 there is no doubt that this provision in the articles is enforceable by the members see *Rayfield v Hands* (1958)). The difficulty is that the article merely requires the shares to be sold to existing members without specifying how to resolve a situation where more than one member wishes to purchase the shares. The attitude of the courts is to treat the articles as a business document and construe them so as to give reasonable business efficacy (*Holmes v Keyes* (1959)) so that it would seem appropriate to regard this provision as offering shares to all shareholders. Whether the offer is accepted by the first person to reply is doubtful – it would be more appropriate to hold that the vendor offers the shares to existing shareholders in proportion to their existing holding. If the directors acquire further shares they are required to report the addition to their existing holdings to the company in writing; this information would be entered in the Register of Directors' Interests. Failure to disclose renders the directors liable to a fine and/or imprisonment. The price payable for any shares purchased from existing shareholders is fixed by the contracting parties but in this case the articles require it to be a fair price.

If shares cannot be purchased to bring the directors up to their desired holding, they could seek to allot the unissued 5% to themselves (bringing their holding to 50%). In addition, or in substitution, they might try and increase the company's share capital and then allocate the new shares to themselves. To make their position impregnable, any new shares could have a weighted voting provision from the outset since it is unlikely the court will treat the articles of the company as unfair and contrary to s 459. Creation of further shares is authorised (for companies whose articles so permit, Table A, art 32 does permit) by s 121 provided the increase in share capital is approved by ordinary resolution. The directors again need support from other shareholders to achieve a majority and may be well advised not to try and create shares with weighted voting rights which may well arose suspicion in the minds of the non-director shareholders.

If the directors propose to allot the existing unissued shares and/or any new shares to themselves they face a number of legal difficulties. The power to allot relevant securities (defined in s 94 and including ordinary shares) is vested in the general meeting even when, as is usual, the power to run the company is vested in the board (s 80). However, s 80 provides that the shareholders can give the power to allot shares to the board either in the articles or by ordinary resolution. Originally, the shareholders had to vote to give the power to allot shares to the directors at least every five years but s 80A allows a private company (by elective resolution in accordance with s 379A) to give the authority for an indefinite period. It is unlikely that an elective resolution has been passed since all shareholders must agree to it. Thus, the directors should consider whether they have the power to allot shares by consulting the articles of the company or any resolution already devolving the power to them. The authority to allot may be general or limited (eg only applying to some classes of share, or to a maximum number of shares at any one time). The directors can be advised that if they break s 80 and allot shares without authority they are liable to a fine but the allotment is valid. Assuming the directors are authorised to allot shares (or are willing to contravene s 80), they must still be wary of s 89 which provides a right of pre-emption for existing shareholders. Section 89 states that where a company is proposing to allot equity securities (defined in s 94 and including ordinary shares) wholly for cash, the shares must first be offered to existing shareholders in proportion to their existing shareholding. Thus, s 89 allows the directors to offer only 45% of any increase in share capital (or of the unissued 5% of existing shares), which they are allotting, to themselves. A private company, such as Bombay Ltd, can exempt itself from section (s 91) but appears not to have done so. However, if the directors break s 89 and allot all the shares to themselves, the allotment remains valid although the directors are liable to compensate shareholders to whom shares were not offered for any loss suffered thereby (s 92, there is a two-year limitation period). The directors can avoid any difficulties with s 89 by allotting the shares other than wholly for cash (see below).

The directors might think that if they comply with (or avoid) all he statutory regulations any allotment made by them would be unimpeachable. They would be wrong. The greatest hurdle to any scheme by the directors to allot shares (old or new) to themselves is the imposition on them of the fiduciary duty to exercise any power of allotment *bona fide* for the benefit of the company and for a proper purpose. The obligation to act *bona fide* (and for the benefit of the company – probably) is subjective so that provided the directors honestly believe they are acting properly in allotting themselves shares they are not in breach of this limb of their fiduciary duty. However, the directors must exercise their powers not only honestly but also for a purpose consistent with that for which the powers were conferred on them, ie for a 'proper purpose'. A leading case is the Privy Council decision in *Howard Smith Ltd v Ampol Petroleum Ltd* (1974). In *Ampol* the directors of HS, a company in need of further finance, issued shares to members who held a minority interest in the company but offered none to the majority shareholder (A) who had made an unwanted take-over bid. This allotment of shares reduced A's shareholding to below 50% and was challenged by as an improper use of the directorial power to issue shares. The Privy Council ruled that when a use of power is challenged, the court should first consider the nature of the power, ie why was this power conferred on the directors whose exercise thereof is in question, and then examine the substantial purpose for which it was exercised. If the power was not exercised for the proper purpose the exercise of the power was void. The court stated that the decision as to whether the power was properly exercised is determined objectively. In this case the court ruled that the power to allot shares is given to directors to raise funds for the company and that while the directors intended this allotment to raise capital the primary purpose of the issue was to defeat A's bid and not to raise money. Consequently, this allotment was void. Other cases on this area have held that an improper use of directorial power can be ratified by ordinary resolution (*Bamford v Bamford* (1970)) but the directors of Bombay cannot guarantee they will be able, without shareholder support, to pass such a resolution. Whether the directors can convince the court that a proposal to increase their own shareholding is a proper use of directorial power depends upon why they were given the power to allot shares. Perhaps if the directors proposed to allot shares to themselves in return for an agreement to work for the company this could be seen as beneficial to the company (even though no cash was raised which is what the cases seem to say is the only proper purpose underlying an allotment) and hence an allotment for a proper purpose. Note that the power to raise the proper purpose point is technically a matter for the company (ie *Foss v Harbottle* (1843) applies) but the courts have been prepared to allow a minority shareholder to raise the issue (*Hogg v Cramphorn* (1967)) unless and until the impropriety is ratified by the company in general meeting.

Finally, the directors should consider how they are going to pay for any shares they decide to allot to themselves. They could pay in cash. There is no requirement that the shares be issued at a price in excess of their nominal value (*Hilder v Dexter* (1902)) but the price which the directors agree to pay cannot be less than the nominal value (s 100). If shares are allotted at a discount the allotment is valid but the allottee (and in some cases any subsequent holder) is liable to pay the amount of the discount, with interest, to the company (ss 100, 112). The directors might prefer to pay other than in cash and s 99 provides that shares can be paid for in money or money's worth. This may be an attractive proposition in that the directors do not have to pay cash and it evades the pre-emption rule. Since Bombay is a private company there is no requirement that the non-cash consideration be professionally valued and it is common practice in private companies for directors to pay for shares by agreeing to work for the company. Provided the non-cash consideration is not wholly illusory (for example when the agreement to work is given by a director who is incapable of work) and the company (manifested by the directors) honestly regard the consideration as approximating in value to the nominal value of the shares allotted, the court will not examine too closely the valuation of non-cash consideration (*Re Wragg Ltd* (1897)).

Undoubtedly the simplest means of acquiring control of the company is to purchase shares from the existing shareholder but if this is not possible then the directors should enlist the support of sufficient shareholders to be able to pass an ordinary resolution, create more shares and allot them to themselves and then ratify any breach of directors' duty.

Question 34

The elaborate provisions of company law designed to ensure that a company does not issue shares at a discount and maintains its share capital thereafter are designed to protect the creditors of the company. Creditors would be better protected by a requirement that a company must have a minimum share capital which has been fully paid up in cash.

Comment on this assertion.

Answer plan

The question suggests that the rules relating to capital maintenance are ineffective in achieving their designated aim – the protection of creditors. Thus, three issues arise. First, what are the rules and second are the rules designed to protect creditors. Finally, having analysed the rules relating to capital maintenance, consider the minimum share capital requirements and comment on whether amendment of these rules would better protect creditors.

Answer

Shares in companies are not government issued bonds and directors are not trustees, consequently, Parliament and the courts have always acknowledged that investors in, and creditors of, companies face some degree of risk. The directors cannot be expected to try and maximise profits without taking risks and their attempts may be unsuccessful either because of bad luck, or incompetence, or general trading conditions, or changes in government policy or for any number of other reasons. Parliament has sought to strike a balance between regulation of companies in pursuance of the general good and allowing businesspeople to conduct their affairs as they see fit with a view to maximising profit. In addition, Parliament has tried to ensure that company insiders (directors and shareholders) do not protect their own position at the expense of the company's creditors. Consequently, the current system is designed to be a balance – risk is not eliminated but is subject to management, and creditors, who have no control over how the company is run, have some protection from insiders. The way the rules on capital maintenance operate may incidentally benefit shareholders (who arguably need less protection than creditors since they have more control over the company) but the rules on capital maintenance are traditionally acknowledged as designed to protect creditors. In *Flitcroft's Case* (1882), Jessel MR characterised a company creditor as person who gives credit to the company on the basis of a representation that the company would maintain its share capital, not misuse it and not return it to shareholders albeit his (ie a creditor's) right is enforceable ultimately only by winding up. Nowadays, the share capital (plus undistributable reserves) is often called the creditors buffer. This gives the impression that the funds subscribed by investors remain in a locked account available to be distributed to creditors if the company does not pay its debts. This is not the case. As the House of Lords readily accepted in *Trevor v Whitworth* (1877), the money subscribed for shares can be used in the course of the business. All a creditor is entitled to expect is that the money subscribed for shares has been used in the legitimate course of business. Thus, capital maintenance can be seen as a means of creditor protection – the efficacy of this protection will now be examined.

There are two aspects of capital maintenance; first the company must raise share capital and second, the company must not return it, except when authorised so to do, to the shareholders prior to winding up.

Raising share capital

A private company limited by shares has no minimum share capital set out in the Act. All that is required is one subscriber (there can be more) to its memorandum and he must take at least one share. Shares must have a nominal value of a fixed amount (s 2) hence a private company must have a share capital of at least 1p (1 x 1p shares). A private company need not issue a minimum number of shares, all that is required is one for the (or each) subscriber to the memorandum (s 1). A private company need not issue shares fully paid, ie with the full nominal value paid (in cash or otherwise) on issue, although most shares are issued fully paid. Where shares are not issued fully paid up, the company can make calls (demands for all or some of the nominal value not yet paid by the current or a former shareholder) upon the current holders of the shares for further sums up to the full amount of a share's nominal value (and any agreed premium). If the nominal value of issued shares (plus any premium) has not been paid at the time of winding up, the shortfall is recoverable from the then holders of those shares if the company is unable to meet its liabilities. In practice the majority of private companies have a total share capital of £1,000 or less and individual shares have a nominal value of 10p or £1. Since most companies formed in the UK are private companies, the share capital subscribed at the outset (or claimable on an insolvent winding up) is not likely to be a large sum so that it offers no real protection to creditors even if it the cash obtained remains unspent rather than simply forming an entry in the books of the company. A persistent criticism of UK company law is that it allows grossly under-capitalised companies to be formed. It is true that most companies formed in the UK survive for less than 10 years but since companies can use money subscribed for shares (so long as used legitimately) it is not the lack of share capital which leaves companies vulnerable to cash flow problems but a lack of *cash*. Public companies are subject to a marginally more rigorous regime. A public company must have a minimum share capital of £50,000 (s 118) of which at least one-quarter must have been subscribed (s 101) plus the whole of any premium, before the company can commence trading. In practice most public companies (certainly quoted companies) have a share capital way in excess of this sum.

The Act lays down elaborate rules to ensure that shares are not issued at a discount (s 100), that is at a price below the nominal value of the share. Note, however, that the full nominal value need not be paid on issue provided the contract of sale provides that the price which the company may at some point demand (now or in the future) exceeds the specified nominal value (plus any premium provided for in the contract of issue). If shares are issued at a discount, the allotment is still valid although the original allottee is liable to make good the discount (plus interest) and subsequent holders of the shares may also incur liability for any shortfall (ss 100, 112). Where the discount is not recovered from a shareholder, the directors are liable to make good the shortfall. In *Ooregum Gold Mining Co of India v Roper* (1892), the company's existing £1 shares were trading on the market for less than their nominal value. The company wished to sell more shares and allowed people to subscribe for £1 nominal value shares for 25p which was specified in the contract of sale as the only sum payable. The House of Lords ruled that shareholders who had purchased these shares were liable to pay a further 75p on the winding up of the company despite the shares being described by the company as 'issued partly paid' since to issue a share partly paid is to issue at a discount. However, there is a major loophole in the 'no discount' rule; a company can accept payment for shares (other than those taken by the subscribers to the memorandum, s 106) in money or *money's worth* (s 99). Thus, non-cash consideration is acceptable and the courts make little inquiry into the value of non-cash consideration unless it is illusory or manifestly inadequate (*Re Wragg Ltd* (1897)). The ability to outflank the no-discount rule by allotting shares other than for cash has been restricted in respect of public companies. Section 99 provides that an undertaking to work for a public company (or another) is not good consideration and the holder must pay the nominal value of the shares (plus interest). Section 102 prohibits the allotment of shares by a public company in consideration of an undertaking which is to be, or may be performed more than five years after the date of allotment – an undertaking to be performed so far in advance is akin to being illusory. Section 103 provides that a public company shall not allot shares in return for the acquisition of a non-cash asset unless the asset has been professionally valued (there are exceptions, eg when there is a take-over and payment is by a share swap). The Act then elaborates the valuation procedure at length. Breach of these provisions renders the allottee liable to pay the nominal value of the shares (plus any premium and interest). Subsequent holders of the shares are jointly and severally liable (s 112) unless they are purchasers for value without actual notice (or acquired the shares from such a holder). The courts can relieve a holder from liability where it is just and equitable so to do (s 113). Consequently, in *Re Ossory Estates plc* (1988), a shareholder, who had partly paid for shares by means of non-cash consideration (land) which had not been properly valued, and was thus liable to pay the full nominal value of the shares, was relieved from liability when it emerged that the company had sold part of the land for a price far exceeding the notional value of all the land transferred to it. Relief was appropriate since there was manifestly no issue at a discount. The rules on the issue of shares have been called 'a pretty large sledgehammer to crack a fairly small nut'.

Maintaining share capital

Having obtained its share capital the company must maintain it. This sounds as though the company must squirrel the money away or at least deposit it in some extraordinarily safe investment. This is not the case. A company can use the money it has garnered provided it is used legitimately (for example not in an *ultra vires* activity). In particular, a company should not return this share capital to the shareholders for to do so would illegitimately exhaust the funds available for creditors. To ensure the proper maintenance of share capital a company cannot:

- pay dividends to shareholders other than out of distributable profits (ss 263–281);
- buy its own shares (s 143 – no new capital and old capital used up improperly);
- provide financial assistance to others to buy its shares (s 151 – again the company's money is simply recycled);
- reduce share capital without court approval (s 135).

The rules on what constitutes distributable profits which are available for payment as dividends (a company need not declare a dividend even if it has such profits) are now determined by statute and are a clarified version of those developed by the judges over a hundred years. The statutory rules aim to ensure that unrealised profits, for example when land is revalued, are not used to justify dividends and that profits made in one year cannot be paid out as dividends when the company has made substantial losses in previous years. Consequently, there is little opportunity for a company to pay a dividend unless it has generated a profit. However, there is nothing to stop a company paying directors or director shareholders large fees or salaries for acting as a director of the company whether the company has made such profits or not. Obviously, where director shareholders have paid themselves large sums, despite the lack of profits, and the company has gone into insolvent liquidation, the directors may incur liability for fraudulent or wrongful trading and be required to contribute to the assets of the company. There has been considerable concern expressed about the level of directors' salaries/fees in some companies, particularly when the company has not generated any or many profits. Many public companies have adopted the recommendation of the Cadbury Committee that the directors remuneration be fixed by a special committee without a majority of directors but as yet no appreciable difference is salaries has been noted.

The rules which prohibit a company from buying its own shares or providing financial assistance to another to purchase shares in the company were until 1980 subject to few exceptions. Since 1980, the number of exceptions has increased, underpinning the new exceptions are certain general principles – adequate publicity, shareholder approval and, where the funds used by the company are not distributable profits (which could have been paid to the shareholders as dividends anyway), but payments out of capital (only open to private companies), protection of creditors. These exceptions were part of a package of measures introduced to help companies, particularly private companies, raise money. Consider, the purchase by a company of its own shares. Prior to 1980 a private company wishing to raise outside investment faced two difficulties – issuing new shares diluted existing shareholdings thus affecting the control of the company (unattractive to current shareholders particularly in a family company) and new investors would obtain a minority shareholding which would be, effectively, unmarketable. The provisions allowing a company to issue redeemable shares or to buy back its own shares were designed to provide sufficient flexibility to permit existing shareholders to retain control while increasingly the marketability of shares and continuing to protect creditors. Creditors are protected by the requirement that directors issue a statutory declaration that the company can in their opinion pay its debts (and will be able to do so for the next 12 months) before a resolution to allow self-purchase out of capital or financial assistance can proceed. The auditors of the company must then comment on the directors' opinion in a report and must confirm that, having looked at the company's state of affairs, they are not aware of anything which would render the director's opinion unreasonable (ss 156, 173). Section 176 allows a creditor to object to a purchase of shares by the company funded out of capital (five-week time limit from date of resolution) and s 177 sets out the court's powers when an objection has been lodged; the court can, among other things, affirm, reject or modify the proposal and can order the objectors to be paid off. Where a company goes into liquidation within 12 months of a statutory declaration, the directors may be liable to contribute to the assets of the company (s 76 Insolvency Act 1986). Apart from the excessively complicated nature of the provisions, these rules seem to provide adequate protection for creditors.

Section 135 permits a company to reduce share capital provided that the articles of the company permit a reduction, a reduction has been authorised by special resolution and the court has approved the reduction. Section 135 does not limit the circumstances in which a company may seek to reduce capital but it does specify three possible grounds for so doing. Where one of these three grounds is the basis of an application a court is likely to approve the reduction provided the position of the company's creditors is secured (ss 136 and 137 provide rules for dealing with creditors unhappy with the reduction).

Conclusion

Creditors, particularly unsecured creditors, are adversely affected when a company goes into insolvent liquidation – the current rules do not prevent such losses. However, it is by no means clear that requiring companies to have a larger share capital would prove an acceptable solution. Are the rules on non-cash consideration to be changed, is there to be a minimum subscription for private companies, would such changes stifle new businesses? Surely, an effective balance between encouraging business initiative and protecting creditors is to encourage efficient directors rather than further complicating the rules on capital maintenance.

Question 35

You have recently become company secretary of Glitz Ltd a moderately successful company owned and run by various members of the Sparkle family. The board has decided to undertake a major acquisition of new machinery which cannot be financed from the company's reserves. The machinery is likely to enhance production efficiency and capacity for a number of years. The directors do not wish to dilute their voting strength within the company and are uncertain whether the shareholders will support this major purchase. The board is keen to ensure that whatever means of financing is adopted it will attract the necessary funds.

Outline the possible sources of finance and the extent to which these methods meet the requirements of the board.

Answer plan

First analyse the requirements of the board, then consider possible sources of finance – particularly, loans and shares (ordinary and preference) – in the light of them. Draw a conclusion on suitability.

Answer

The board wish to raise finance for a long-term project designed to increase the profitability of the company. They wish to ensure that the money is raised so the proposed source of funding must be sufficiently attractive to potential investors. However, the directors do not wish their voting strength to be diluted and, given the possible disquiet among existing shareholders, the board will need to ensure that their shareholdings and benefits are not diminished. Possible sources of finance will be examined bearing in mind these constraints. It may be noted in passing that the unease of the shareholders does not preclude this project proceeding. The directors run the company (subject to the giving of directions by special resolution) and need not bow to the wishes of the shareholders although the risk of being dismissed if too many shareholders are upset cannot be ignored (s 303, ordinary resolution required). Possibly the unease of the shareholders could be quietened by the circulation of some explanation for the new scheme pointing to the possibility of enhanced profits even if there is a temporary reduction in distributable profits.

What are the relative merits of shares and loans in this context.

(a) *Shares and loans*

The issue of further shares may be attractive to a company from a financial point of view in that dividends must be paid only if the company has made a distributable profit and the directors have declared a dividend. Thus, shares provide a means of raising capital without any continuing payment obligation on the part of the company. Nor is a company required to repay the capital acquired by means of an allotment of shares (unless they are redeemable shares) so the funds raised for the machinery need not be repaid by the company. Consequently, to an investor the purchase of shares can be seen as a risky investment. There is no guarantee of income and the capital invested is, at best, recoverable on winding up. Indeed on winding up, a shareholder has claims on the assets of the company only when the creditors have been paid in full. While the company is a going concern, and particularly if the machinery is as useful as suggested, there is the possibility of capital growth within the shares but in a private company this growth is hard to realise, the shares are not freely marketable and the attitude of the Sparkle family to new shareholders may not be accommodating if the allottee wishes to sell out subsequently. Hence seeking new shareholders (even if the practical problems of issue can be overcome – see below) from outside the company may not be successful. Of course the board can always offer shares to existing shareholders to raise further funds. Indeed, a further issue of shares to outside investors may be unattractive to existing shareholders who see the pool of money available for the payment of dividends being available to a greater number of participants than previously. Further, extra shareholders would diminish the proportion of shares held by existing shareholders, including the directors, which the board wish to avoid if it dilutes their voting strength. Loans, on the other hand, do not dilute existing shareholdings but do carry a continuing financial commitment. The interest payable on the loan must be paid even if the company has not made any profits, although interest payments can be deducted from income to determine the company's net profits. In addition, the loan will have to be repaid in accordance with the loan particulars and failure to meet repayments could lead to the lender initiating action against the company. A loan may be secured or unsecured, the latter will carry a higher rate of interest, and for a potential investor the secured loan is more attractive. A lender may have power to intervene in the affairs of the company if the loan contract so authorises but a secured lender has statutory and common law powers to seize the charged asset or appoint a Receiver to act on his behalf if his security is at risk. The obvious lenders the company should consider approaching if this is the preferred route are the existing shareholders, especially in a family owned company, and the company's bankers.

One way of reconciling some of the advantages of shares and those of loans could be to attract investment into a new class of shares which do not have voting rights and, thus, do not affect the current voting position within the company. However, non-voting ordinary shares would not be very appealing to an investor and it might be necessary to consider the creation and allotment of preference shares.

(b) *Preference shares and loans*

Preference shares (voting or non-voting) have the attraction from the company's point of view that the financial commitment to pay the preference dividend is, like interest on a loan, a pre-determined sum – assuming the company has profits to sustain any dividend. As with ordinary shares, there is no obligation to repay capital while the company is a going concern although many preference shares are created as redeemable shares and the company will have to redeem them at some future date. Unlike loans, preference shares cannot be issued at a discount (s 100) so that the contracted purchase price cannot be below the nominal value of the shares so that there can be no question of investors buying preference shares of £100 nominal value for £70 and obtaining £100 on redemption. However, Glitz could sell loan notes with a face value of £100 for £70 with the contract providing that when the loan is discharged the loan-notes would be redeemed in full so that the holder would receive back £100. Glitz should be told that it is possible to redeem shares at a premium if the articles so permit and a person buying a share from an existing shareholder may be able to pay a price below the nominal value of the shares although such is hardly a hopeful sign. Preference shares might be unattractive to Glitz for several reasons. First, the shares may be issued at a time of high interest rates thus requiring the company to issue them with a relatively high fixed dividend which remains a continuing commitment even when interest rates fall; this problem is obviated by the use of redeemable shares. Second, a preference shareholder is a member of the company and has, unless the articles provide otherwise, the right to vote and otherwise participate in the running of the company; this is easily overcome by issuing the shares without any or with limited voting rights but unless this is done the directors may find their voting strength diminished. Third, extra classes of shares complicate the share structure of the company and can give rise to problems if the company wishes to vary class rights. Again in common with ordinary shares, preference dividends are paid out of taxable profit and cannot be set against profits. While a lender is not a member of the company and has no direct influence over its affairs which might be attractive to the company, Glitz might still feel the necessity to listen to a major creditor and the documents creating the loan might confer rights on a lender, eg to appoint a director. A lender who seeks to influence the company from outside runs the risk of being classified as a 'shadow director' with consequent director's duties but the same could apply to an influential shareholder.

(c) Practical issues

The board might be able to retain voting control even if further shares are issued even without using non-voting shares. For example, it is possible to alter voting rights of existing shares by the insertion in the articles of a weighted voting clause. Unfortunately for the directors, alteration of the articles requires a special resolution (s 9) and obtaining a majority of three-quarters of those present and voting, given the likely opposition of existing shareholders, seems doubtful. Alternatively, the directors could seek to sub-divide their shares into two or more shares each of which carries a vote. Section 121 permits a company, whose articles so authorise (Table A, art 32 provides authority), to sub-divide shares into shares of smaller nominal value than that fixed in the memorandum. The decision to sub-divide must be made by the company in general meeting, ie an ordinary resolution is required. If the directors decide to raise the necessary capital by allotting shares they can allot any existing unissued shares but if there are no such shares they would have to create a new class and then allot them. Creation of further shares is authorised (for companies whose articles so permit, Table A, art 32 does permit) by s 121 provided the increase in share capital is approved by ordinary resolution. The directors may need support from other members of the Sparkle family to achieve a majority. If the directors propose to allot any existing unissued shares and/or any new shares they face a number of legal difficulties. The power to allot relevant securities (defined in s 94 and including ordinary but not preference shares) is vested in the general meeting even when, as is usual, the power to run the company is vested in the board (s 80). However, s 80 provides that the shareholders can give the power to allot shares to the board either in the articles or by ordinary resolution. Originally, the shareholders had to vote to give the power to allot shares to the directors at least every five years but s 80A allows a private company (by elective resolution in accordance with s 379A) to give the authority for an indefinite period. As company secretary you should be able to discover whether such a resolution has been passed. The authority to allot may be general or limited (eg only applying to some classes of share, or to a maximum number of shares at any one time). The directors can be advised that if they break s 80 and allot shares without authority they are liable to a fine but the allotment is valid. Assuming the directors are authorised to allot shares (or are willing to contravene s 80), they must still be wary of s 89 which provides a right of pre-emption for existing shareholders. Section 89 states that where a company is proposing to allot equity securities (defined in s 94 and including ordinary but not preference shares) wholly for cash, the shares must first be offered to existing shareholders in proportion to their existing shareholding. Thus, s 89 would require the directors to offer any new issue of shares to members of the Sparkle family before seeking outside investment but the section also provides that breach of it does not invalidate the allotment. Breach does, however, expose the directors to liability. The power to organise loans falls within the remit of the board and there is no need to involve the shareholders in any way so there are practical advantages for a board with sceptical shareholders using loans to raise funds for expansion. Further, the allotment of shares, but probably not the raising of loans, is subject to the fiduciary duty to exercise any power of allotment *bona fide* for the benefit of the company and for a proper purpose. The obligation to act *bona fide* (and for the benefit of the company – probably) is subjective so that provided the directors honestly believe they are acting properly in allotting shares to raise funds for the machinery they are not in breach of this limb of their fiduciary duty.

Conclusion

You might tell the board that, from the potential investor's viewpoint both preference shares and loans offer a fixed rate of return but while loan interest must be paid, a dividend is not always covered or declared so that if the company wishes to be sure of success a loan looks more promising. Also the degree of security a loan may offer may attract investors. The right to influence the company by attending general meetings and voting is open only to shareholders and not (directly) creditors but preference shareholders often find their rights curtailed by the articles so that an outside investor might not be influenced by this factor even if the board is. To an investor the benefits of loans appear to outweigh those of shares and the same is probably true for Glitz.

Question 36

Krisp Ltd was incorporated in 1992, its share capital is divided into 5,000 £1 shares – 2,000 6% preference shares and 3,000 ordinary shares. The articles provide that the preference shares confer on the holders thereof:

(a) the right to a dividend of 6% on the paid up value of the shares held; and

(b) the right on winding up to secure the paid up value of the shares in priority to any payment to the ordinary shareholders.

On incorporation Crunch became the sole director of the company the shares of which were all allotted, fully paid, as follows:

(i) 2,999 ordinary shares to Crunch in consideration of his transferring to the company his existing business;

(ii) 1 ordinary share to Mrs Crunch for cash; and

(iii) the preference shares to Mrs Crunch's elderly mother, Mrs Brittle, for cash.

Crunch is paid a generous salary by the company and Mrs Crunch is also paid handsomely for acting as company secretary. The company has made modest profits every year since it commenced trading but has never declared a dividend on either the ordinary or preference shares. Mr and Mrs Crunch have recently separated and there are rumours that Mr Crunch will appoint a new company secretary, Toffee, his new partner. Mrs Crunch she would like to bring an action in Krisp Ltd's name to restrain alleged transfers of assets from Krisp to a new company founded by Mr Crunch and Toffee.

Advise Mrs Crunch and Mrs Brittle as to their entitlements as shareholders while the company is a going concern and on winding up and the likelihood of being able to bring an action on behalf of Krisp against Mr Crunch.

Answer plan

You are directed at two main issues. First, the entitlements of ordinary and preference shareholders while the company is a going concern and the rights of these shareholders if the company is wound up. Second, whether Mr Crunch could incur liability to the company for his actions and, if this is the case, who could commence such an action.

Answer

Before considering the position of the shareholders (other than Crunch) it may be noted that the allotment of shares to Crunch in return for the transfer of his existing business to the company is valid. Section 99 permits shares to be paid for in money or money's worth and there is no requirement that the non-cash consideration be professionally valued (as would be the case if Krisp was a public company). A court has the power to treat shares issued for non-cash consideration as shares issued at a discount (allotment still valid but shares must be paid for and breach of director's duty) but it is exercised very rarely and only when the alleged consideration is manifestly illusory – such is not the case here. Even if the shares had been issued at a discount, the allotment would be valid and Crunch would be liable to make good the shortfall. Thus, there is no doubt that Crunch is the majority shareholder in the company. The extent of his majority depends upon whether the preference shares carry the right to vote at general meetings of the company. Let us consider the position of the minority shareholders.

Shareholder rights

(a) *Mrs Crunch*

While the company is a going concern Mrs Crunch has the usual rights of a member, for example, she can attend meetings and vote and she is entitled to a dividend, if declared. As a minority shareholder with only one share she has no influence within the company although she would be entitled (subject to the discretion of the court) to bring a derivative action on behalf of the company if Crunch was in breach of director's duty and his actions were a

fraud on the minority (on which see below). However, even with
one share she could petition under s 459 if the affairs of the
company were being conducted in a way that was unfairly
prejudicial to her interests as a member. Unfortunately, even if such
is the case the remedy most likely to be awarded is that the
company should buy her share at a fair price which is unlikely to
yield a large return. Has she a s 459 claim? While Mrs Crunch
might object to the absence of dividends she has been paid
'handsomely' for acting as company secretary. Exclusion from the
post of company secretary (should it arise) would not by itself be
unfairly prejudicial but if she had a legitimate expectation that she
would participate in some way in the corporate governance of the
enterprise, albeit not as a director, she might have a remedy.
Further, if the allegations about the asset-stripping are proved this
breach of duty by Crunch would be grounds in itself for a s 459
action. In addition she could seek just and equitable winding up (s
122(1)(g) Insolvency Act) but she would have to establish some
basis for the winding up which seems unlikely on the facts given.
Even if just and equitable winding up was a possibility the court
could deny her this remedy if she had an alternative remedy (s 459
is the obvious one) which it is unreasonable to refuse. Arguably, to
destroy a viable company when her likely entitlement on winding
up is small (£1, ie the nominal value of her share, plus a percentage
of any surplus assets after the claims of the creditors of the
company and her mother have been satisfied) if she can be
adequately compensated for any wrongs done in some other is
unreasonable and is unlikely to be awarded by a court. Crunch
may be equally keen to disengage himself from any business
connection with his estranged wife. He could achieve this by
offering to buy her out which preserves the company as a going
concern or he could choose to initiate a voluntary winding up of
the company. A voluntary winding up requires the passing of a
special resolution and his ability to achieve such a resolution
depends upon whether Mrs Brittle can vote.

(b) *Mrs Brittle*

Her position is very different. In determining her rights the courts
have regard to two canons of construction (ie presumptions drawn
in the absence of evidence to the contrary). First, the House of

Lords in *Birch v Cropper* (1889), in which the issue was whether the ordinary and preference shareholders had equal rights to the surplus assets of a company on winding up, ruled that all shares of whatever class are presumed to carry equal rights unless this presumption is rebutted by words indicating an inequality. Thus where the articles are silent all shareholders have the right to attend all company meetings and vote on all resolutions. The courts have tended to find words sufficient to rebut the presumption of equality with relative ease. However, on the facts of this case, there seems no reason why Mrs Brittle should not be entitled to vote, consequently she (with Mrs Crunch) controls two-fifths of the votes at a general meeting and has the power to block a special resolution but not an ordinary resolution. The second presumption applied by the courts is that where the articles (or other relevant documents) specify that preference shares carry particular rights that is a statement of maximum entitlement, this presumption is extremely difficult to rebut. Consequently, where, as here the articles of the company provide that the preference shares carry a right to a preferential dividend (6% in this case), the preference shareholder must be paid her dividend (if the company has made profits and declares a dividend) in full before the ordinary shareholders are entitled to a penny. However, having received her 6% (£120 per annum) that exhausts her right to dividend and she has no further entitlement to dividend on those shares. Does this mean that where, as in this case, a company has declared no dividends for some years the company continue to roll up profits and at some point in the future decide to pay a dividend of 6% to Mrs Brittle for that year and then distribute the balance to the ordinary shareholders (this sounds very tax inefficient)? In other words is a preference dividend once missed lost for ever or does the unpaid dividend roll up year on year so that the accumulated sum must be paid before the ordinary shareholders can receive anything. In *Webb v Earle* (1875), the court held that preference dividend is presumed to be cumulative (ie unpaid dividend rolls up) unless there is evidence to rebut the presumption – the articles of Krisp do not appear to render preference shares non-cumulative (but note the position if the company is wound up – see below). Non-payment of dividend, particularly if Crunch could be said to be using the company's profits to enhance his own position (generous salary), could justify a finding of unfair prejudice (s 459, *Re Sam*

Weller Ltd (1989)) which would allow the court, if it wished, to order the dividend be paid or to amend the articles to strengthen Mrs Brittle's rights (s 461).

Mrs Brittle appears to have the power to block a voluntary winding up of the company (Crunch cannot pass a special resolution if she votes against it) but she could not prevent an unpaid creditor petitioning. It might be argued that Mrs Brittle should seek a just and equitable winding up of the company (s 122(1)(g) Insolvency Act 1986) on the ground that this company was a family company, that she invested in the company to support her son-in-law and that, if the Crunches divorce, the relationship of the members is such that had they been partners, a dissolution of the partnership would have been ordered (*Ebrahimi v Westbourne Galleries Ltd* (1973)). If there is a voluntary winding up (on whatever basis) and, after payment of the liquidator and the creditors, there are surplus assets what are Mrs Brittle's rights? The articles plainly displace the presumption of equality – she is entitled to £1 per share (£2,000) if the assets are sufficient but to no more (*Scottish Ins Corn v Wilson & Clyde Coal Co Ltd* (1949)) whatever the size of the surplus. Thus, if Krisp has surplus assets of £2,000, it all goes to Mrs Brittle, if £5,000 then each shareholder receives a pound per share but if £11,000 then Mrs Brittle gets £2,000 and the ordinary shareholders share the remainder (£3 per share). One further point – suppose that at the date of any winding up Mrs Brittle is owed arrears of preference dividend, are these arrears a debt which must be paid off before the shareholders receive anything, or are arrears, not paid off prior to winding up, lost? It appears that, unless the presumption can be rebutted, arrears of preference dividend are lost once winding up commences. This would allow an unscrupulous board to miss dividends for many years, build up surplus funds from profits which could have been paid as dividends, put the company into liquidation and pay the accumulated surplus (less any prior claim to return of capital vested in the preference shareholders) to the ordinary shareholders alone. Not surprisingly, the courts have tended to find words to rebut the presumption that the unpaid dividend is lost on winding up if at all possible (*Re Wharfedale Brewery Co Ltd* (1952)). In this case the wording of the articles might, surprisingly, suffice – 'in priority to any payment to the ordinary shareholders' could be the straw to which a court would cling to avoid the unfairness of denying arrears to Mrs Brittle.

Mrs Crunch and Mrs Brittle would be well advised to pursue the statutory remedies (ss 459 and 122(1)(g)) open to them as members rather than rely on their contractual rights as shareholders. Alternatively, they might seek to sell their shares to Crunch but cannot force him to buy them. It is too late to do anything in this case but, should Mrs Crunch re-marry and Mrs Brittle wish to invest in her new son-in-law's business, she should avoid irredeemable preference shares. Indeed one could argue that everyone should avoid all types of preference share!

Action against Crunch

As the director of the company, Crunch owes a fiduciary duty to the company (not to the shareholders, *Percival v Wright* (1902)) and his obligations include a duty not to allow his personal interests and his duty to conflict. Simply, receiving a large salary is not breach of fiduciary duty although there are certain requirements which must be complied with if a director is to contract with his company (essentially duties of disclosure). Failure to meet these requirements may make certain contracts voidable at the company's option but do not confer any right to sue on Mrs Crunch or Mrs Brittle in their own right or on behalf of the company. However, if Crunch is stripping assets from Krisp and transferring them to a new company he may be also be in breach of the duty cast on all directors not to misuse corporate assets. If he is so engaged, he is unlikely to wish to initiate litigation against himself on behalf of Krisp. Krisp being the proper plaintiff in an action since it is the company's assets which are being removed (*Foss v Harbottle* (1843)). However, while shareholders are not normally permitted to act on behalf of the company in respect of wrongs done to the company an action is permitted where the wrongdoers control the company. Crunch controls Krisp and he, allegedly, is a wrongdoer and it would seem that Mrs Crunch or Mrs Brittle could sue on behalf of the company. However, the right of a shareholder to act for the company is limited by the courts to those cases where the shareholder is acting for the company and not in pursuance of some private agenda and the action is likely to benefit the company. A recent illustration of the operation of these principles is contained in *Barrett v Duckett* (1995). In that case a shareholder, B, owned 50% of the shares of T Ltd and was the mother-in-law of the other shareholder, D, who was the director of the company. D and B's daughter had divorced. The Court of Appeal, ruled that a shareholder who sought to sue on behalf of a company must establish 'to the satisfaction of the court' that he should be allowed to sue on behalf of the company and that 'the shareholder will be allowed to sue on behalf of the company if he is bringing the action *bona fide* for the benefit of the company for wrongs to the company for which no other remedy is available. Conversely if the action is brought for an ulterior purpose or if another adequate remedy is available, the court will not allow the derivative action to proceed'. In this case, as in *Barrett*, there may well be an ulterior motive in seeking to bring an action on behalf of Krisp. There is probably an alternative action (liquidation or s 459) open to the minority shareholders. Liquidation would certainly deprive the alleged wrongdoer of his control of the company and allow an independent liquidator to pursue such remedies against him as he thought appropriate. A s 459 action would also involve exposing Crunch's dealings to the courts and if he has been asset-stripping the court could order him to re-imburse the company, be bought out by another shareholder or compensate the minority shareholders for any losses attributable to his misdealing.

Question 37

Surplus plc was once a large trading concern and has substantial cash assets. Over recent years it has hived off the majority of its activities into new companies, over which it retains control, leaving itself with little in the way of direct trading operations but it continues to generate substantial profits.

The articles of the company provide that rights attaching to any class of shares can be varied provided that holders of three-quarters of the nominal value of the issued shares of that class approve, in writing or at a meeting, the proposed variation. The preference shareholders have no right to vote at general meetings of the company.

The company proposes the following:

(a) To reduce share capital by paying off at par the 'A' preference shares which carry a right to a 10% preference dividend, are preferential as to return of capital and have a right further to participate on winding up to a maximum of £1 per share.

(b) To redeem immediately at £2 over par the 'B' preference shares which carry a right to a 15% dividend and which are redeemable at par in 1996/7.

(c) To reduce the preference dividend payable on the 'C' preference shares (which carry rights of equal participation on winding up) from 12% to 10%. (d) To issue bonus shares to the ordinary shareholders on a one-for-one basis.

Amy, who owns 'A', 'B' and 'C' preference shares objects to these proposals. She believes that the majority of the A and B preference shareholders would accept the proposals. Advise her on the legitimacy of these proposals.

Answer plan

The first two proposals involve a reduction of share capital and Amy may also allege they are a variation of her class rights. The third proposal is not a reduction but may be a variation. The final proposal is not a reduction but indirectly affects the preference shareholders. Finally s 459 may be relevant.

Answer

Amy is faced with proposals for massive re-structuring of the share capital of the company. She is unhappy with the scheme put forward by the management, but believes she will be in a minority in objecting to it. Two, or more, classes of shareholder may be unpopular with the management of the company, who may prefer a simpler share structure, and multiple classes can lead to disputes between classes of shareholder over the rights which each class possess. The Companies Act 1985 allows a company to alter its share capital by ordinary resolution (s 121) but provides special rules for the reduction of capital and the variation of rights attaching to any class of shares. Can Amy avail herself of any of these provisions?

(a) *Reduction of capital*

The proposals concerning the A and B preference shares both involve a reduction of share capital. Reduction of share capital has an adverse effect on the creditor's buffer and may also, as here, be opposed by shareholders whose shares will be abolished. Reduction is possible if it is done in compliance with the Act. Section 135 states that a company can reduce share capital provided:

- it has the power to do so in its articles (Table A, art 34 gives such a power); and
- it passes a special resolution to do so; and
- the court confirms the reduction.

The creditors of Surplus are given *locus* to object to any reduction but it seems none are doing so. It is assumed that the proposed reduction will not reduce the share capital of the company below the minimum specified in the Act (s 117). There are no specific provisions in the Act dealing with the rights of shareholders when a reduction is proposed but the House of Lords determined in the 19th century that the courts have a discretion to confirm or reject a proposed reduction of capital. The definitive view of when the discretion should be exercised was given in *Scottish Insurance Corpn Ltd v Wilsons & Clyde Coal Co* (1916), in which the House of Lords held that the jurisdiction of the courts was not limited to ensuring the technical accuracy of a petition to reduce but extended to ensuring that the reduction was fair and reasonable. However, despite the existence of a broad jurisdiction to reject an application to reduce, the courts have exercised that power very infrequently. In *Re Ratners Group plc* (1988), Harman J ruled that, assuming the reduction was not a 'hollow and pointless act', the court would confirm a reduction where three principles had been satisfied. First, all shareholders should be treated equitably (which generally means equally unless some shareholders have agreed to being treated differently). Second, the proposals should have been properly explained to the shareholders so that they could exercise an informed judgment on them. Third, creditors must be adequately protected. As a gloss on Harman's view it must be added that where a scheme is supported by the company, creditors and the majority of shareholders it is unlikely to be rejected by the court. Consequently, Amy should be advised that the procedures for reduction of capital may be satisfied. What may cause a court to pause before confirming the proposals for the A and B shares is the fact that the preference and ordinary shareholders are being treated differently *and* there is perhaps a variation of class rights.

(b) *Reduction and variation of class rights*

In determining whether to confirm the reduction of share capital, the courts will decide if the proposal treats the preference shareholders equitably. Where the reduction involves a variation of the class rights of the relevant shareholders the court will not treat the proposal as fair and equitable unless the relevant class have consented to the proposal. The court will ascertain if there is a variation of class rights by comparing the rights of the preference shareholders on winding up (or redemption in the case of the redeemable shares) with their rights under the proposed reduction. This literal approach has been much criticised but remains the norm for variation of class rights cases. An extreme example of the literal approach is *Re Mackenzie* (1916) discussed below.

In this case the company is seeking to repay the preference shareholders the par value of their shares with, in the case of the B shares a £2 bonus. The B shareholders are being deprived of their income (the dividend) but are receiving that which they would get on redemption plus a bonus. The A shareholders are obtaining a preferential right to return of capital but are losing their right to dividend and the right to participate on winding up to the extent of a further £1 per share. What will the courts do in such cases? Amy should be advised that the courts have generally been reluctant to treat the abolition of preference shareholders (with consequent loss of an assured income) as a variation of class rights. In *Re Saltdean Estate Co Ltd* (1968), Buckley J said that where a company wished to pay off capital as surplus to its requirements *prima facie* it should repay first those shareholders who would be repaid first on winding up. The A and B shareholders would appear to have rights which would require them to be repaid before the ordinary shareholders and thus to pay them off would not be regarded as unfair. In the same case, Buckley J said that no doubt the preference shareholders hope to retain their interest in the company but this expectation is always vulnerable to a future winding up or reduction of capital, 'this vulnerability has always been a characteristic of the preferred shares. Now that the event has occurred [reduction], none of the preferred shareholders can assert that the resulting state of affairs is unfair to him'. The decision in *Saltdean* was approved by the House of Lords in *House of Fraser v ACGE Investments Ltd* (1987) but these case left open the problem of the preference shareholder whose rights on winding up extended beyond a preferential right to return of capital.

The A shares have a limited participatory right on winding up (£1 per share over par – assuming sufficient surplus assets) which abolition will destroy. In *Re William Jones & Sons Ltd* (1969), the court confirmed a reduction by which the preference shareholders with such a participatory right were abolished. However, the preference shareholders made no objection to the scheme which involved them being paid off at par when the market value of the shares was below par. The judge, Buckley J again, treated the right of participation as ephemeral given there was no prospect of the company being wound up. Whether the lack of an immediate prospect of winding up justifies the refusal to treat the abolition of the preference shareholders rights as unfair seems doubtful. Clearly, when winding up is imminent an attempt to implement a reduction of capital which abolishes preference shareholders with participatory rights is a variation which could lead to a rejection of a capital reduction proposal (*Re Old Silkstone Collieries Ltd* (1954)).

It seems probable that these proposals will be confirmed by the court. However, if the reduction of the A shares is a variation of class rights it is likely that the company would be required to comply with its own variation clause in order to obtain confirmation of the reduction. It is possible that the articles of the company provide that *any* reduction of share capital is a variation of the rights of a class of shares which is subject to the reduction. If this is so then the usual rules for variation apply (see *Re Northern Engineering Industries plc* (1994) where the articles were so construed). Where the company has to consult its shareholders about a proposal because it is a variation, s 127 provides an unhappy shareholder with a further line of attack.

(c) *Variation without reduction*

Is the proposal to reduce the C preference dividend a variation of the class rights of holders of those shares? The courts adopt a narrow view of variation in that a comparison is drawn between the right which would attach to a share before and after the proposed amendment of the class right – if the right is literally the same there is no variation. Hence, in *Re Mackenzie & Co Ltd* (1916), the company had 4% preference shares with a nominal value of £20 thus paying a dividend of 80p per share. The company amended its articles to reduce the nominal value o the preference shares to £12 thus reducing the preference dividend to 48p per share. The court held that since the preference shareholders had the same right both before and after the amendment (4% dividend) their class rights had not been varied. However in this case the proposed amendment is a variation (reduction of dividend from 12% to 10%). That being the case, the company must comply with the appropriate procedures for the variation of class rights. It is not clear if Amy's class rights are conferred by the memorandum or the articles – the latter is more usual. Class rights contained in the articles can be varied if the company has a class rights variation clause (whenever included in the articles) and complies with it. There is no such clause in Table A but Surplus plc has a clause. Consequently, the C shareholders should be consulted to see if they support the proposal and if they do not approve by the necessary majority (consent seems improbable) the variation cannot take effect. Even if the relevant shareholders do approve the variation, s 127 allows a dissentient shareholder(s) who holds 15% of the relevant class of shares and who did not vote for the variation to apply to the court to have the variation set aside. The application must be within 21 days of the vote unless and until the court confirms the variation it has no effect. The court can will refuse to confirm a variation if it would unfairly prejudice the shareholders of the class represented by the applicant. There are very few cases on this provision so that it is difficult to advise Amy as to what might constitute unfair prejudice. If the class rights are contained in the memorandum, s 125(3) provides that they can be varied if the company has a class rights variation clause in the articles *which was included in the articles at the time of incorporation* and the company complies with its own rules. Hence, Surplus could seek to amend the dividend rights but the proposal is subject to approval by the C shareholders. If the C shareholders agree, Amy, provided she has the requisite number of shares, can apply under s 127. If the variation clause did not form part of the original articles then s 125(5) applies. Section 125(5) provides that in such a case class rights can be varied only if all shareholders in the company (not just of the relevant class) agree to it. Where the company proposes to hold a class meeting to vote on the variation, the Act lays down rules for the amount of notice etc required.

The proposed allotment of bonus shares to the ordinary shareholders will not, it seems, be treated as a variation of the rights of the preference shareholders even if, as here, the preference shareholders (at least the A shares until abolished and the C shares) have a right to participate if the assets of the company so that any increase in the number of shares potentially reduces the amount of surplus assets payable in respect of each share (*Dimbula Valley (Ceylon) Tea Co v Laurie* (1961)).

Given that Amy believes the majority of preference shareholders will support these proposals she is unlikely to be successful in her applications to court even where she has *locus*. Perhaps she is best advised either to bring an action under s 459 alleging unfair prejudice – however, the likely remedy would be to be bought out at a fair price, ie she would not be able to retain her stake in the company. It might be argued that since many public companies provide that on a reduction of capital in circumstances such as these, the company will pay the former shareholders the market value of their shares, for Surplus to seek to do otherwise is inherently prejudicial. If the reduction in dividend was seen as unfairly prejudicial the court could order the dividend to be restored (s 461) or grant such other remedy as it saw fit. The issue of bonus shares is unlikely to be unfairly prejudicial without some other element of impropriety.

Question 38

Teddy has recently taken over as company secretary of Bear plc an unlisted public company and has been investigating the administration of the company. He has discovered the following and seeks your advice:

(a) Six months ago, Rupert, purchased shares in the company and applied to be registered as a shareholder. The directors have just decided to refuse to register Rupert but have given no reasons. The articles of the company provide that, 'The directors may choose to refuse to register as a member any person to whom shares have been transferred'.

(b) Paddington, the registered holder of 1,000 shares, claims that his share certificate was stolen and that a forged transfer of shares was made in favour of Bungle. Bungle is seeking registration as a shareholder.

(c) Bear plc has recently paid a dividend and it has come to light that payment was made to six members who had sold their shares in the previous year. This occurred because the names of these members had not been removed from the register.

(d) It has just emerged that the previous company secretary, X, forged a share transfer from a member, Fred, and issued a share certificate in respect of the shares so 'transferred' to his wife. Winnie innocently purchased shares from X's wife, was registered as a shareholder and was issued with a share certificate by X. Fred wishes to be re-instated on the register of members.

All the shares in Bear plc are fully paid up.

Answer plan

The question, on various aspects of share transfer, is broken down into four single issue parts. The issues raised are, the right (if any) of the directors to refuse to register a transferee of shares, the effect of a forged share transfer, the effect of non-removal from the register of members and whether the company is bound by an act of forgery committed internally.

Answer

All companies are required to have a company secretary (s 283) who may be a natural legal person or a company and who may also be a director of the company but not the sole director (s 283). Public companies like Bear plc are encouraged to appoint as company secretary a person of appropriate qualification and experience (s 286). Teddy, as company secretary, is likely to carry out many of the administrative tasks imposed on companies by the Companies Act and supervise the general administration of the company including the maintenance of the company's registers. One register which is required to be kept is a register of members (s 352) which must be kept at the company's registered office (s 353). In this case, Teddy appears to have discovered some problems in respect of the register of members and seeks your advice about four particular cases.

(a) Rupert

Shares in a company are freely transferable (s 182). The basic transfer procedure is that the registered holder completes and signs an instrument of transfer and delivers it with his share certificate to the transferee (Rupert) who completes the instrument of transfer, has it stamped, and then delivers it with the share certificate to the company. However, agreeing to a transfer does not make Rupert a member of the company. He must be registered as a shareholder if he is to be a member of Bear plc and until registration the company will not issue a share certificate in his name. Table A, art 24 entitles the directors to refuse to register *partly* paid shares but no discretion to refuse to register fully paid shares unless the articles so provide, the articles of this company do so provide. If Bear was a *quoted* public company the Stock Exchange listing requirements (which require shares in quoted companies to be freely transferable other than in exceptional cases) would preclude the articles empowering its directors to refuse transfers. However, an unquoted company can have such a provision. The courts will construe the power to refuse to register narrowly since the shareholder has a *prima facie* right to be registered. If the directors, as in this case, are given an absolute discretion to refuse to register, they need not give reasons for the refusal even if legal proceeding as are brought (*Berry and Stewart v Tottenham Hotspur FC Ltd* (1935)). However, a refusal to register can be challenged if the directors were not acting *bona fide* for the benefit of the company in the interests of the company (*Re Smith & Fawcett Ltd* (1942)). The burden of proving a lack of *bona fides* falls on those challenging the refusal to register which, given no reason may be given, is a heavy burden. In this case the directors decision to refuse to register Rupert appears to be unchallengeable. However, when directors decline to register a shareholder they must notify the shareholder of their decision within two months of an application to be registered and failure so to do renders the company liable to a fine and the directors liable to a fine and/or imprisonment (s 183). More importantly for Rupert, the courts have determined that a refusal to register must be taken within a reasonable time and treat the two month period as reasonable period (*Re Swaledale Cleaners Ltd* (1968), the period can be extended if there are special circumstances) so that Bear plc would seem to have exceeded the time limit. Thus, Rupert can apply to the court for rectification of the register (s 359) and the issue of a share certificate.

(b) *Paddington*

Shares in a company are transferable (s 182) but in this case it is alleged that the share transfer was forged – who is entitled to be registered as a member of Bear plc, Paddington or Bungle? A share certificate is *prima facie* evidence that the named member has title to the shares (s 186) so that, Paddington should be regarded as having title unless the shares have been validly transferred to another person. Thus, Bungle bears the burden of proving his entitlement to be registered as a shareholder. Section 183 requires a transfer of shares to be made in writing by a proper instrument of transfer. The Stock Transfer Act 1963 sets out forms of transfer document for fully paid shares and it is assumed that an appropriate form was used. If the signature of the holder is forged on an instrument of transfer of those shares then the instrument is void (*Dixon v Kennaway & Co* (1900)). Consequently, the shares are not transferred and Paddington remains the holder of the shares. Bungle's remedy is against the person who purported to transfer the shares to him – if he can be found. Indeed, even if Bungle succeeded in being registered the company could remove him from the register because the only basis for registration is the forged transfer (*Sheffield Corpn v Barclay* (1905)).

(c) *The six members*

Section 361 states that the register of members is *prima facie* evidence of its contents. Thus, the six members to whom dividends were paid were *prima facie* members and entitled to the payment. However, the register is not conclusive evidence and s 359 provides that it can be rectified and s 359(1) states that if there is any unnecessary delay in entering on the register the fact that a person has ceased to be a member, the person aggrieved or any member of the company can apply for rectification. While rectification of the register would correct the register for the future it does not determine the fate of the past dividend payment. It is assumed that the transferees of the shares were also paid a dividend and if they were not they are entitled to a payment from the company whether the company can recover the money from the former shareholders or not. Section 359(3) authorises the court to decide any question necessary or expedient to be decided for rectification of the register. The ability of the company to recover dividends wrongly paid is arguably not a question 'necessary or expedient to be decided for rectification of the register' so the court would not have the power to order the return of the money under this section. It is assumed that the quasi-contractual (restitutionary) rules on money paid by mistake operate and the dividends may be recoverable by reference to the general law.

Whether rectification can be arranged by agreement between all relevant parties, ie the company and transferors and transferees, is as yet unsettled with cases supporting and denying the efficacy of informal rectification.

(c) *Winnie*

Winnie has been issued with a share certificate. A share certificate is *prima facie* evidence of title (s 186). However, the presumption raised by the share certificate, that Winnie owns the shares, can be rebutted. Where there is evidence in rebuttal the presumption will still prevail if the company is estopped from relying on that evidence. Thus, in Winnie's case there are three issues. First, can the company disclaim the share certificate altogether, second can it produce evidence to rebut the presumption that the person in possession of the share certificate is the rightful owner of the shares and third, is the company estopped from relying on that evidence.

The company might seek to disclaim all liability for the share certificate on the basis that the person who had issued it on behalf of the company, X, was not authorised so to do. For example, in *Ruben v Great Fingall Consolidated* (1906), the company secretary forged a share transfer and issued to Ruben a share certificate, which was signed by the secretary and bore the names of two other directors of the company. The signatures of the directors had been forged by the company secretary. The issue for the House of Lords was whether the company could deny the validity of the certificate. The House of Lords stated that the forged certificate was a complete nullity and could not bind the company. The House held that a company secretary had no authority to guarantee on the company's behalf the genuineness or validity of a document. While this decision may have been appropriate in 1906 it is surely the case that nowadays the company secretary does have authority (actual or ostensible) to guarantee the validity of document such as a share certificate. However, if X was not so authorised the company can deny the validity of the share certificate issued to X's wife. That being so it could be argued that the wife had nothing to transfer and the subsequent transfer to Winnie was a nullity. It seems very odd that Bear plc should be able to deny liability or the acts of their employee and it can be hazarded that *Ruben* would not now be followed particularly since the role and authority of a company secretary has been greatly enhanced since 1906 (see, for example, *Panorama Development Ltd v Fidelis Furnishing Fabrics Ltd* (1971)).

The evidence that the transfer to X's wife was forged is evidence on which the company could rely to rebut the presumption of title raised by the share certificate. However, it appears that since Winnie has paid for the shares on the faith of a share certificate, albeit one issued as the result of a forged transfer (to the wife), the company is estopped from denying the genuineness of its own issued certificate (subject to the previous paragraph). Winnie is entitled to say – you issued a certificate, I believed what it said (ie that X's wife was the owner) so I am entitled to rely on it (*Re Bahia & San Francisco Rly Co Ltd* (1868)). If the company is estopped from denying Winnie's right to be a member and has to re-instate Fred, it can seek compensation from X's wife even if she was not party to the fraud (*Sheffield Corpn v Barclay* (1905)). Should X's wife be found liable she can seek a contribution from the company if it was negligent in registering the transfer although this seems unlikely unless it should have spotted and curtailed X's fraudulent activities earlier. Estoppel allows Winnie to assert her rights against the company but it does not affect the validity of Fred's title, unless perhaps he knew of the original forged transfer and failed to denounce it with reasonable speed. If Fred was tardy once he discovered the truth in asserting his rights, he would be estopped from raising the forgery and might not be able to demand re-instatement on the register of members.

Public companies generally insure themselves against the consequences of acting on a forged transfer.

Question 39

A   Section 143(1) Companies Act 1985 provides that 'A company limited by shares shall not acquire its own shares, whether by purchase, subscription of otherwise'.

Why might a company wish to (or have to) acquire its own shares?

B   Prof Ltd was formed as a subsidiary of a large computer conglomerate. Subsequently, it was the subject of a management buyout by Brain and Drain. Brain now wishes to reduce his involvement in the company and it has been suggested that Prof Ltd acquire 100,000 of its own £1 shares at par from Brain. The proposal is that the purchase will not be accompanied by a fresh issue of shares but will involve the transfer of all the company's distributable profits (£58,000) to a capital redemption reserve and a permissible capital payment to make up the shortfall.

Student plc has just warned the company that unless all outstanding invoices (totalling some £25,000) are paid it will consider putting Prof Ltd into liquidation.

Comment on any legal issues arising from the above facts.

Answer plan

As with all two-part questions time management is important and, unless there is a mark allocation to the parts of a question, try to allow equal time for each part. Part (a) does not require an essay on the rule but rather a consideration of cases when (and why) it does not apply – do not answer unless you know what you are talking about because guessing is difficult in this area although the statute (s 143) gives some help. Part (b) requires consideration of whether the proposed payment to Brain is valid and if not what could be alternatives open to the company and/or Drain. Also note the consequences where there is an insolvent liquidation with in 12 months of a permissible capital payment (a PCP).

Answer

A The rule contained in s 143, that a company may not acquire its own shares, re-states the common law decision in *Trevor v Whitworth* (1887). The House of Lords in that case showed the courts concern for the interests of creditors and held that since a creditor effectively 'lent' money to the company (by allowing credit) he has a right to expect that the company will retain its capital and not use it improperly (including not returning it to the shareholders). The share capital (plus undistributable reserves) can be called the creditors buffer. Consequently, s 143 provides that a company cannot reduce its share capital (nominal value of shares subscribed by shareholders) by buying its own shares (no new capital provided and existing capital used). This does not mean that the money subscribed for shares cannot be used and must be locked away in the bank – the money can be used in the course of the business. All a creditor is entitled to expect is that the money subscribed for shares has been used in the legitimate course of business. There are, however, a number of exceptions to s 143.

Section 143(3) provides that a company can acquire its own shares when:

(a) the redemption or purchase of shares is made in accordance with ss 159–181; or

(b) the acquisition is part of an authorised reduction of capital; or

(c) the acquisition of shares is ordered by the court pursuant to its powers under s 5 (alteration of objects), or s 54 (re-registration of public company as private), or s 461 (remedy for unfair prejudice); or

(d) the shares are forfeited by the company because the acquirer has not paid for them.

Exceptions (b), (c) and (d) have existed for a number of years and the reasons for such exceptions are generally obvious (less so in the case of reduction of capital). Moreover, (b) and (c) are subject to judicial control in that a reduction of capital must be confirmed by a court (s 135) and the Act provides for the protection of creditor interests and the exceptions in (c) arise only when the court orders the acquisition. The exception in (a) is of recent origin and its use and operation are more controversial. Why then might a company wish to (or be required to) purchase its own shares?

(a) *Redemption or purchase of shares*

Both public and private companies may redeem or purchase their own shares provided that the company maintains the creditors' buffer. Indeed private companies can reduce the creditors' buffer and make a permissible capital payment (a PCP) provided that they comply with the strict procedures laid down in the Act. This exception was part of a package of measures introduced in the early 1980s to help companies, particularly private companies, raise money. Prior to 1980 a private company wishing to raise outside investment faced two difficulties – issuing new shares diluted existing shareholdings thus affecting the control of the company (unattractive to current shareholders particularly in a family company) and new investors would obtain a minority shareholding which would be, effectively, unmarketable. The provisions allowing a company to issue redeemable shares or to buy back its own shares were designed to provide sufficient flexibility to permit existing shareholders to retain control while increasingly the marketability of shares and continuing to protect creditors. The ability to issue redeemable shares means that a company increases its capital and the investor knows that he will be locked in only for a determinable period. The ability to re-purchase shares allows a company to re-organise its share structure as and when (and if) required and gives an investor some possibility of releasing his investment even if the company does not go public. The facility to re-purchase allows a company to buy out a founder-shareholder when he wishes to retire (assuming other shareholders lack the funds or the desire to purchase the shares), or to buy out a troublesome shareholder. Alternatively, re-purchase may have financial benefits, for example to enhance the earnings value of the remaining shares (this has been the principal reason public companies have used the re-purchase provisions) or reduce future dividend payments (by abolishing preference shares, for example). A public company might also seek to purchase its own shares to preclude a take-over bid (but this might involve a breach of directors' duty – breach of the proper purpose doctrine – and should be carefully scrutinised before proceeding).

When a company wishes to redeem redeemable shares or purchase its own shares there are extremely onerous procedural requirements designed to ensure that only certain funds are used for these purposes and that an appropriate amount of publicity for the proposed scheme is provided. However, a court order is not required. Any attempt to redeem or re-purchase other than in compliance with the Act leaves the company open to a fine and every officer of the company in default liable to a fine and/or imprisonment. Further, the acquisition will be void (s 143(2)).

(b) *Reduction of capital*

Section 135 permits a company to reduce share capital provided that the articles of the company permit a reduction, a reduction has been authorised by special resolution and the court has approved the reduction. Section 135 does not limit the circumstances in which a company may seek to reduce capital but it does specify three possible grounds for so doing. Where one of these three grounds is the basis of an application a court is likely to approve the reduction provided the position of the company's creditors is secured. Section 135 lists as possible grounds for reduction:

- the extinction or reduction of unpaid share capital (no self–acquisition by company);
- cancellation of paid up share capital which is lost or unrepresented by available assets; and
- payment off of any paid up share capital in excess of the company's wants.

Cancellation of paid up share capital is designed to reflect reality. There is little point in a company having a high nominal capital when trading losses have reduced its net assets to a lower figure. Reduction of capital here would allow a company to resume dividend payments; this might be regarded as a sensible basis for reduction. Paying off unneeded share capital involves returning money to the shareholders and is most often encountered when a company is scaling down its trading activities (commonly encountered in the past following nationalisation). In all cases of reduction the court has to be satisfied that the creditors of the company are adequately protected before confirming the reduction.

B There are two matters of concern to Prof. The threat of liquidation (probably designed to get the debt paid) which is also a useful reminder of some of the issues involved in a share acquisition by a company.

Liquidation

Student plc is threatening to put Prof Ltd into liquidation. Section 122(1) Insolvency Act 1986 provides that a company may be put into liquidation if it is unable to pay its debts and s 123 of that Act provides that a company is deemed unable to pay its debts if, inter alia, it has failed, within three weeks of receiving a written demand in prescribed form, to pay a debt in excess of £750. Thus, in this case, it seems likely that Student plc has the ability to seek compulsory liquidation of Prof. Compulsory winding up is both lengthy and expensive and, if liquidation is really likely, it would be better if Student plc could persuade the directors of Prof Ltd to initiate a creditors' voluntary winding up if the company really is insolvent. This would require Prof to pass an extraordinary resolution (three-quarters majority of those present or voting required) in favour; the winding up would be subject to close supervision by the creditors.

A liquidator, who must be a licensed insolvency practitioner, has both to swell the assets of the company and pay such money as the company has to the creditors in order of priority. In seeking to swell the assets, a liquidator can try to recover funds from directors who have broken any of their duties and can, where apposite, pursue actions for fraudulent or wrongful trading. In addition the liquidator should seek to have set aside or re-opened certain transactions entered into within the periods specified in the Act. For example, floating charges granted within 12 months of the winding up are *prima facie* invalid (s 245, two years for a charge in favour of a connected person). Student should be warned that if Prof were to pay them, and then go into insolvent liquidation within six months of the payment, a liquidator might seek to have the payment set aside as a 'preference' (s 239) although there are strict requirements for the operation of this provision. However, the threat by Student may be just a means of galvanising Prof into paying its debts and have no effect on the proposed acquisition of shares. Of course, if the proposed acquisition goes ahead and liquidation (whether initiated by Student or another) did ensue within 12 months there are consequences for Prof and its directors.

Share acquisition

The proposed share acquisition must be approved by the board of Prof which must exercise its decision whether or not to purchase Brain's shares *bona fide* for the benefit of the company. Breach of duty would render the directors liable to re-imburse the company for any loss and the recipient of corporate funds (Brain) might also be liable to refund the money under the principles of constructive trusteeship. If the scheme is acceptable, the shares must be paid for. Obviously existing shareholders may be prevailed upon to buy the shares but it seems that this is not likely in this case. Perhaps the shareholders have no funds and no desire or ability to borrow the necessary sums. However, the company is willing to buy the shares. How can it pay Brain? A new share issue has been rejected, perhaps because it would dilute the ownership of the company, and it is proposed to fund the acquisition partly by a payment out of income (£58,000 from distributable profits) and partly from capital (£42,000). Private companies (Prof Ltd is private) are permitted to purchase their own shares provided certain conditions are complied with and may use the funds proposed in appropriate cases. Does the purchase by Prof comply with the statutory provisions?

These provisions are complex but are designed to ensure that the shareholders approve the purchase, that only appropriate funds are used for the purchase and that there is adequate publicity for the purchase. First, the company must have authority to purchase its own shares – Prof is authorised (Table A, art 35). Section 162 then sets out conditions for payments for shares made out of corporate 'income'. The conditions are that the contract to purchase was approved in advance by special resolution (s 164, a written resolution would suffice and Brain must not have voted) and that the purchase so authorised was paid for out of the company's distributable profits (s 168, or a fresh issue of shares made for the purpose, ss 160, 162 – which does not apply here). Thus the payment of £58,000 would appear to be acceptable (made out of distributable profits, defined in s 263). Further, s 170 requires a transfer of a sum representing the share-purchase price from distributable profits to the capital redemption reserve (the CRR). These sections appear to be satisfied. However, a purchase made in compliance with s 164 must also be given appropriate publicity for the purchase (s 169, notice to Registrar, copy of contract at registered office etc). Turning to the balance of the payment. Section 171, which applies only to private companies, allows companies to purchase their own shares out of capital – such a payment (which may represent all or part of the purchase price) is a 'permissible capital payment', a PCP. Needless to say, there are strict rules for the use of a PCP. Section 173 provides that the payment must have been approved by special resolution (at a meeting or unanimously by written resolution) obtained *after* the directors of Prof Ltd had made a statutory declaration. This statutory declaration by the directors must specify:

- the amount of the PCP;
- that the directors, having made full inquiries into the affairs and prospects of the company, are of the opinion that the company will be able to met its debts immediately after the PCP *and* it will continue as a going concern for the next 12 months after the PCP and be able to pay its debts as they fall due.

The auditors must have commented on the statutory declaration to the effect that, having inquired into the company's affairs, they were not aware of anything which would render the directors' opinion unreasonable (s 173). After a special resolution approving a PCP has been passed the decision must be publicised (s 175). The publicity must mention the power of members and creditors to object. If Prof complies with all these rules the payment of £42,000 will also be valid. However, even if a PCP is valid at the time it is made the directors and Brain can incur liability to any subsequent liquidator of Prof Ltd. Section 76 Insolvency Act 1986 provides that where a company goes into insolvent liquidation within 12 months of the payment out of capital being made, the directors who signed the statutory declaration are liable to contribute to the company's assets. The directors can escape liability if they can establish they had reasonable grounds for their opinions, it seems probable that the auditors' approval would be a 'reasonable ground', provided the directors had not concealed any information from the auditors. Section 76 would also render Brain liable to contribute to the assets of the company to the extent of the PCP.

Question 40

In 1993, A and B formed a company, Shark Ltd. The shares in Shark Ltd were allotted to A and B equally in return for the transfer to the company of the business which they have been operating as a partnership. A and B were the sole directors of the company. In 1994, A and B agreed to purchase from C, for £10,000 all the shares in an existing company, Lamb Ltd which C controlled. A and B become the directors of Lamb Ltd and paid C £5,000 in cash and the balance by the issue of a redeemable, interest-bearing debenture secured by a floating charge on Lamb Ltd's stock. Both companies traded successfully but A and B now find that they have different views on how to expand their business enterprises. Thus, they formulated a scheme to split the companies. The scheme required A to transfer his 50% shareholding in Shark to Wolf Ltd (a company controlled by B) in return for B transferring his shares in Lamb to A and agreeing to pay A £50,000 over the next 5 years. This debt was to be secured by a charge over the assets of Shark. Subsequently, B refused to transfer his Lamb shares claiming that he overestimated the value of the Shark shares and that he is not prepared to proceed without an amendment of the agreement. A is seeking specific performance of the agreement as originally drawn.

Comment on any legal issues which arise from these facts.

Answer plan

It is not clear who, if anyone is seeking advice on the affairs of these companies so the legal issues cannot be tailored to any particular client. The principal matter that arise appear to relate to the initial purchase of Lamb shares from C and the proposed scheme to divide the companies between A and B. Other issues include the allotment of Shark shares and other possible ways of splitting the businesses between the protagonists. In some ways a narrow question but it does demand familiarity with the complicated provisions on financial assistance.

Answer

There are a number of legal issues which arise from the facts outlined in the question. First, it should be noted that the allotment of shares in Shark Ltd to A and B is not contrary to the Act. In common with many traders who incorporate their business they have transferred that business to the company in return for an allotment of shares. Section 99 provides that the consideration for shares may be provided in money or, as here, in money's worth. Section 100 states that shares must not be issued at a discount but where the consideration for shares is not in the form of cash it is unlikely that the shares would be treated as anything other than fully paid. There is no statutory requirement that the consideration for shares in a private company be valued and the courts will not treat consideration such as this as other than full payment unless it is manifestly inadequate or illusory (*Re Wragg* ((1897)). Indeed in the classic case of *Salomon v Solomon & Co Ltd* (1895) where the promoter transferred his boot business to the company the House of Lords refused to investigate too closely the value of the business transferred by S in return for shares and a secured loan even though the value appeared to have been, at best, a wildly optimistic figure. Indeed, who suffers if the business is over-valued; A and B who are the shareholders anyway.

A and B subsequently agree to purchase from C his shares in Lamb Ltd. There can be no objection to a shareholder selling his shares in a company since shares are supposed to be transferable (s 182). However, the method of payment may cause problems. A and

B paid C partly in cash and partly by means of redeemable, interest-bearing debenture, ie by means of a loan secured on the stock of Lamb Ltd, the very company whose shares are being purchased. Section 151 provides that where a person is acquiring shares in a company it is not lawful for that company to give financial assistance directly or indirectly for the purposes of the acquisition before during or after the acquisition. The arrangement whereby A and B, once they become directors of Lamb Ltd, authorised Lamb to grant a debenture (a secured loan) over its stock is plainly such assistance (see *Carney v Herbert* (1985)). This is so despite the fact that courts have bound themselves to look at the commercial realities of a situation, ie is there really financial assistance, rather than strain to try and bring transactions within the scope of the section (*Charterhouse Investment Trust Ltd v Tempest Diesels Ltd* (1986)). There are exception to s 151.

Two of the exceptions to s 151 are clearly irrelevant. These are when the company lends money in the ordinary course of business, for example where a bank customer borrows money to buy shares in the bank, and where the financial assistance is authorised by some other provision of company law. Section 153 also lists various circumstances which do not seem to be within the ambit of s 151 simply to avoid argument on the point. The remaining group of exceptions, ss 153(1),(2) and 155, is designed to ensure that the broad scope of the prohibition does not unintentionally ensnare genuine commercial transactions which are of benefit to the company. Section 155 does not apply to A and B but they might seek to argue that s 153(1) or (2) does. Section 153 states that a company can give assistance if its principal purpose in so doing is not to give financial assistance to facilitate the acquisition or to reduce or discharge any liability incurred by a person (A and B here) for the purpose of the acquisition of the shares but is an incidental part of some larger purpose of the company *and* it is given in good faith in the interests of the company. The ambit of this exception is uncertain. In *Brady v Brady* (1989), the House of Lords expressed the view that this provision required those responsible for authorising the financial assistance to have acted in the genuine belief that it was being done in the company's interests. Could A and B argue that C's management is so poor that the scheme represented the only way in which the company could be saved (the larger purpose) so that their intervention was beneficial to present and future creditors (whom these sections are designed to protect by ensuring the company does not squander its share capital) and present employees? The difficulty is that A and B appear to have benefitted to a greater degree than anyone else so that on might query their *bona fides* in authorising the financial assistance and thereby cast doubt on the reality of any larger purpose. The meaning of 'larger purpose' is discussed below when considering the break up scheme.

The civil consequences of breach of s 151 are dependent on the common law but the section provides that any company which breaks this provision is liable to a fine and the officers of the company who authorised the financial assistance, A and B in this case, are liable to a fine and/or imprisonment. A and B, as the directors who authorised the breach of s 151, are in breach, thereby, of their duties to the company and must compensate the company for any loss it has suffered in consequence. In this case the interest on the debenture would be recoverable as would any capital payments which have been made. An action against A and B could be initiated by Lamb Ltd but, in the circumstances, this is most unlikely since A and B control Lamb and are hardly likely to authorise it to sue them. Once the relationship of A and B deteriorates, B may seek to bring a derivative action on behalf of Lamb in respect of the breach. However, B may find himself precluded from bringing an action on behalf of Lamb since he was party to the illegality of which he later seeks to complain (*Nurcombe v Nurcombe* (1985) prevented a shareholder bringing a derivative action when she had, knowingly, benefitted from the conduct of the director of which she later sought to complain on behalf of the company). Indeed, C the recipient of the debenture may find that he is a constructive trustee of the benefits received as a consequence of the unlawful financial assistance since he was well aware of the breach of duty having benefitted from it. Alternatively, C may discover that the purchase of shares (or at least the method of payment) by A and B is void owing to the breach of s 151. The issue of the effect of breach on the transaction for which the assistance was given arose in a number of cases concerning the forerunners of s 151. In *Victor Battery Co Ltd v Curry's Ltd* (1946), the facts of which resemble the present case, Roxburgh J said that the granting of a debenture could not, in law, be financial assistance unless the debenture was valid and consequently concluded that breach of s 151 did not invalidate the financial assistance. Later cases, while not overruling *Victor Batteries*, have looked at the commercial realities and concluded that, where the financial assistance has the effect in fact of underpinning the acquisition, it is financial assistance (whether it is legal or not) and is void (*Heald v O'Connor* (1971) and *Carney v Herbert* (1985) are two examples). However, this leaves open the question of whether the debenture is void or the purchase is void. In *Carney v Herbert* (1985), the Privy Council determined that where the unlawful assistance was ancillary to the overall transaction *and* its elimination would leave unchanged the subject matter of the transaction, it could be severed leaving the remainder of the transaction enforceable. In *Carney*, the court felt able to sever from a contract for the sale of shares a guarantee of the purchaser's debt given by the company whose shares were being sold. In this case severance seems less likely since part of the consideration for the contract of sale is unlawful and the courts will not re-write contracts under the guise of severance.

Turning then to the scheme formulated to split the existing businesses between A and B. In passing it should be noted that A and B might have been wise to enter into a scheme of arrangement under s 425 which allows a court to sanction a proposal which might otherwise be breach of s 151. Alternatively, the procedure whereby a private company can give financial assistance by complying with s 155 could have been contemplated. Section 155 provides that a private company, eg Lamb, can give financial assistance for the acquisition of its own shares if it has net assets (ss 154, 155) which are not reduced by the assistance or, if reduced, the assistance is provided out of net profits. In effect a company can make a loan etc if it gets its money back (no reduction of net assets) or if the loan comes out of money payable to shareholders (net profits) so that the creditors of the company are not adversely affected by the scheme. Unfortunately neither of these was adopted and it is probable that the proposed scheme is in breach of s 151. First, A agrees to transfer his Shark shares to Wolf Ltd — nothing objectionable in that. This leaves Wolf indebted to A for the value of the Shark shares. A third party, B, discharges Wolf's liability by agreeing to pay A — nothing objectionable so far. B discharges Wolf's debt by transferring the Lamb shares to A (a share swap) and agreeing to pay A £50,000. If the scheme stopped there the transaction would be unimpeachable. Unfortunately, B's agreed payment of £50,000 was to be secured and the security provided was to be a charge over the assets of Shark the very company whose shares were being acquired by Wolf. Thus, there is an apparent breach of s 151 and a court would not order specific performance of the contract unless the financial assistance provided, indirectly, by Shark, is within an exception to s 151 or this part of the agreement can be severed. Does the exception in s 153(2) apply? As mentioned above, this requires the assistance to be an incidental part of a larger purpose of the company and the assistance must be given in good faith in the interests of the company. The good faith and interests of the company part is satisfied here – the scheme is needed to break the deadlock between the parties. What constitutes a larger purpose was discussed by the House of Lords in *Brady v Brady* (1989).

In *Brady*, the facts of which are rightly characterised by Farrar as 'labyrinthine', two brothers, who had fallen out, sought to split a family business, which operated through a series of interlinked companies, in two main spheres (haulage and soft drinks). A plan was evolved which was designed to leave one brother with the haulage based business and the other brother with the soft drinks based business. The plan (in simplified form!) required M to purchase all the shares in Brady (the holding company) from O leaving M with a debt due to O. This debt was partly paid by the transfer to O of assets belonging to Brady. Clearly Brady was contributing financial assistance to the purchase of its own shares. It was argued that the assistance was simply incidental to a larger purpose – the reorganisation of the family business – and that it was in the interests of Brady since the only alternative, given the rancour between the brothers, was to wind Brady up. The House of Lords accepted that the plan was in the best interests of the company (as in this case). However, the House, reversing the Court of Appeal, found no larger purpose to which the financial assistance was merely incidental. The House ruled that the financial assistance in this case was driven by a more important reason than the provision of the assistance – the reorganisation plan – but said that purpose and reason were different. Simply because there is an important reason underpinning the scheme did not make it incidental to a larger purpose. On the facts, the scheme was designed to facilitate the purchase of shares in Brady, even if the reason was to split the family businesses, and there was no larger purpose to which it was incidental. This narrow interpretation of s 153, ignoring the commercial context and focusing on the disputed transaction, seems likely to apply to this case so that A would not obtain his order for specific performance. It should be noted in passing that in *Brady* it was ultimately accepted that s 155 could apply and the plan (and the one here) could be implemented by use of that section. As Gower remarks, it would have been a great deal cheaper for everyone if the s 155 route had been explored earlier.

Question 41

Christie, James, Rendell and Sayers hold all the issued share capital of Detective Ltd of which they are the executive directors. Christie has indicated that she would like to retire from the business and sell her shareholding. James, Rendell and Sayers would like the company, which is highly profitable, to pay Christie £100,000 for her past services (she has received a salary and has a company pension). The memorandum and articles of the company permit the company to make gratuitous payments.

Christie is willing to sell her shares in the company when she retires, the remaining directors would prefer these shares to be retained within the company. None of the remaining shareholders have sufficient funds on their own to purchase all of Christie's shareholding.

Advise the directors how to proceed in order to achieve their aims.

Answer plan

Two issues arise, the payment to Christie – is it legal, if so how can it be achieved – and keeping the shares in the company. In respect of the purchase can it be by the company or existing shareholders and how is it to be funded.

Answer

Payment to Christie

The proposed payment on retirement does not appear to be *ultra vires* (the company has power to make gratuitous payments) and the board, it can be assumed, is authorised to make such payments (they are also the shareholders). Thus, the payment would seem to be valid provided the directors were not in breach of their fiduciary duty in authorising it and s 312 (payment to directors on retirement) has been complied with. There should be no difficulty in complying with s 312 since all that is required is approval in advance by the shareholders and the remaining directors are also the shareholders of Detective Ltd. There is still some doubt as to the ability of the directors to give away the company's money even where the company is authorised to make gratuitous payments but where some benefit, however elusive, to the company can be discerned such payments are valid (*Re Horsley & Weight Ltd* (1982) took a more generous view and did not require any benefit to the company). Certainly, a gratuitous transaction decided on by the directors other than *bona fide* for the benefit of the company would presumably be invalid as well as being a breach of duty by the directors (see *Aveling Barford Ltd v Perion Ltd* (1989), sale of asset to company controlled by a director at gross undervalue was breach of director's duty – an attempt to defraud the company). If Detective remained solvent, this transaction is unlikely to be challenged since all the shareholders were party to the decision. However, if the company went into insolvent liquidation the liquidator might wish to challenge its validity. If the company failed to make the payment it is unlikely Christie would have a contractual claim to the money since she has not provided any consideration for the agreement. Perhaps she should suggest that the price of the shares is augmented by £100,000 and she forgoes the retirement gift.

Sale of shares

Although the remaining directors do not wish Christie's shares to be sold to an outsider, Christie is not debarred from selling her shares to anyone who wants to buy them unless the articles of the company limit their transferability. Table A contains no such restriction so it can be assumed that this company has no such provision although an attempt could be made to insert such a clause since the remaining shareholders could change the articles (s 9) by special resolution (they control three-quarters of the votes). Any attempt by the majority to change the articles in this way might be challenged by Christie as being an abuse of majority power in that it was not *bona fide* for the benefit of the company (*Allan v Gold Reefs of West Africa Ltd* (1900)) although this not an area where the courts have proved very interventionist. Alternatively, Christie could seek to challenge any proposed amendment by a petition alleging unfair prejudice (s 459). On the facts, it appears that the remaining shareholders and Christie are on good terms so that the insertion of such an article is unlikely to be sought. The board of Detective Ltd do not have a power to refuse to register a new fully paid up shareholder so that indirect pressure cannot be put on Christie by a threat to refuse to register any transferee. However, an outsider who purchased the shares would not be a director, unless appointed by the board (to fill a casual vacancy) or the shareholders. Consequently, an outsider would be unlikely to wish to purchase a minority shareholding unless this was a scheme acceptable to the remaining shareholders. Christie might prefer, as the remainder of the board would, to sell her shares to the company or to the existing shareholders.

Section 143 appears to preclude the simple solution that the company purchase the shares. The inability of a director-shareholder to retire and sell his shares to the company was one of the reasons put forward to permit, in prescribed cases, a company buying its own shares. There are two ways of approaching the issue, either Detective could seek to buy the shares out of income or out of capital (only private companies can purchase shares out of capital). The statutory provisions are complex but are designed to ensure that the shareholders approve the purchase, that only appropriate funds are used for the purchase and that there is adequate publicity for the purchase. On any vote to approve a purchase the shareholder who is intending to sell to the company cannot vote. If Detective does purchase the shares they are cancelled thereby reducing the issued share capital (and reducing capital if the purchase is made out of capital). The resolutions that must be passed to approve the purchase (sometimes ordinary, sometimes special) may be obtained by holding a meeting or, since

Detective is a private company, by means of a written resolution (s 381A, unanimous support of those entitled to vote required). Consider first purchase with payment out of income. Section 162 allows a company to buy its own shares if authorised to do so by its articles (Table A, art 35 applies here) and the conditions set out in the Act are complied with. The conditions are that the contract to purchase is approved in advance by special resolution (s 164) and any purchase so authorised to be made must be paid for out of the company's distributable profits (s 168) or a fresh issue of shares made for the purpose (ss 160, 162). The distributable profits of a company are determined by reference to s 263, and are, in essence, the company's accumulated, realised profits (not previously distributed or capitalised) less its accumulated, realised losses (not previously written off in an authorised reduction or re-organisation of capital). Effectively, the fund used to pay for the shares must be money which could have been paid to the shareholders or constitute new capital. Since Detective is 'highly profitable' it seems likely that the directors could decide to pursue this method of purchase and have the funds to do so. If a purchase is made in compliance with s 164, s 169 requires appropriate publicity for the purchase (notice to Registrar, copy of contract at registered office etc) and s 170 requires a transfer of a sum representing the share-purchase price from distributable profits to the capital redemption reserve. The capital redemption reserve forms part of the share capital of the company and can be reduced only by compliance with the usual rules (s 135) for the reduction of share capital. There is one exception to the rules on reduction in respect of the capital redemption reserve – it can be used to pay up unissued shares to be allotted to members as fully paid up bonus shares.

The board of Detective could be advised that if the company has insufficient distributable profits to apply for the purchase of Christie's shares, the company might still be able to buy the shares. Section 171, which applies only to private companies, allows companies to purchase their own shares out of capital – such a payment (which may represent all or part of the purchase price) is a 'permissible capital payment', a PCP. Needless to say, there are rules for the use of a PCP. Section 173 requires the payment out of capital to be approved by special resolution after the directors of Detective have made a statutory declaration. This statutory declaration must specify:

- the amount of the PCP
- that they have inquired into the financial situation of the company and that in their opinion
- that after the company has purchased the shares it will be able to pay its debts and the company will continue business as a going concern for a full year.

The auditors must comment on the statutory declaration to the effect that, having inquired into the company's affairs, they are not aware of anything which would render the directors' opinion unreasonable (s 173). After the special resolution approving the PCP has been passed the decision must be duly publicised (s 175) which notification must inform the creditors of their right to object to the payment. Section 176 allows a member or creditor to object to a PCP (five–week time limit from date of resolution) and s 177 sets out the court's powers when an objection has been lodged; the court can, among other things, affirm, reject or modify the special resolution and can order the objectors to be paid off. In this case all three shareholders would have to vote for the proposal so only creditors would be able to object. The directors might prefer not to use a PCP because, if the company goes into insolvent liquidation within 12 months of the payment out of capital being made, s 76 Insolvency Act 1986 provides that the directors who signed the statutory declaration are liable to contribute to the company's assets unless they can establish they had reasonable grounds for their opinions (the auditors' approval?). Christie would also incur liability to the extent of the PCP.

If the company seeks to purchase Christie's shares other than in accordance with the Act, the purchase is unlawful and the director's are in breach of duty (there are also criminal penalties).

While no single shareholder may be able to afford Christie's shares, the shareholders might be able to afford a block each or to purchase the total block jointly. Either scheme could preserve the existing share balance between the remaining shareholders and not allow any one of them to obtain a dominant position within the company. However, even if one shareholder purchased all of Christie's shares she would still have only 50% of the votes, ie insufficient on her own to pass a resolution. Alternatively, all or some of the directors could seek to borrow money from the company to allow them to purchase Christie's shares. This gives rise to two problems. First, the loan by a company to a person to enable him to purchase shares in the company is prohibited by s 151 and second, a company cannot make loans to a director (s 330). While s 151 provides that a company cannot provide financial assistance (loans are included, s 152) to a person for the purchase of its own shares (there are criminal penalties for so doing and the assistance is void), private companies can do so provided they are solvent and adhere to the statutory procedure provided. Section 155 provides that Detective could give financial assistance for the acquisition of its own shares if it has net assets (ss 154, 155) which are not reduced by the assistance or, if reduced, the assistance is provided out of net profits. In effect Detective can make a loan if it gets its money back (no reduction of net assets) or if the loan comes out of money payable to shareholders (net profits) so that the creditors of the company are not affected by the self-dealing.

The procedural hurdles which must be surmounted to allow financial assistance are similar to those applicable to a purchase of shares by the company – approval by special resolution (a written resolution can be used) and a statutory declaration by the directors which is supported by the auditors. The statutory declaration is not identical to that required for a PCP but requires the directors to declare that in their opinion that following any proposed financial assistance the company could pay its debts and will be able to do so in the next year following the assistance (or if the company is to be wound up in that period will be able to pay all debts). The auditors report must confirm that, having looked at the company's state of affairs, they are not aware of anything which would render the director's opinion unreasonable (s 156). There are provisions for shareholders to object which would be inapplicable here given that all the remaining shareholders would have to approve the assistance (assuming all vote or a written resolution is used). A director who makes a statutory declaration without reasonable grounds for his opinion is liable to a fine or imprisonment (but no civil liability in the Act). There are onerous publicity requirements. If financial assistance is provided other than in accordance with the Act, a director who authorised the assistance is in breach of duty – in this case the directors, being the recipients of the loan, would have to return the money. Assuming the provisions for the granting of financial assistance are complied with, there is still the difficulty that the proposed loan is to the directors.

Section 330 provides that a company cannot make a loan to a director and that any loan made is voidable at the company's option (s 341). However, since the directors are the shareholders they are unlikely to seek to avoid the loan. Consequently, the loan would not be challenged unless the company went into liquidation and the liquidator sought to recover the loan on behalf of the company. Presumably the shareholders can approve the loan and thus render the loan unimpeachable even if liquidation ensues (it is not clear if simple inaction is approval). A liquidator might then argue that the breach of duty by the directors in authorising the loan in the first place enabled him to sue the directors (unless breach ratified by shareholders?). There are exceptions to s 330 where loans to directors are valid and if one of these apply there is no wrongdoing of which the company can complain. For example, s 334 allows small loans (up to £5,000).

There seems little doubt that one way or another the remaining shareholders will be able to purchase Christie's shares if she is willing to sell them either to them or to the company.

Chapter 7

Loan Capital

Introduction

Loan capital is the rather grand name attached to a company's borrowings (so remember your overdraft is your loan capital); borrowing is an important method of financing for many companies. Loan capital can be divided into two categories. First, sums owed by the company as a specific debt, eg a loan from X, the most common example of which is the company's overdraft and second, marketable loans. Marketable loans are in essence potential debts which may be issued (sold) to investors. These loans will be issued on strict terms and conditions relating to date when the interest is due, date of redemption and other rights attaching. A company could create 1 million pounds of marketable debt divided into £1 units bearing interest at x% which it can sell as and when required and for whatever price it will fetch (there is no prohibition on issuing a loan at a discounted price unless it is convertible into shares). If £1 of redeemable debt is sold at a discount, the owner at redemption, who receives the face value of the debt and not the issue price, will make a capital profit. Marketable loans are frequently known as bonds. Individual loans or marketable loans may be secured by a charge or unsecured; much of the law in this area concerns company charges. Fashions in marketable loans vary. The highly specialised rules relating to international or Euro bonds fall outside the scope of a company law syllabus.

Any document which states the terms on which a company has borrowed money may be called a debenture (s 744) whether or not it carries security but in the business world an unsecured loan is likely to called an unsecured loan note rather than a debenture. Charges have to be registered to be valid against other creditors of the company but the position on registration is presently something of a mess. The registration of company charges is currently subject to the 1985 Act but its provisions have been prospectively replaced by the 1989 Act. However, no date for the substitution of the 1989 system has been set and it looks increasingly likely that these 1989 change will not be implemented but will be replaced by some alternative amendments. Until some change is executed the 1985 Act prevails.

Loan capital raises general issues – the ability of the company to borrow, the powers of the directors to borrow and the issue of marketable loans – and specific provisions relating to company charges. Questions on loan capital often involve a company which has gone into insolvent liquidation and requires the liquidator to be advised on the validity and priority of certain debts. In all questions of this type, two issues arise – how can the liquidator maximise the company's assets (eg sue directors for wrongful trading, have some charges set aside) and how should he determine priorities between competing creditors.

In this chapter the Insolvency Act 1986 is referred to as IA.

Question 42

Resurgam plc is a company specialising in intensive study courses for candidates re-sitting professional examinations. The Chairman of the board has asked you brief him on the advantages and disadvantages to the company, to Resurgam's current shareholders and to potential investors, of three alternative means of raising the finance necessary to fund the company's projected expansion, namely:

(a) creating and issuing further ordinary shares; or
(b) obtaining a loan secured by a fixed charge; or
(c) obtaining a loan secured by a floating charge.

Answer plan

A question on which it is hard to shine since little analysis is required, but equally hard to go disastrously wrong. No detail can be given in the time likely to be available so a broad overview is adequate. Do, however, note that the three groups, the company, future investors and current shareholders may not have identical interests and, where appropriate should be given different information.

Answer

There are a number of issues which Resurgam should consider before deciding how best to fund its future expansion. The board should bear in mind that factors which might be perceived as advantages to the company may not be so regarded by the current shareholders (or likely investors). The initial decision which the company must make is whether to raise further funds from shareholders or whether to borrow the money thought necessary. Resurgam will be aware that increasing share capital lowers the gearing ratio of the company making it easier to use loan finance in the future.

Loan capital versus share capital

The differences between the two methods of financing can be sub-divided into a number of categories.

(a) *Risk/return*

For the company – shares do not carry a continuous commitment in that a dividend need not be declared even if distributable profits are made by Resurgam. However, loans are likely to be interest bearing and the interest is payable even if the company has not made a profit albeit interest on a loan is an allowable expense for tax purposes thereby reducing the corporation tax liability, if any, of the company. Dividends are paid out of profits and are not tax-deductible.

For the investor – shares carry more risk for the purchaser since they may yield no return and can become valueless if the company is unsuccessful but if the company is successful the shareholders are likely to receive a good return and there is the potential for capital profits. Loans are likely to bear a fixed rate of interest so that an income can be guaranteed but the interest will not increase if the company is profitable and a loan may have no potential for capital growth (some loans, for example bonds issued at a discount which carry no interest, 'zeroes', have growth potential in that at redemption they are redeemed at face value). Some loan stock is convertible into shares allowing an investor to start off with a fixed return (from the loan) and, if the company seems successful, convert into shares. Both dividends and interest are usually paid twice-yearly.

For the current shareholders – increasing the number of shares reduces the value of current shares and increases the pool of shareholders among whom dividends must be spread. Consequently, shareholders to whom a rights issue is offered would be wise to consider subscribing. The current shareholders would have to approve an increase in share capital (s 121).

(b) *Issue*

For the company – shares can be offered at a premium but cannot be offered at a discount (s 100) whereas loans can be issued at a premium or a discount (unless convertible into shares when they cannot be issued at a discount). Shares are rarely redeemable so that if the company wishes to reduce share capital it must comply with the statutory procedures for reduction including court confirmation (s 135). Loan stock can be irredeemable but is generally redeemable and redemption is not a reduction of capital allowing the company more flexibility in its financing.

For the investor – shares issued wholly for cash are subject to statutory pre-emption rights, ie new issues must be offered first to existing shareholders in proportion to their current holdings (s 89), although this right can be excluded or easily evaded (eg by issuing them other than wholly for cash). Debentures are not subject to statutory pre-emption rights.

For the current shareholders – the right of pre-emption, unless excluded by Resurgam, is an attractive option. Shares are freely transferable and may be quoted on the Stock Exchange whereas this is not always the situation with loan stock.

(c) *Security*

For the company – if the company fails to pay dividends the shareholders have no immediate remedy (although it may constitute unfair prejudice contrary to s 459, *Re Sam Weller Ltd* (1990)) whereas a lender with a secured loan may be able to seize the charged asset if his interest remains unpaid or he regards the security as in jeopardy.

For the investor – shares are not secured on any assets of the company and ownership of a share does not make a shareholder an owner of any portion of the company's assets (*Short v Treasury*

Commissioners (1948)). A secured loan gives an investor rights in respect of the asset charged as security. On winding up shareholders receive the nominal value (or more) of their shares only if there are surplus assets available after the payment of all creditors. Even creditors may find themselves ranked behind certain statutory debts (preferential debts) on winding up, but a secured creditor, provided he has checked the value of his security, is likely to receive his money back.

(d) *Company participation*

For the company – ordinary shareholders are likely to have votes (non-voting shares can be issued but the Stock Exchange is not enthusiastic about such shares) and must be consulted to some degree about the running of the company. In practice the directors control the company and in a public company need pay little heed to the wishes of all but a few large shareholders. Creditors, in theory, play no part in the running of the company. A glance at the financial pages will show that substantial creditors, eg banks, wield considerable influence particularly if a company needs to re-schedule a loan.

For the investor – a small shareholder has a vote but no influence over the way a company is run although he will get tea and biscuits at the AGM. A small creditor is equally without influence (and no tea and biscuits). Large investors of either type, pension funds or other institutional investors, are likely to be listened to by the board (investors should beware becoming shadow directors if they wield too much influence, s 741). Creditors may be entitled to attend special creditor meetings.

(e) *Practicalities*

For the company – apart from considering the effect of borrowing on the company's economic standing, the company should consider the costs of raising money. Indeed the company might be well-advised to see its bankers privately and arrange a loan rather than seeking finance from the market. The power to borrow is an implied power of every trading company (*General Auction Estate & Monetary Co v Smith* (1891)) and the negotiation of loans will fall within the remit of the board.

Fixed versus floating charges

If the company decides to borrow to expand its business any creditor is likely to require security. Companies have two forms of security they can deploy – fixed charges, ie a charge over a specified asset or property, or floating charges, ie a charge over a class of asset, and current shareholders are largely unaffected by the type preferred. Both types of charge are subject to registration and if not registered are void (s 395) although the underlying debt is unaffected by non-registration. Both types of charge may be set aside if the company goes into insolvent liquidation within a statutory period of the charge being created and the charge was designed to prefer one creditor over another (s 245 IA). Resurgam and future creditors should note the differences between fixed and floating charges.

(a) Fixed charge

A fixed charge may be legal or equitable. For example if the company charges its real property to its bank by means of a mortgage, the bank has a fixed legal charge over that property. The bank will obtain the title deeds to the property which effectively precludes the company dealing with the property without the knowledge and consent of the bank. A fixed equitable charge is less formal and can be achieved by the deposit of title deeds. The holder of a fixed charge can, on winding up or if the security is at risk, seize the charged property and sell it to discharge the indebtedness thereafter accounting for any surplus to the company. A fixed chargeholder does not claim against the general assets of the company on winding up, he simply claims against 'his' asset and provided he has ensured it is of adequate value he is not in competition with the other creditors for the assets of the company unless the same asset has been used as security for a further loan when a question of priority will arise. A fixed charge, generally prevents the company dealing with the charged asset without the consent of the chargeholder and is, thus, an inappropriate form of security for assets which are constantly changing, eg stock, but inept drafting can lead to the creation of a fixed charge over such assets (see for example *Re Cimex Tissues Ltd* (1995)).

(b) *Floating charge*

A floating charge, which cannot be created by a sole trader or a partnership, is an equitable charge on a class of assets, present or future, or over the whole undertaking, rather than being over a specified asset. Thus, a floating charge could be granted over goods to be produced or book debts. In theory a floating charge can be granted over a wider range of assets than a fixed charge but the courts have recognised a fixed charge over book debts (*Siebe Gorman v Barclays Bank* (1987)) and goods in the course of production (*Re Cimex Tissues Ltd* (1995)) so this difference may be illusory. The essence of a floating charge is that it leaves the company free to deal with the charged asset as it sees fit (but note the effect of a negative pledge clause and automatic crystallisation, below) without consulting the chargeholder.

Since a floating charge is over a class of assets, the chargeholder is uncertain as to the value of his security at any moment before the charge crystallises (transmutes into a fixed charge on the happening of certain events, eg receivership, liquidation or the giving of notice by the chargeholder). If there is a fixed and floating charge over the same asset the fixed charge (being fixed and legal) will generally have priority over the floating charge even if created later than the floating charge. Floating chargeholders, to protect themselves, may include in their charge notification that they take priority over later chargeholders (even if fixed), ie a negative pledge clause, but such a clause is effective only if the later chargeholder has *actual* notice of the clause. It can be argued that this restriction on the company's ability to deal with its asset, ie by double charging, is contrary to the whole nature of a floating charge which supposedly allows a company freedom to deal with the charged asset. Floating chargees are also experimenting with automatic crystallisation clauses which seek to provide that if a company attempts to charge an asset subject to a floating charge the charge automatically crystallises (ie without any intervention on the part of the chargeholder) and becomes fixed thus retaining its priority over the new charge – the efficacy of such clauses is not yet settled.

There are three further drawbacks of a floating charge. First, a floating charge ranks behind preferential debts on winding up. Second, it attaches only to assets of the relevant class which *belong* to the company. Consequently, where a floating chargee has a charge over raw materials to be used in production he may find that the supplier of the goods has retained title to them until he is paid (a retention of title clause) thus allowing him to remove them, if not paid, from the company's premises and out of the grasp of the floating charge. Similarly, goods are not company assets susceptible to the clutch of a floating charge if they are subject to a lien or a trust or have been leased. Third, a floating charge created within 12 months of winding up (or two years if the chargeholder is a connected person) is invalid (s 245 IA) unless the company was solvent at the time the charge was granted. If a charge is *prima facie* invalidated by s 245 it will remain valid to the extent of any consideration provided for the charge. Hence, if a company negotiates a loan facility of £100,000 secured by floating charge six months before liquidation and at liquidation the company has used £30,000 of the facility then the charge is valid to the extent of £30,000. In contrast if the company owed X £100,000 and six months before liquidation granted a floating charge to secure that loan all the security would be invalid – no new consideration would have been provided by X.

There is little doubt that a fixed charge provides greater security than a floating charge but it may be inappropriate for the needs of the company and the creditor and the advice as to the preferred security will depend upon those needs.

Question 43

Conservative Ltd had been experiencing severe financial difficulties since early 1994 but its directors, John and Kenneth, continued to trade hoping that the company's trading position would improve although they thought it unlikely the company would be able to pay its debts unless there was a massive upturn in business. They have now given up the struggle and have called a meeting for 1 June 1995 to wind up the company.

Conservative Ltd has assets of £34,000, additionally its plant and machinery has an estimated value of £22,000. The company's liabilities are:

(a) £25,000 loan owed to Big Bank plc secured by a fixed charge, created in March 1994 and duly registered, over plant and machinery;

(b) £15,000 overdraft owed to Small Bank Ltd secured by a floating charge over the company's assets and undertaking, created in August 1994 and duly registered;

(c) £20,000 owing to employees (one month's salary for 20 workers); and

(d) £21,000 owed to sundry trade creditors.

In November 1994, Kenneth negotiated the sale of property to the company for which he was paid a commission by the vendor of sold property to the company thereby making a profit of £8,000; he has not, so far, disclosed this profit to John or the shareholders.

Liquidation costs are likely to be around £5,000.

Advise the liquidator on any relevant issues of company law and indicate which creditors will be paid.

Answer plan

The usual issues arise – how can the assets of the company be augmented (actions against directors etc) and how should the assets be distributed. Consider each debt in turn to determine its validity and conclude with a rank order for payment.

Answer

On the appointment of a liquidator the powers of the directors of a company cease except insofar as they are permitted to act either by the company in general meeting or the liquidator. The liquidator has to comply with a complex web of procedures but his principal obligation can be summarised by reference to s 143 (albeit this section only applies to companies being wound up by the court), it is 'to secure that the assets of the company are got in, realised and distributed to the company's creditors and, if there is a surplus, to the persons entitled to it'. In carrying out this duty the liquidator must maximise the assets before determining who receives any money.

Swelling the assets

In addition to seeking contributions from shareholders who hold partly paid shares and pursuing legal actions against third parties, the liquidator of this company might wish to consider whether he can recover any sums from the directors of the company. Consider first the contract negotiated by Kenneth. The House of Lords in *Aberdeen Railway Co v Blaikie Bros* (1854) ruled that a director could not benefit directly or indirectly from a contract made by his company. This has been modified to provide that a director cannot benefit from a contract between himself and his company or between his company and a third party without making *adequate disclosure* of his own interest. Disclosure in this company could have been achieved by disclosure to the board (because the company has Table A, art 85) but the consequences of failing to disclose to the shareholders or, where permissible, the board, are the same. If there has been inadequate disclosure, the company is allowed to rescind the contract (where the director has received a direct benefit and rescission is still possible) or make the director liable to account for any indirect benefits (as in this case). In this case, the liquidator should seek to recover the £8,000 from Kenneth.

Another possibility which the liquidator might pursue is an action against the directors for wrongful trading. The concept of wrongful trading was introduced by s 214 IA and it allows a court to declare a director liable to contribute to the assets of the company if the director knew, or ought to have concluded, that there was no reasonable prospect of the company avoiding insolvent liquidation and he did not take every step he ought to have taken to minimise the potential loss to the company's creditors. Thus, if this is an insolvent liquidation the liquidator can seek a court order for one or more directors of the company to contribute to the assets of the company. Section 214 does not authorise an order requiring a director to contribute towards the costs of liquidation or post-liquidation debts. An order is to contribute to the assets of the company and the section does not authorise an order that a particular creditor be paid nor only those creditors whose debts were incurred after the director should have known that the company would go into insolvent liquidation (*Re Purpoint Ltd* (1991)). John and/or Kenneth cannot be liable under s 214 unless he both knew or ought to have concluded that insolvency could not be avoided *and* he failed to take every step to minimise loss to creditors which he ought to have taken. The section only envisages the imposition of liability on a director who has both not realised what he should have done and has not done what he should have done. In determining whether a director has met the standard expected of him s 214 provides guidance. Sub-section (4) says that a director is to be judged by what a reasonably diligent person with the 'general knowledge, skill and experience that may reasonably be expected of a person carrying out the same functions as are carried out by that director' (ie the director potentially subject to an order) and the 'general knowledge, skill and experience' of the director whom it is sought to make liable. This somewhat obscure provision seems to mean that what a director should have known or done is to be judged by reference to a theoretical director who possesses those skills that may 'reasonably be expected' of a director unless the director is better qualified than this theoretical director when he is to be judged by reference to his own qualifications. Assuming John and Kenneth have no special skills they are to be judged by reference to the theoretical director who possesses those qualifications which can reasonable be expected from a director; the Act is silent as to what qualifications one can reasonably expect a director to possess and the courts have been reluctant to list what can be expected. It could be argued that cases suggest one cannot reasonably expect a great deal, certainly in *Re Elgindata Ltd* (1991) the judge concluded that poor management was one of the risks which an investor had to bear although in some cases on s 459 mismanagement has been deemed to be unfair prejudice (see *Re Macro (Ipswich) Ltd* (1994) for example).

In determining whether John and Kenneth did all that could be expected of them there is one case (the only case on the section so far) to consider – *Re Produce Marketing Consortium Ltd* (1989), hereafter *PMC*. In *PMC* the company had traded successfully for some nine to 10 years and remained profitable until 1980. Thereafter, between 1980 and 1984 the company built up an overdraft, and in 1984 had an excess of liabilities over assets and a trading loss. Between 1984 and 1987, when insolvent liquidation ensued, the trading loss continued as did the excess of liabilities over assets but the overdraft approximately halved due to an increase in indebtedness to the company's principal supplier. By February 1987 one of the directors realised that liquidation was inevitable but the company was allowed to trade until October the decision being justified as allowing disposal of the company's supplies of perishable goods which were held in cold-store. Knox J found that the directors should have concluded by July 1986 that liquidation was inevitable because, although accounts were not available until January 1987, their knowledge of the business was such that they must have realised that turnover was down and that the gap between assets and liabilities must have increased. Since the Act provides that the directors are to be judged by reference to what they know and what they ought to know Knox J held that they ought to have known the financial results for the year ending 1985 in July 1986 at the latest so that the fact that these results were not known until 1987 was no excuse. Moreover, the directors had failed to take all steps to minimise loss – the directors had not limited their dealings to running down the company's stocks in cold-store even if this was a justified step. Knox J held that both directors must contribute £75,000 to the assets of the company, this being the loss which could have been averted by speedy liquidation. It could be argued that John and Kenneth were even more reprehensible since they seemed to be aware that the company was unable to meet its obligations and seem to have done nothing to minimise the company's debts. The loans taken out in 1994 were presumably to prop up the business and there seems to have been no rational business plan operated by the directors to improve the company's position. Assuming John and Kenneth have funds, an action for wrongful trading seems appropriate. The liquidator might conjoin such an action with an application to disqualify them from acting as directors.

Paying the creditors

Let us assume that some money has been recovered from the directors, to whom should it, and the other corporate funds, be paid? Consider the four competing claims. Note that if any of them should have been registered and were not then they become unsecured debts (s 395), that transactions at undervalue or constituting a preference may not be enforceable (ss 238–241) and that a floating charge created within a specified period of winding up may be void (s 245). In practice secured creditors dispose of the asset to which their charge relates and account for any surplus to the liquidator but, in theory the realisation of a charged asset can be left to the liquidator.

Big Bank plc lent the company £25,000 secured by a fixed charge, duly registered, some 14 or 15 months before liquidation commenced. If this charge is valid the proceeds of the sale of plant and machinery will be paid to Big Bank leaving them with a projected shortfall of £3,000 in respect of which they are an unsecured creditor. There seems no evidence that this charge was a preference and even if it was the Insolvency Act only permits the setting aside of preferential transactions entered into in the six months prior to liquidation (unless the bank was a connected person, which it is not). Big Bank drop out of the liquidator's sums except to the extent of £3,000.

Small Bank lent the company £15,000 (the overdraft), secured by floating charge duly registered, some nine or 10 months prior to the liquidation. Section 245 provides that a floating charge created within 12 months of insolvent liquidation (the bank is not a connected person, if it were the period would be two years) is invalid (the debt remains valid but unsecured) *except* to the extent of any money paid to the company after the creation of the charge and in consideration for the charge. Since Small Bank lent money to the company it seems likely that they fall within the exception and that the charge is valid. Thus, the only issue for the liquidator to determine is whether the overdraft arose after the charge and is thus secured or whether all or part of it arose prior to the charge in which case that part would be unsecured. It seems unlikely that the overdraft arose prior to August 1992. Even if the company had an overdraft at that date of £15,000 or more, the case of *Re Yeovil Glove* (1965) would probably protect the bank. In *Yeovil Glove*, the company had an overdraft of around £66,000 and the company's bank sought security which the company granted by creating a floating charge over its assets. Within a year the company went into insolvent liquidation having at that time an overdraft of around £66,000. The issue for the court was whether the overdraft at liquidation and at the time the charge was created should be treated as the same overdraft – if they were then the charge was invalid (created within 12 months of winding up and no new money provided to the company). The Court of Appeal held that since the company had been allowed to operate its bank account during the period between the granting of the charge and the liquidation (some £110,000 had been paid in and drawn out) the overdraft existing at the time of liquidation was not to be regarded as the same debt as the overdraft in existence at the granting of the charge. The money paid in after the charge was granted and before liquidation paid off the original overdraft even if the company then drew out an equal amount of money from its account – those drawings created a new debt. Hence, the liquidation overdraft was a post-charge debt which provided new money to the company and was secured. Thus in this case, if the overdraft existed prior to the charge and the company was allowed to continue using its account after the charge was granted, *Re Yeovil Glove* would apply so that as money flowed through the account the old (unsecured) loan would be discharged to be replaced by a new (secured) loan. Thus, Small Bank have a claim over the assets of the company to the extent of any consideration provided for the charge – probably the full sum.

Small Bank would, however, be paid after any preferential creditors. The employees of the company are preferential creditors in respect of unpaid wages up to a maximum of £800 per employee. Thus each employee must be paid £800 (£16,000 total) before any other creditors are paid by the liquidator. The balance of their unpaid wages is an unsecured debt.

Thus the liquidator should pay the costs of the liquidation (£5,000) then the employees (£16,000), making a total of £21,000. This leaves assets of £13,000 which must be paid to Small Bank (owed £15,000) leaving Small Bank £2,000 out of pocket. If the liquidator obtains any money from John and Kenneth, this is used first to pay Small Bank its £2,000 and the remainder is divide between Big Bank (£3,000), the employees (£4,000) and the unsecured trade creditors. The unsecured creditors rank equally each will receive the same percentage of their debt if there are inadequate funds to pay them in full.

Question 44

In May 1992, Funfood Ltd, a company engaged in the manufacture of snack foods, borrowed £20,000 from D, the brother of one of the directors, which loan was expressed to be repayable on demand. In August 1994 the company created a floating charge over the company's assets and undertaking in favour of the ABC Bank to secure the company's overdraft (then standing at £48,000) up to a maximum of £100,000. The floating charge, which was duly registered, prohibited the company from granting a further floating charge over all or any part of its assets or undertaking without first giving notice to the ABC Bank and further provided that the granting of any such floating charge entitled the bank to give notice to Funfood which notice would crystallise the bank's charge. In December 1994, the company borrowed £60,000 from E which loan was secured by a fixed charge over the company's factory; the charge was duly registered. In January 1995, D threatened to recall his loan unless it was secured. The company repaid the loan and D then lent the same amount of money to the company; the loan was secured by a floating charge which was duly registered.

On 1 June 1995, the Inland Revenue, who are owed £16,000 in unpaid PAYE contributions, presented a petition to wind up the company. At that date the company's overdraft stood at £104,000, the extra £4,000 over the agreed limit having been borrowed to pay staff wages. The company's factory is worth £85,000 and the other assets of the company are likely to realise about £42,000. Liquidation costs are estimated at £6,000.

Advise the liquidator.

Answer plan

In any question this type the possible issues – how can the assets of the company be augmented (actions against directors etc) and how should the assets be distributed. Primarily, this question addresses the second issue. When considering the payment of creditors, the liquidator must check the validity of each claim and where two creditors claim a charge over the same asset, which is insufficient to satisfy both debts, determine which has the prior claim.

Answer

While the obligations of a liquidator are two-fold, to gather in the assets of the company, and where possible augment them, and to pay out the assets to the appropriate claimants, this question does not appear to raise any particular issues relating to the acquisition or augmentation of the company's assets. It may be that the directors were reckless in trading in a parlous state for so long so that an action for unfair trading (s 214 IA) might be apposite but the main thrust of the question is towards distribution of such assets as there are. In practice secured creditors dispose of the asset to which their charge relates and account for any surplus to the liquidator but, in theory the realisation of a charged asset can be left to the liquidator and if the liquidator disputes the validity of a charge the chargee cannot simply seize the asset and sell it.

Validity of claim or charge

Before considering any question of payment, the liquidator must check that all the claims lodged, and any charge relied upon, are valid. Consider each claim in turn. It can be assumed that, since the company is a trading company, it has an implied power to borrow (*General Auction Estate & Monetary Co v Smith* (1891)) so that, even if the company has no express power to borrow, the borrowings are not *ultra vires*. It can be assumed that the board have the power to initiate borrowings and there seems no question of unauthorised loans being entered into. If the loans were *ultra vires* or negotiated by a person lacking authority, the creditor would probably be protected by ss 35 and 35A.

First in time (May 92) is D's loan which appears to be valid but is unsecured, D is, provisionally, an unsecured creditor and ranks at the bottom of any list of creditors when the assets are being distributed. D re-appears later.

Second, is the floating charge granted by the company to the ABC Bank to secure the overdraft facility (August 94). The charge was registered so that the loan and the charge appear to be valid. However, s 245 IA, provides that a floating charge created within the relevant period is invalid unless the company could pay its debts at the time the charge was granted (ie was solvent) or s 245(2) applies. The relevant period is within 12 months of the winding up (s 245(3)) so that the charge of August 1994 falls within it and unless the company was solvent at that date the charge is invalid except to the extent that s 245(2) applies. This section says that a charge granted within the relevant period is valid to the extent that money was paid to the company in consideration for the creation of the charge. Consequently, £56,000 is secured by the charge (£104k–£48k) which gives the bank a claim on the assets of the company in priority to an unsecured creditor. Indeed, since the £4,000 over the agreed overdraft limit is used to pay wages it is a preferential debt insofar as it was used to pay employees who could have claimed any unpaid wages as a preferential debt, ie the bank is subrogated to the position of the employees (Sched 6 para 11). The remaining £48,000 may also fall within s 245(2) even though the company's overdraft stood at that sum when the charge was granted if the principle enunciated in *Re Yeovil Glove Ltd* (1965) applies. In *Re Yeovil Glove*, the company had an overdraft of around £66,000 and the company's bank sought security which the company granted by creating a floating charge over its assets. Within a year the company went into insolvent liquidation having at that time an overdraft of around £66,000, ie the facts resemble the current case. The issue for the court was whether the overdraft at liquidation and at the time the charge was created should be treated as the same overdraft – if they were then the charge was invalid (created within 12 months of winding up and no new money provided to the company). The Court of Appeal held that since the company had been allowed to operate its bank account during the period between the granting of the charge and the liquidation (some £110,000 had been paid in and drawn out) the liquidation overdraft was not to be regarded as the same debt as the overdraft in existence at the granting of the charge. The money paid in after the charge was granted and before liquidation paid off the original overdraft. This was the case even if the company had then drawn out of its account a sum equal to that it had paid in – those drawings created a new debt. Hence, the liquidation overdraft provided new money to the company and the charge was valid. Thus in this case, if the company has paid at least £48,000 into its account after the charge was granted, and was then allowed to draw that sum out before liquidation commenced, *Re Yeovil Glove* would apply. Consequently, as money flowed through the account the old (unsecured) loan would be discharged to be replaced by a new (secured) loan. It seems that £100,000 is secured by the floating charge. The bank's floating charge contained a restriction on the company's freedom to deal with the assets subject to the charge. This restriction, if broken, entitled the bank to serve notice and thereby crystallise the floating charge, ie turn it into a fixed charge. However, this restriction applies only to future floating charges so that it is unaffected by the fixed charge in favour of E. Moreover, the ability of the bank to crystallise its charge on the creation of future floating charges is not an *automatic* crystallisation clause – it merely gives the bank power to serve notice and thus crystallise its charge. The bank appear not to have exercised this power in respect of D's floating charge. The effect of having two floating charges over the same property (if D's charge is valid) is discussed below.

Third in time is the charge in favour of E. The charge was registered, being fixed it does not fall within s 245, and appears to be valid. The only doubt about the validity of E's security is raised by s 239 IA. This Act provides that where a company has, within the relevant period given a preference to a person, the liquidator can apply to the court challenging the alleged preference. The court, if its finds a preference has been given, can make such order as it sees fit for restoring the position which would be operative but for the preference. Thus, if this is a preference the liquidator could seek to have the security set aside. The charge is within the relevant period – six months prior to the onset of winding up (s 240) – but is it a preference? There is scanty case law on this provision but it seems that the liquidator must establish that the company desired to prefer E, ie wished him to be treated more favourably than other creditors. Since E would no doubt have refused to make the loan but for the charge he is not being preferred over other existing creditors – it simply a condition of the loan (see the parallel case of *Re MC Bacon Ltd* (1990)). Thus, E can sell the factory to discharge his loan and give any surplus to the liquidator where it will form part of the assets of the company. E can be ignored by the liquidator in determining priorities since he has been paid in full.

In January 1995, D threatened to recall his loan which the company duly repaid but replaced with an identical loan secured by floating charge. The loan, like the 1992 loan, is a valid debt but is the charge valid. It is a floating charge created within 12 months of winding and is invalid unless the company was solvent, which is doubtful, except to the extent of any consideration provided for the creation of the charge. While, technically, D has lent the company money he has simply re-cycled the existing loan and not provided any new funds. In such a case the court has the power to disregard the alleged consideration as not being *bona fide* (*Re Destone Fabrics Ltd* (1941) is similar to this case) and invalidate the charge. Thus, D remains an unsecured creditor. Had the floating charge been validated by s 245(2) IA, it might anyway have been regarded as a preference contrary to s 239 IA. If D's charge had been valid, he would have been in competition with the bank which also has a floating charge over the assets and undertaking of the company which assets etc are insufficient to satisfy both claims - in such cases the first charge has priority provided both charges are over identical assets (*Re Benjamin Cope & Co* (1914)).

The final sums to be considered are the unpaid PAYE contributions and the liquidation costs – both are valid.

Priority of payment

Having determined which claims are valid, the liquidator must determine whom he should pay and in what order. E has dropped out of the picture leaving the liquidator with £67,000 at his disposal and claims of £140,000 so that those at the bottom of the rank order will receive nothing unless all claims are required to abate equally. Funfood Ltd in collecting PAYE contributions from its employees was acting as a tax collector for the government. Withholding taxes of this type are treated as preferential debts and preferential debts are payable in priority to all other debts (s 175 IA) – thus £16,000 is payable to the revenue leaving £51,000 of which £4,000 is payable to the bank as a subrogated creditor which leaves £47,000. The liquidator can then deduct his costs which leaves £41,000 (*Re Barleycorn Enterprises Ltd* (1970) established that liquidation costs take priority over floating charges) which is payable to the ABC Bank in respect of its floating charge over the assets of the company. This leaves the bank £59,000 out of pocket and D will receive nothing at all. Had there been any surplus after payment of all creditors that sum would have been repaid to the shareholders.

Question 45

You have been appointed liquidator of an insolvent company, Reindeer Ltd, which was founded by Rudolf and which has been engaged in the manufacture of novelties for festivals. The majority of the issued share capital of Reindeer is owned by Rudolf, who was the sole director of the company, with the remainder being owned by his brother, Gandalf.

What, if anything, should be done about the following which the liquidation has revealed:

(a) A year prior to the commencement of liquidation, Reindeer sold its factory to Elk Ltd for £110,000 (which was its book value) and then leased the premises back from Elk. Elk Ltd, which is controlled and run by Gandalf, has recently contracted to sell the property for £0.75 million.

(b) Shortly before your appointment the company redeemed a floating charge which had been granted to Christmas Bank plc six months earlier as security for the company's overdraft which was guaranteed by Gandalf.

(c) The company collected substantial amount of income tax from the employees which should have been remitted to the Inland Revenue; at Gandalf's suggestion, the money was used to pay off other creditors of the company who were pressing for payment.

Answer plan

A number of issues for the liquidator to consider which, as is usual, include swelling the assets of the company (sale of property, redemption of floating charge) and determining the distribution of the assets (preferential debts). In addition, appraise the conduct of Rudolf and Gandalf and consider whether an action for disqualification should be commenced and its impact if successful.

Answer

As liquidator you have been asked to consider a number of issues which have emerged in the course of the liquidation of Reindeer. The substantive issues can be treated separately.

(a) *Sale of property*

One duty cast upon a liquidator is to augment the company's assets available for distribution to creditors. In this case, the company has sold an asset at a price which appears to be an undervalue. A number of possibilities arise. Can this transaction be set aside, can the profit on the resale be recovered from Rudolf, Gandalf or Elk or can damages be recovered for a foolish commercial decision or for any other reason?

First, it must be seen whether the rise in value of the property sold is attributable to some external factors, if such is the case, the company was unlucky but the transaction is not actionable. If, however, the difference between the sale price and the new price is not so assignable, you may wish to pursue the issue of the sale further. A sale by a company to a third party cannot generally be rescinded merely because the company could have got a better price for the asset but if the sale falls within s 238 IA a court can make an order to restore the company to the position it would have been in had it not entered into the transaction. Section 238 covers the situation where the company sells an asset at an undervalue but the section is applicable only if the transaction falls within the relevant period defined in s 240. The relevant period, for a transferee who is a connected person is two years whereas in other cases it is six months. Thus, the critical issue is whether the purchaser, Elk Ltd, is a connected person. Section 249, which defines connected person, treats directors and shadow directors and associates as connected to the company. Elk is neither a director or shadow director of Reindeer although Gandalf may well be a shadow director (a person in accordance with whose directions the directors of the company are accustomed to act, s 741) since he seems to play a large role in the affairs of the company. If Gandalf is a shadow director it might be that the court would lift the veil of incorporation and treat Elk and Gandalf as one and the same for the purposes of s 238 (a similar approach was manifested in *Aveling Barford v Perion Ltd* (1989)). Alternatively, if Elk is an associate of Reindeer the two-year statutory period will also operate. Section 435 IA, defines associate in some detail but the upshot is that if Rudolf controls one company and Gandalf another then Elk is an associate of Reindeer either because hey are brothers or because Gandalf is a shadow director of Reindeer. Thus, the sale at the undervalue can be set aside unless Reindeer could pay its debts at the time of the sale. This seems the simplest way of dealing with the sale of property but if, for some reason s 238 is inapplicable, other routes may be open to you.

A liquidator may sue a directors if he has broken the duties cast upon him (there is no *locus* problem since the power to run the company passes to the liquidator on winding up), although it will not be worth so doing if Rudolf has no money. Is selling an asset at an undervalue a breach of duty? Rudolf in authorising the sale may have been negligent but it is unlikely that simple negligence from which he has not benefitted would render him liable for breach of the common law duty of care and skill. The conventional formulation of the nature and extent of this duty is that given by Romer J in *Re City Equitable Fire Insurance Co Ltd* (1925) in which he held, *inter alia*, that a director need display only such skill as may reasonably be expected from a person of his knowledge and experience. It is plain that if Rudolf has made a mis-guided but foolish decision he will not be negligent. Arguably, trying to raise funds by selling an asset if perfectly sensible although failure to have the property re-valued seems very mis-guided. The sale is not to a director and so the sale itself it cannot be a breach of fiduciary duty by Rudolf (it is not clear if shadow directors owe a fiduciary duty) if he acted *bona fide*. However, directors are supposed to exercise an independent judgment and if it can be shown that Rudolf simply implemented Gandalf's instructions without paying proper regard to the interests of the company that might be a breach of duty.

Whether Gandalf can incur liability if s 238 does not apply is uncertain. He may well be a shadow director. There are no cases discussing whether the common law rules on company contracts benefitting directors apply to shadow directors but if they do apply there can be no question of approving this sale if it is a misappropriation of a corporate asset. If a director does so appropriate he is liable as a constructive trustee and must return the property; constructive trusteeship could also be imposed on Elk Ltd if it had knowingly received misappropriated property. While the common law position is uncertain, there is no doubt that the statutory provision on substantial property transactions are applicable to such persons. Thus, if, as seems possible, he is a shadow director s 320 will apply to any sale of property to Elk Ltd if that company is 'connected' with Gandalf since the asset is a non-cash asset of requisite value (over £100,000). Section 346 defines a connected person (the definition differs from the provision in the Insolvency Act); it includes a company with which a shadow director is associated so there is no doubt that, since he controls Elk, Gandalf and Elk are connected for the purposes of s 320. Section 320 does not prevent Gandalf (via Elk) from buying a corporate asset from Reindeer but does require the transaction to be approved by the shareholders in general meeting and the apparent lack of such a resolution in this case *prima facie* renders the sale voidable (s 322). While all the shareholders in Reindeer knew about the transaction this is probably not a case where knowledge would be regarded as approval. While there are bars to the operation of s 320 there is no statutory time limit on the ability of the company to rescind an improper transaction (a possible advantage over s 238 IA). Further, s 317 requires a director or shadow director to make adequate disclosure of his interest in any contract between himself and his company. Failure to disclose his interest in Elk, even though known to Rudolf, appears to be a breach of s 317 which certainly gives rise to a criminal penalty and may give the liquidator a civil remedy (the position on this is unclear).

It should also be noted, that in the case of *Aveling Barford v Perion Ltd* (1989), the facts of which resemble this case, the sale to a shareholder at a gross undervalue was held to be an unauthorised return of capital which was incapable of ratification.

(b) *Redemption of the floating charge*

A floating charge granted within 12 months of the commencement of a winding up is invalid, unless the company was solvent at the time, except to the extent of any consideration provided for the charge (s 245 IA). Consequently, the floating charge in favour of the bank was potentially invalid. However, by the time of winding up, the debt which the charge was designed to secure had been repaid. While the charge would have been invalid the underlying debt would not have been affected by s 245 so that where, as here, the debt has been repaid the potential invalidity of the charge is irrelevant (*Mace Builders Ltd v Lunn* (1987)). However, a debt paid within six months of winding up may be challenged as being a preference contrary to s 239 IA. This section provides that where a company has within the relevant time given a preference to a person, the liquidator can apply to the court which can make such order as it sees fit for restoring the position which would be operative but for the preference. Thus, if this repayment is a preference the liquidator could seek to have the security set aside. Is this a preference? There is scanty case law on this provision but it seems that the liquidator must establish that the company desired to prefer a creditor *or* a guarantor of one of the company's debts, ie intended that person to be treated more favourably than other creditors. It seems not improbable that Gandalf would be regarded as having been preferred and the court could make such order as it saw fit, eg recover the money paid to the bank and leave it to pursue Gandalf if Reindeer does not pay. As noted above, Gandalf is probably a shadow director and his conduct in seeking to prefer himself is a factor to be considered in deciding whether to seek his disqualification.

(c) *Non payment of withholding tax*

Juggernaut in collecting income tax from employees (under the PAYE scheme) was acting as a tax collector for the government. Withholding taxes of this type are treated as preferential debts and preferential debts are payable in priority to all other debts (s 175 IA) – thus the sums collected but not remitted are a first charge on the assets of the company. Failure to account for taxes already deducted has been treated as an important, but not a crucial, factor in determining whether a director should be disqualified. Section 1 Company Directors Disqualification Act 1986 (CDDA), permits a court to disqualify a person from being a director, or being directly or indirectly concerned in the management of a company, in a number of prescribed circumstances. The majority of reported cases involve s 6 which provides that a person shall be disqualified (for a minimum of two years) from corporate management where he is or has been a director (or shadow director) of a company which has become insolvent *and* his conduct as a director of that, or any other company, makes him unfit to be concerned in company management. Acting as a director etc while disqualified is a criminal offence punishable, on indictment, by a fine and/or imprisonment for up to two years.

Judges determining cases on s 6, have stressed that the Act, while designed to protect the public and while not a purely penal statute, can result in penal consequences for a disqualified person in that a person may be precluded from trading through a limited company – Gandalf, for example, if disqualified would have, unless exempt, have to give up his directorship of Elk. Consequently, it is not surprising that judges have recognised these possible practical consequences, while seeking to give effect to Parliament's intention to limit the activities of unfit directors, in interpreting the Act's provisions. Factors taken into account (see also Sched 1) include breach of fiduciary duty, misuse of assets, responsibility for breaches of mandatory requirements and where the company is insolvent (necessary for s 6), the extent of the director's responsibility for the insolvency. The leading case on s 6 is *Re Sevenoaks Stationery (Retail) Ltd* (1990) in which the Court of Appeal held that the words 'unfit to be concerned in the management of a company' should be treated as ordinary English words which should be simple to apply in most cases. Each case turned on its own facts said the court but a director need not display total incompetence to be unfit. The court approved earlier cases which had held that simple commercial mis-judgment should not merit disqualification while a lack of commercial probity and an appropriate degree of incompetence could do so (see, for example, *Re Lo-Line Electric Motors Ltd* (1988)) – this points to these two being on the list for possible disqualification. In *Sevenoaks* five years disqualification ensued. Since each case turns on its own facts it is impossible to state definitively that Rich (or any member of the board) will be disqualified but his conduct seems to warrant the penalty. The appropriate period for disqualification was discussed in *Sevenoaks* in which Dillon LJ suggested that 10–15 year disqualification should be reserved for particularly serious cases (eg where this was a second disqualification) and two to five years for not very serious cases leaving six to 10 years for serious cases which do not merit the top bracket.

Question 46

Quince Ltd, which manufactures jellies and jams, is seeking to expand its business. The company secretary, Oberon, has recommended to the board that it take up a loan being offered by an individual, Flute, with whom he is acquainted. Flute has proposed that his loan be secured by a floating charge over the assets and undertaking of Quince Ltd which charge would automatically crystallise into a fixed charge if Quince Ltd seek to create a fixed charge over any of its assets subject to the floating charge. Flute has also requested that the company shall not create a subsequent floating charge over all or any of the assets to which his charge relates which would rank in priority to or *pari passu* with his floating charge. Oberon, has assured the board, who are experts on jam but not law, that this is all perfectly in order and that he will negotiate everything on their behalf.

The board would like to know what all this means before authorising Oberon to proceed. Elucidate.

Answer plan

After a brief introduction about financing, secured loans and floating charges in general, there are two matters which must be explained in detail. First, the impact of the clause providing for automatic crystallisation and second, the effect of a negative pledge clause.

Answer

The background

In advising you as to the meaning of the clause proposed by Flute it is necessary to give a little background. A company such as Quince is able to borrow money (it is an implied power even if not an express provision of the memorandum) and the board is likely to be empowered to negotiate a loan in accordance with the powers vested in them (Table A, art 70) so that the loan is neither *ultra vires* nor beyond the authority of the board. It is noted that the actual loan is to be negotiated by Oberon, the company secretary. While a company secretary would not have usual authority (ie authority deriving from his position) to negotiate loans, there is no reason why the board cannot delegate their authority to him – they invest him with actual authority to act for the company. The terms of, and need for, a loan are a matter of commercial judgment rather than subject to elaborate legal provisions but the board in negotiating a loan (or delegating others to do so) must act *bona fide* in the interests of the company and for a proper purpose – it is assumed that such is the case and that alternative methods of financing have been explored. If the loan is designed to prop up a failing company, you should note the provisions of the IA relating to wrongful trading. Loans may be unsecured or secured and if the company continues to trade and pays any interest on the loan the difference between them is irrelevant. However, if a company goes into liquidation a secured creditor has a claim upon the particular asset of the company to which his charge relates and can remove that asset (or more probably arrange its sale) from the clutches of the company's other creditors. The terms of a charge may also confer contractual rights on a chargeholder, eg the right to appoint a director or to attend certain company meetings. A chargeholder such as Flute can appoint a receiver to deal with the charged asset on his behalf in defined circumstances, eg if a liquidator is appointed. Charges fall into two categories, fixed and floating. A fixed charge, which may be legal or equitable, relates to a specific asset of the company, eg land owned by the company, and will preclude the company dealing with that asset without the consent of the chargeholder. A floating charge, which is equitable, is not specific but relates to a class of asset with which the company generally remains free to deal. On the happening of certain events, eg liquidation, or when the chargeholder gives notice in compliance with a provision in the charge which renders the security enforceable, the floating charge is said to crystallise. On crystallisation, the floating charge becomes a fixed charge attaching to such assets as currently make up the charged class.

There is no statutory definition of a floating charge and what the parties call the charge is not conclusive evidence of its status (see *Re New Bullas Ltd* (1993)) but judicial pronouncements have isolated certain factors which are likely to be present if a charge is to classified as floating. These factors (see *Government Stock Investment Co v Manila Rly Co Ltd* (1897) and *Illingworth v Houldsworth* (1904)) are that the charge is over a class of assets both present and future, that the class is one which, in the ordinary course of business, changes periodically and that the charge leaves the company free to deal with the charged asset in the ordinary course of conducting the company's business (this freedom need not be absolute). The type of asset frequently subject to a floating charge is goods in the course of production but there is no reason why, as here, a floating charge cannot embrace the whole corporate enterprise. Cases since the important decision in *Siebe Gorman & Co Ltd v Barclays Bank Ltd* (1979) have stressed that the courts will not seek to classify charges too rigidly and will allow companies considerable licence to tailor the terms of their loans as they see fit. The attraction of a floating charge to Quince is that it can allow the company to deal with its assets without the need to consult the chargeholder. The basis of this freedom to deal is disputed as is the notion of the ordinary course of a company's business but there is little doubt that selling, leasing or further charging a charged asset is *prima facie* 'in the ordinary course of business'. Hence, Quince would normally be free to deal with its assets, despite the charge, until crystallisation. When, on crystallisation, a floating charge is transformed into a fixed charge, chargeholder approval would be required for any disposition of the charged asset.

Automatic crystallisation clause

Certain events, eg winding up and the appointment of a Receiver, automatically crystallise a floating charge but the charge becomes fixed only from that moment and is not retrospectively transformed into a fixed charge from its inception. This has important consequences on winding up. A floating charge being, until crystallisation, an equitable charge, is ranked in the order of priorities after a fixed legal charge over the same asset *even if it was created after the floating charge.* Thus, if Flute was proposing a normal floating charge he would be vulnerable if the company went into insolvent liquidation in that any fixed chargeholder would have a prior claim over a corporate asset subject to both a fixed charge and his floating charge. Floating chargeholders have sought to protect themselves against the risk of being overtaken by a newer fixed charge by means of an automatic crystallisation clause, ie a clause which crystallises the floating charge without any action on the part of the chargeholder and designed to effect the transformation before priority is lost. The validity of a clause such as the one proposed, designed to preserve the priority of a floating charge by automatically transforming into a fixed charge just prior to the creation of the second charge, is not entirely settled. An early case, *Evans v Rival Granite Quarries Ltd* (1910), seems to reject – but with contrary dicta – the validity of such clauses but in the New Zealand case of *Re Manurewa Transport Ltd* (1971), such a clause was upheld (although the judge gave an alternative ratio). *Manurewa* has been followed in Australia but rejected in Canada. The most recent English decisions on the point (*Re Brightlife Ltd* (1986) and *Re Permanent House (Holdings) Ltd* (1989)) both decided by Hoffman J (as he then was) appears to accept the validity of an automatic crystallisation clause. Hoffman J treated a charge as a contract between the company and the chargeholder and saw no reason why company law should intervene in the parties freedom to put such terms in their contract as they saw fit. While this argument has much power there is a counter view. It can be argued that to allow Flute to rely on his contractual rights is unfair to a third party (a second chargeholder) who has no means of knowing about the automatic crystallisation clause. It is true that a prudent third party would inquire of the company whether his charge would crystallise any prior floating charges but the company might provide an inaccurate answer. It is open to the Secretary of State to make regulations relating to such clauses, for example it could be required that such a clause is registered. What is certain, is that an automatic crystallisation clause, if upheld, will be construed strictly against the party who seeks to rely on it and that Flute's clause will protect him only if it is sufficiently clear. Clauses of this type are of greater concern to third parties than to the company which grants the initial charge.

Negative pledge clause

Since a floating charge leaves a company free to deal with its assets, and dealing may include the creation of further charges, a company may grant a second fixed or floating charge over charged assets. This raises a question of priorities between such charges. As we have seen a fixed charge will generally obtain priority even if there is notice (which registration provides) of the existence of the prior floating charge since one of the features of a floating charge is that the company is free to deal with its charged asset. Logically the same must be true where the second charge is also floating. However, in *Re Benjamin Cope Ltd* (1914), Sargant J held that a company's freedom to deal did not extend to permitting a company to create a second floating charge over charged assets which ranked in priority or *pari passu* with the first charge. His reasoning was on the basis that to allow a second charge priority was contrary to received commercial wisdom. However, in *Re Automatic Bottlemakers Ltd* (1926), the Court of Appeal (which included Sargant J) held that a second floating charge over *part* of the charged assets could obtain priority if the first charge had permitted the creation of a second charge with priority. It is not clear if *Automatic Bottlemakers* would justify a second charge obtaining priority when it was over part of the assets subject to the first charge but the first charge had not specifically authorised the creation of later charges with priority. It could be argued that where there is no restriction on the creation of later charges the company's general freedom to deal with a charged asset allows the creation of a later floating charge with priority. Since there is the risk of a later charge obtaining priority, prudent chargeholders (whom Flute seeks to join) commonly insert negative pledge clauses in their agreements with companies. A negative pledge clause being a clause specifically precluding the creation of a second charge with priority. Such a clause restricts the company's freedom to deal with the charged asset but since the restriction does not prevent all dealings, but merely one, it is not thought to render the first clause fixed. However, the validity of the clause does not necessarily make it effective. It can be argued (see Farrar for example) that for the company to ignore such a clause and grant a further charge would be a case of equitable fraud and thus the second charge would be void. However, if a second charge is not ruled to be void, the first charge will retain priority only if the second chargeholder has notice of the first charge (which is provided by registration) *and* of the restriction on the freedom to deal. There is no constructive notice, it seems, of a restriction (a restriction need not, at present, be registered other than when the company charge requires registration in Scotland) and even if a chargeholder has actual knowledge of a floating charge this seems not to be notice of a restriction or to require the potential chargeholder to make inquiries (*English and Scottish Mercantile Investment Co Ltd v Brunton* (1892)). Where, however, a potential chargeholder searches the Register of Charges, and thereby obtains actual knowledge of the charge he will also obtain actual knowledge of any restriction registered with the charge. Thus, Flute's negative pledge clause will only work if a potential chargeholder searches the register and thereby obtains actual knowledge of the restriction.

There seems no reason for a company such as Quince Ltd to object to such a clause.

Chapter 8

Administering the Company

Introduction

The administration of companies is a wide-ranging topic covering such issues as the conduct of meetings, votes and resolutions, the maintenance of statutory registers and the role of the company secretary. Administration is everyday company law which goes on all the time in the background. It is not one of the spectacular areas concerning dispute and dissension which arise less frequently. Some aspects of administration have arisen in previous chapters — the qualifications and powers of a company secretary for example — and some is inherent in most questions — the passing of resolutions nearly always arises. This chapter seeks to consider some basic areas of the administration of companies ending with a brief outline of administration of a failing company.

It should be noted that you either know the material relating to administration or you do not — waffle is impossible. Even if you do know, it is the type of question where it is impossible to display anything better than competence.

Question 47

Henry and Wendy operate a niche market business which they have recently incorporated as Comp-u-Clean Ltd; they are the sole directors and own between them 51% of the shares. They do not anticipate becoming a public company or the issue of further shares in the near future. They have sought your advice on whether they need undergo an annual audit and whether they can limit the amount of accounts and reports they need to produce. They would also like to dispense with company meetings and conduct any necessary business between shareholders in writing or informally.

Advise them.

Answer plan

The question imposes its own plan — a discussion of the need for an auditor, the content and presentation of reports and accounts, the ability, if any, to dispense with meetings and informal conduct of shareholder business provisions.

Answer

The promoters of Comp-u-Clean are concerned about the accounting, reporting and decision-making processes applicable to a company as opposed to the unincorporated business they have been operating. They have no doubt heard that the government is pledged further to reduce the administrative burden upon entrepreneurs and hope to benefit from any previous lifting of the burden. Are they to be disappointed?

(a) *Reports and accounts*

Section 221 requires all companies to keep accounting records and failure to comply is a criminal offence. Since 1908, companies have been required to circulate members with the annual accounts of the company and members are now also entitled to receive a copy of the profit and loss account. The original basis underlying the requirements relating to reports and accounts was that those who have invested in the company should be kept informed of the state of the company and, thus, their investment. These rules on disclosure are immensely detailed but assume that if the directors have to tell the shareholders certain things this will, even if shareholder approval is not required, constrain the behaviour of the directors to avoid shareholder disapproval. As explained below, a small company may be able to avoid some of the more onerous reporting requirements. However, the reports and accounts which are required are also designed to provide information for interested third parties, eg employees and creditors so that their provision can be justified even for a company where there are few shareholders and the directors control the company. Reports and accounts are presented not just to the shareholders but must also be available, via submission to the Registrar of Companies (s 242), to the wider public (listed companies also have to disclose information to the Stock Exchange). Small and medium sized companies can deliver to the Registrar abbreviated accounts. There are strict time limits for the preparation of accounts and their delivery to the Registrar. Late submission renders the company and its directors liable to a fine (ss 242, 242A). In this company it has 10 months from the end of the company's accounting reference period to file the accounts etc.

Since the purpose of these accounts is to inform the shareholders of the state of financial health of the company and provide an account of the directors' stewardship in the previous year, these accounts must present a true and fair view of the company's financial position and must comply with Sched 4 of the Act (s 226). Section 241 requires the directors to lay the accounts before a general meeting of the company. However, a private company, as this is, can elect to dispense with the laying of accounts before a general meeting if such election is in compliance with s 252 (an elective resolution is required, see below). The election to dispense with the laying of accounts lasts indefinitely (it can be revoked by ordinary resolution) but an auditor or shareholder can require the company to hold a general meeting for the purpose of laying accounts (s 253). If no meeting is held the members must be circulated with the relevant accounts. Whether or not a meeting is held all reports etc must, within a specified time, also be sent to all debenture-holders (s 238).

The Companies Act requires four documents to be presented to the shareholders and the Registrar annually. These are the balance sheet, the profit and loss account, the directors' report and the auditor's report. Generally the accounts presented to shareholders will also include a statement of source and application of funds in accordance with SSAP (Statement of Standard Accounting Practice) 10 unless the turnover of gross income is less than £25,000. Directors may also choose to issue other reports, eg a chairman's report, but are not required so to do. Comp-u-Clean must prepare a profit and loss account for each financial year (s 226) and a balance sheet as at the last day of the year (s 226). The profit and loss account, which shows such things as the company's trading record, other income and expenditure, is a temperature chart of the company's financial health throughout the year. The balance sheet is a snapshot of the company's financial position on a particular date. Both documents must give a 'true and fair view' of the company's profit and loss for the year and the position at the end of the year (s 226). The Act specifies the content, format and valuation rules to apply to the balance sheet and profit and loss account (there are various format prescribed — Comp-u-Clean is probably a 'small' company). There is no legal requirement that the company complies with SSAPs in preparing these documents but compliance with SSAPs gives rise to a presumption that the accounts give a 'true and fair view' and deviation there from gives rise to a presumption that they do not. The Act also lists various disparate items which must be included as notes to the accounts.

Failure to comply with the statutory requirements relating to accounts has civil and criminal consequences. Section 245 allows, but does not require, the directors to issue revised accounts (or a directors' report) if the original accounts did not comply with the Act — the absence of compulsion is designed to encourage openness and compliance rather than relying on punishment which may induce concealment.

The whole system is aimed at providing the best possible information to shareholders and others. However, the Secretary of State can require the directors to explain the deviation from the statutory provisions and he can instruct the directors to revise the accounts and, if the directors fail so to do, he (or others authorised to act on his behalf, eg the Financial Reporting Review Panel) can seek a court order instructing the directors to issue revised accounts.

In addition it is a criminal offence for directors to approve annual accounts which they know do not comply with the Act or are reckless as to whether they comply or not (s 233). Failure to produce proper accounts is a matter which would be of concern to a court if the company went into insolvent liquidation and it was considering a disqualification order against Henry and Wendy. In a recent case the Court of Appeal said that failings in this area are 'serious matters' and went on to stress that the privilege of limited liability carries with it responsibilities. Directors, the court held, must be punctilious in observing the safeguards laid down by Parliament for the benefit of others who have dealings with their companies. They must prepare proper books of account and prepare annual accounts; they must file their returns and accounts promptly; and they must fully and frankly disclose information about deficiencies in accordance with the statutory provisions although isolated lapses in filing documents may be excusable. However, persistent lapses which show overall a blatant disregard for this important aspect of accountability are serious and cannot be condoned even if they do not involve any dishonest intent.

The minimum content of the directors' report is set out in the Act (s 234). It must include such items as information about the directors, for example the size of their shareholding, and information about the company's business, for example the principal activities of the company, any significant changes from the previous year and any likely future developments. The directors' report must also include information about employment and any charitable or political donations (no approval is required for such donations but they should be *intra vires*). The directors' report, unlike the accounts, is not audited.

There can be no question of Henry and Wendy dispensing with the statutory accounting and reporting requirements even though they are reporting to themselves.

(b) *Audit*

Traditionally, all companies are required to appoint auditors (s 384) in accordance with s 385 (or s 385A). However, the Companies Act (Audit Exemption) Regulations 1994 amended the Companies Act 1985 to exempt small companies from the requirement to hold an annual audit. Comp-u-Clean will qualify as small if it is not part of a group, has a balance sheet total of less than £1.4 million and a turnover of not more than £90,000. If its turnover is between £90,000 and £350,000 will be exempt if the directors send a special report to the shareholders (in compliance with s 249C). An exempt company must hold an audit if a member or members holding at least 10% of any class of shares demands one (s 249B).

If an audit is required, s 385 provides that the members appoint the auditor at each general meeting at which accounts are laid; if the company has elected not to hold such a meeting, the auditors must be appointed at another meeting of the company. However, since the company has up to 10 months before it need hold a meeting at which accounts are laid, the section also provides that the first directors, Henry and Wendy, can appoint auditors who remain in office until the conclusion of the first relevant general meeting. To appoint auditors at every general meeting may be thought cumbersome, even if the same auditors are just nodded through, and the company may wish to use s 386 to dispense with annual appointment. Section 386 permits a private company to dispense with the annual appointment of an auditor and provides that the auditors, once appointed, continue in office until a resolution is passed to terminate the appointment (s 393) or the company becomes dormant (s 250). To take advantage of this section, the company must pass an elective resolution in accordance with s 379A (see below). The auditor must be a member of a recognised supervisory body (s 25 CA 89) and be qualified under that body's rules for appointment as an auditor, be independent of the company (s 27 CA 89) and hold appropriate qualifications (Sched 11 CA 89). To remove an auditor requires an ordinary resolution (s 391) but special notice of any such resolution is required (s 391A).

The function of the auditor is to report to the members on the financial statements made by the directors particularly as to whether they comply with the Companies Act and give a true and fair view of the state of the company's affairs and results for the period under consideration (s 235). In preparing their report, the auditor must satisfy himself that proper accounting records have been kept and that the annual accounts agree with the underlying accounting record. If the auditor is not satisfied that records etc are accurate he must so state in his report. In order to prepare his report, the auditor has a right of access at all times to the books and accounts of the company and can require the company, its subsidiaries and its directors to provide any information required for the performance of his duties. Any failure to provide information must be reported in the auditor's report and it is a criminal offence for an officer of the company to make, knowingly or recklessly, a false statement to an auditor. Where information is not provided, the auditor has a duty to try and remedy the omission. Henry and Wendy should be advised that, in addition to the statutory duties, the accountancy bodies have laid down a number of guidelines relating to the auditor's report (SSAPs) which should be complied with unless the company can justify departure from them.

Henry and Wendy will seek to avoid the ongoing costs of the audit if possible.

(c) *Meetings and resolutions*

We have seen that a private company can dispense with the need to hold a meeting for the laying of accounts and appoint auditors. Henry and Wendy would be well advised to adopt s 379A which would permit other deviations from the usual requirements to have formal resolutions. An elective resolution can be used to confer authority to allot shares on the directors (for an indefinite period in a private company) and to dispense with the holding of an AGM. An elective resolution, which is part of an attempt by government to lighten the administrative load on smaller companies, must be approved by all the shareholders, in person or by proxy, at a meeting (21 days' notice of resolution required). It can be revoked by ordinary resolution.

Where meetings are apparently required, the Act and Table A try to balance the need for proper democracy with the practicalities of running small companies where to hold formal meetings of very few shareholders (who may be related) seems unrealistic. To avoid unnecessary meetings, s 381A allows much shareholder business to be conducted by written resolution although such resolutions must be properly minuted (s 382A). Written resolutions must be unanimous, ie Henry and Wendy will have to agree but while they remain on good terms use of this procedure effectively dispenses with the need to hold meetings. The only resolution which cannot be made in written format is one to remove a director or auditor.

Question 48

Write short notes on:
(a) the qualifications, rights and duties of a company secretary; and
(b) the location and function of a company's registered office; and
(c) the purpose and contents of the register of substantial shareholdings; and
(d) the Annual Return.

Answer plan

No plan is needed — the question simply demands notes on the specified topics.

Answer

(a) *The company secretary*

All companies are required to have a company secretary (s 283) who may be a natural legal person or a company and who may also be a director of the company but not the sole director (s 283). The directors generally appoint the secretary, determine the terms of his or her appointment and have the power of dismissal — although dismissal in breach of contract gives rise to a claim for damages in accordance with normal contractual principles. Public companies are encouraged to appoint as company secretary a person of appropriate qualification and experience (s 286) but private companies can pick anyone they like. The company secretary, who may be an artificial legal person, is likely to carry out many of the administrative tasks imposed on companies by the Companies Act and supervise the general administration of the company including the maintenance of the company's registers, for example the register of members (s 352) which must be kept at the company's registered office (s 353). Certain statutory duties are imposed directly on the secretary by the Companies Act. These duties include the submission of statutory declarations, for example a declaration of compliance when a private company re-registers as a public company, and the Annual Return.

The company secretary, in common with the directors, owes a fiduciary duty to the company so that he cannot, for example, take bribes or make a secret profit from his office. The status of the company secretary has increased since the position was first recognised and he is no longer seen as a humble minion but as master of his field — the administration of the company. This enhanced status means that the company secretary has the power to bind the company to contracts falling within his usual authority even if not expressly authorised to act. For example, in *Panorama Development Ltd v Fidelis Furnishing Fabrics Ltd* (1971), the company was bound by contracts to hire cars entered into by the company secretary even though these cars were not, as intended, used to transport clients of the company but for unspecified purposes of the secretary himself. It must be stressed that his authority does not extend to commercial matters (unless expressly authorised) so that a secretary cannot, for example, negotiate loans on behalf of the company.

(b) *The location and function of a company's registered office*

Every company registered in England and Wales must have a registered office (s 2(1)(b)). If the company is registered in England, the registered office can be in England or Wales, but a company registered in Wales must have its registered office within Wales and companies registered in Scotland must have their registered office in that country. The address of the office must be notified to the Registrar as must any change of address and the address must be displayed on all business letters (s 351).

The function of the office is two-fold. First, it is the company's official address so that documents delivered to the registered office are deemed to have been delivered to the company whether or not collected, read or understood by any human agent of the company. Second, the registered office is the place at which the company is obliged to keep certain records which it is required to maintain under the Companies Act. These records may sometimes be open to inspection by members only but generally statutory registers are open to all. Records which must be kept at the registered office include the register of members, unless it is compiled and kept elsewhere in which case its location must be revealed to the Registrar, the register of directors, the register of directors' interests in the company's shares and the register of charges attaching to the company's property.

(c) *The purpose and contents of the register of substantial shareholdings*

Companies are required to send assorted information about themselves and their shareholders to Companies House where it is open to public inspection. In addition, information about the affairs of a company may be obtainable from the company itself. However, access to information about a company and kept by the company is not open to public inspection and even a member has a right to inspect only such information as the Act specifically provides. The Act sets out a number of registers and documents which must be kept by a company which are open to member or public inspection (members generally have a right of access without payment). One such register is the register of substantial shareholdings which must be kept by *public* companies. This contains valuable information in that it lists the beneficial owners of shares whose holding exceeds the statutory minimum. This information could reveal to a searcher (and the company) a possible take-over bid and can aid attempts to attack insider dealing and the register is open to inspection by members and the public.

The regulations relating to substantial shareholdings require notification and registration of ownership of voting shares in excess of the prescribed minimum, which is currently 3% of aggregate nominal value of the company's issued voting shares (the notifiable percentage, ss 198-200). Where there are classes of voting share, interest in 3% of any class must be notified. The regulations apply to directors (who are also subject to special rules) and non-directors. A shareholder is required to disclose his ownership of the relevant class when his interest exceeds 3% or when, having reached the 3% barrier, there is a known increase or decrease of more than 1% in the interest. The requirement to notify the company that one's shareholding exceeds the notifiable percentage is cast upon the share owner and disclosure must occur within two days of the share owner becoming aware of the change. If the company is listed, it must notify the Stock Exchange of any notifications it has received on the day of receipt. In addition, the company must record the details of the notification on the register within three days of receiving the notification. Failure to notify is a criminal offence.

There are considerable difficulties with these provisions and share owners may be unaware that their percentage has changed. For example, if a shareholder owns 2.8% of the issued share capital of a company, this percentage may increase to over 3% without any action on his part — the company may buy its own shares. Again, if the share owner has 4.9% of the issued share capital this may decrease to 3.9% if the directors issued more shares. It is for this reason that notification is required when the share owner becomes aware of the size of his holding (s 202). The Act determines what must be notified (s 209) and the content and form of the register (ss 211, 217 and 218). The lot of the share owner is further complicated by the fact that shares owned by others may be deemed to be owned by him for the purposes of notification. For example, shares owned by a person's spouse or minor child, or by a company in which he has one-third of the voting power, or by a trust of which he is a beneficiary, or by himself and another are all deemed to be owned by that person. Further, shares owned by different people may be aggregated for the purposes of the disclosure rules if they are members of a 'concert party'. Sections 204 to 206 which deal with concert parties have rightly been called 'tortuous' (Gower). The sections provide that a concert party is an agreement, which need not be legally binding, between two or more parties to acquire shares in a public company so long as the agreement provided for that purchase, there are restrictions on the use of the shares (eg restrictions on disposal) and the person acquiring the shares did so in pursuance of the agreement. If a concert party exists, each member is required to notify, within two days, the company and each other when the members' collective holding (ie all shares not just those acquired in pursuance of the agreement) reaches 3% (or increases or decreases by 1%). The concert party rules are designed to prevent manipulation of markets and to provide information on, and aid investigation of, market movements.

(d) *The Annual Return*

Certain documents have to be delivered to the Registrar shortly after the occurrence of the events which they record; for example, changes to the memorandum or articles or the directors. In addition every company is required to make an Annual Return (s 363). The Annual Return serves two purposes. First, it provides a convenient summary of information and, second, it acts as a means of alerting the Registrar that the company may have effectively, even if not legally, ceased to exist. If a company fails to make an Annual Return, the Registrar, after due notice, can take steps to remove the company from the register. Many more companies are removed from the register than are ever wound up since winding up is appropriate only where the company has assets to gather in and then distribute.

The Annual Return must be in the prescribed form and must be delivered to the Registrar made up to its return date, which is usually the anniversary of its incorporation, within 28 days of that date. Failure to make the return renders the company, the directors and the company secretary liable to a fine and a daily default fine. However, many companies fail to make returns at the appropriate time and until recently it seems probable that over half the registered companies were in arrears. Of late, the Registrar has been trying to tighten up the system with greater use of criminal actions or striking off of companies (restoration to the register can arise if the return eventually arrives). Section 713 permits any member or creditor to serve notice on the company requiring it to file an Annual Return and, if the company fails to do so, seek a court order instructing the company to make the return.

The content of the return falls into two categories. First, general information such as the address of the registered office, details of the directors and the company secretary, whether the company has elected to dispense with an annual general meeting etc. Second, if the company has a share capital, particulars of share capital and shareholders must be listed. This information is as at the return date and is necessarily out-of-date so that the Annual Return must also give the location of the company's membership register to allow anyone interested to obtain up-to-date information on the current membership of the company. In practice the Registrar issues a 'shuttle document' — that is a pre-printed form containing all the information relevant to the Annual Return and the company merely has to confirm or amend the form before sending it back to the Registrar. Section 365 allows the Secretary of State to amend the information required in the Annual Return.

Question 49

Reading plc is a small unlisted public company with an issued share capital of £60,000 divided between three shareholders, Whiteknights and Bulmershe, who each hold 40% of the shares, and Earley who holds the balance. Whiteknights and Bulmershe, who are also the directors of the company, would like to dispense with the holding of meetings but are uncertain how to achieve this aim and how, if achieved, resolutions could be passed. Earley rarely attends meetings or replies to letters and the directors would like to acquire his shares.

Advise them.

Answer plan

A question in which a specific administrative problem is addressed
— once the right route is identified, re-registration as a private
company — it is simply a straightforward question on how to re-
register, dispensing with meetings and non-meeting resolutions
and a broader question, acquisition of Earley's shares, also arises.

Answer

(a) *Meetings*

The management of companies is in the hands of the directors
particularly the executive directors, in this case Whiteknights and
Bulmershe (W and B), who conduct the day-to-day running of the
company. However, certain matters, predominantly constitutional
issues such as amendments to the memorandum and articles, can
be implemented only with the agreement of the shareholders. The
agreement of shareholders can be obtained by obtaining individual
assents from *each* of them (*Re Duomatic Ltd* (1969)) but is more
usually procured by passing a resolution at a company meeting. A
resolution passed at a general meeting binds all shareholders,
whether they attended or not and whether they voted for or against
the resolution, and the company. A resolution, unlike a decision
reached informally by all shareholders, will (subject to registration)
bind third parties. A meeting of shareholders, a general meeting,
also has a residual power to run the company when the directors
are incapable of so doing and it can sack the directors. Decisions
taken at meetings, ie resolutions, may require a simple majority of
those present and voting, or a simple majority of those voting in
person or by proxy (an ordinary resolution), but a three-quarters
majority of those voting (in person or in person and by proxy) is
required to pass a special or extraordinary resolution. The
underlying reason for requiring companies to hold meetings is that
members can attend to debate, and perhaps be influenced by
others, and vote.

Companies have two types of general meetings — annual
general meetings (AGM) and extraordinary general meetings
(EGM) — and, for both types, the Companies Act requires

adequate notice to be given. Reading plc must hold an AGM in each calendar year (s 366) and not more than 15 months should elapse between meetings. The AGM provides a means for members to receive reports and assessments on the company's performance. However, when a company has only three shareholders it might be thought, as W and B do, that the holding of an AGM so that the directors (W and B) can report to themselves (and perhaps Earley) is not very sensible and, in practice, many smaller companies fail to comply with the rules on meetings. In response to a proposal by the Institute of Directors, s 366A permits *private* companies to dispense with the holding of an AGM by the passing of an elective resolution.

An elective resolution, which is part of an attempt by government to lighten the administrative load on smaller companies, is a resolution which must be approved by all the shareholders, in person or by proxy, at a meeting (21 days' notice of resolution required, s 399) and the resolution must be registered within 15 days (s 380). An elective resolution can be revoked by ordinary resolution. However, Reading plc being a public company cannot adopt this route. As to EGM — the directors can call an EGM whenever they see fit (Table A, art 37) although the shareholders could remove this power by amending the articles (s 9, special resolution required). Further, s 368 permits the shareholders to require the directors to convene a meeting provided the requisitionists hold at least one-tenth of the paid up share capital carrying voting rights and they have deposited at the company's registered office a signed requisition stating the objects of the meeting and the resolutions that will be proposed by them. If the directors fail to call an EGM the requisitionists can call the meeting and recover their expenses. The court can, on the application of a director or member, call an EGM and the directors of a public company must call an EGM if the company's net assets fall to below half of the amount of its called up share capital (s 142) to report that fact to the shareholders. The majority of matters which might be the subject of a resolution at an EGM could be dealt with by a written resolution if Reading was a private company. Consequently, it seems that the procedures within Reading plc would be somewhat simplified if it became Reading Ltd, ie the company re-registered as a private company.

(b) *Re-registration*

A public company may re-register as a private company under the procedure laid down in ss 53 to 55. Reading plc must pass a special resolution (three-quarters majority of those present and voting), alter its name by deleting plc and substituting Ltd and amend its memorandum of association to omit any features which identify it as a public company. W and B can achieve this change without the support of Earley. The company must then apply to the Registrar for re-registration and, subject to any application by Earley, the Registrar issues a certificate of re-registration. Earley, if he did not vote in favour of the change, has the right to petition the court to cancel the re-registration since he holds in excess of 5% of a class of share capital, provided he applies within 28 days of the passing of the special resolution. Minority shareholders are given this right because the conversion of a company from public to private may result in diminished marketability of the shares although this is unlikely in this case given the size of Reading and the fact that it is unlisted. Instead of striking down the re-registration, a court can postpone a hearing to allow the other shareholders in the company, or the company itself, to buy out the dissentient shareholder or holders. As indicated above, once Reading was a private company it could, by elective resolution (Earley would have to agree) dispense with an AGM. However, the company cannot contract out of its power to hold an EGM and Earley holds sufficient shares to requisition a meeting if he so desires.

(c) *Written and informal resolutions*

If the company had elected to do without an AGM, and neither the directors or Earley called an EGM, how would the shareholders in Reading Ltd reach binding decisions? There are two possibilities. First, s 381A provides that anything which could be done by a resolution in general meeting, *except* dismissing a director (s 303) or the company's auditor (s 391), may be done by written resolution. A written resolution must be signed by all members who would have had a right to attend and vote on the matter in hand had a meeting been held. Assuming all members do sign, a written resolution is effective from the date of the final signature and the signatures need not all be on the same document, ie several copies of a resolution could be circulated among members. Section 381A permits the written resolution procedure to operate whatever the type of resolution required. Section 381B provides that a company's auditors can require a meeting to be held to discuss and vote on a resolution which concerns them as auditors. Thus W and B could conduct the business of the company, insofar as shareholder approval was needed, by written resolution provided they felt confident that Earley would sign up. If Earley refused to sign, an EGM could be called by W and B who could out-vote Earley. Note that s 381A provides a method for passing resolutions by written agreement and it does not validate a decision agreed by all the members informally, ie not in compliance with written resolution requirements. However, s 381C states that the written resolution procedure does not affect the common law so, if the common law permits unanimous non-written decisions to bind the company, that remains the law and there are two parallel procedures for passing resolutions without formal meetings. Note that the common law is not limited to private companies.

In a series of cases, the courts have accepted that decisions unanimously approved by the shareholders who are entitled to attend or vote at a meeting, whether they all agreed at the same time or consecutively, bind the shareholders and the company (from *Re George Newman Ltd* (1895) to *Re Halt Garage Ltd* (1982)) even if made informally. Difficulties arise when the shareholders purport to give unanimous informal consent to a matter which the Act provides must be agreed by a special or extraordinary resolution, particularly when the Act says that such a resolution is the only way to achieve a particular end. The general view is that where the Act provides that a special etc resolution is required to do X, such a resolution may be regarded as *a* means of achieving a decision and that a unanimous informal agreement is an equally valid means — although an un-registered informal decision will probably not bind third parties. However, where the Act says that X may be done by special resolution, some writers argue that it can *only* be done by a proper resolution and not informally (see Farrar for example). Additionally, it is obvious that an informal agreement cannot overcome absolute prohibitions imposed on a company — the shareholders cannot, even unanimously, alter unalterable provisions of the memorandum. In *Re Bailey Hay & Co Ltd* (1971), the judge even held that informal consent could be assumed from acquiescence and in this case he treated the company as bound by an informal decision which had been positively approved by only two out of five shareholders (the majority had abstained) although it must be said that the three were happy to go along with the consequences of the decision for five years.

Thus, even if Earley remains a shareholder, there is scope for W and B to dispense with many company meetings and solicit shareholder approval in writing or informally.

(d) *Acquiring Earley's shares*

If W and B feel that Earley is likely to be too obstructive or absent even if the company goes private, they may seek to acquire his shares either for themselves or with a view to selling them to some third party. They can approach Earley and offer to buy him out or, if the appropriate procedures are followed, propose that the company buy his shares. However, while W and B can propose the purchase, the decision whether to sell is for Earley — though, if the price is right, it would seem foolish to refuse. What W and B cannot do is confiscate or cancel Earley's shares even if the articles permit such behaviour unless it is *bona fide* for the benefit of the company and they are exercising the power for the benefit of the company. Nor could a confiscation clause be inserted unless W and B as shareholders voted to insert the provision in the articles *bona fide* for the benefit of the company which seems improbable. An attempt to expel Earley might trigger a s 459 action on his part which might well suit W and B very well (apart from the cost) since the normal remedy for disgruntled shareholders is an order for their shares to be bought by the majority or the company thereby achieving W and B's aims!

Question 50

Jennifer has recently returned to work as company secretary of Asp Ltd after a career break of 10 years. It soon becomes obvious to her that Asp is in serious financial difficulty and the company's bank, which has a floating charge over the company's assets, is threatening to call in its overdraft. Jennifer has asked you to advise her generally on the legal position of the company and in particular to outline the effects of the following:

(a) receivership;
(b) administration;
(c) liquidation.

Answer plan

Two things are required — an outline of the three types of insolvency procedure which demands knowledge but little thought and a general discussion on the legal position of Asp Ltd which dictates a mental survey of all of company law with advice being proffered an any area which seems likely to arise on the facts given.

Answer

As company secretary of Asp, a company in financial difficulty, you have sought advice about the possible options which could be pursued. There are three options about which you should be aware — receivership, administration and liquidation. Let me outline each one.

Insolvency procedures

(a) *Receivership*

Receivership is a procedure which is not implemented by the company but by a secured debentureholder (or the courts) in accordance with the terms of the debenture. While the procedure cannot be implemented by the company (despite reports in the press which often speak of a company 'calling in the receiver') it may be initiated by the company in conjunction with a creditor when the company recognises that it cannot continue to trade in its current format. This is not to say that the company can veto the appointment of a receiver merely that a more orderly and timely process from the viewpoint of the troubled company may be achieved. Receivers may be appointed by a fixed chargeholder or by a floating chargeholder and, in the latter case, the receiver is called an administrative receiver and must be a licensed insolvency practitioner. The function of a receiver (it can be assumed that the word receiver applies to both types unless otherwise stated) is to receive income or realise property to which the charge attaches to pay off the chargeholder, if the asset charged is of sufficient value. Receivership does not preclude a creditors' or members' petition to wind up the company being presented. Where a liquidator is appointed the receiver remains in office and continues to manage and realise the assets to which the charge attaches but is monitored by the liquidator on behalf of the company's creditors. After the receiver has satisfied his clients (the chargeholder), the liquidator disposes of surplus assets, if any, in compliance with the order of priority for the payment of creditors. If the charged asset is insufficient to meet the claims of the chargeholder the balance of the debt is unsecured.

A receiver appointed by a fixed chargeholder is concerned only with the asset to which his client's charge attaches and he has no general power to run the company. However, a receiver appointed by a floating chargeholder, eg Asp's bank, has the enhanced powers of an administrative receiver. An administrative receiver has considerable powers designed to enable them to keep potentially successful companies afloat — perhaps by selling the enterprise to another company or by re-structuring the company and jettisoning loss-making portions of the business. The enhanced powers of administrative receivers include some of the powers given to liquidators and administrators but not the powers to reopen or set aside preferences and certain floating charges or to initiate proceedings for fraudulent or wrongful trading. An administrative receiver becomes the agent of the company unless and until the company goes into liquidation. It must be stressed that a receiver's principal duty is to his client and he is not obliged to consider, other than as a secondary matter, the interests of other creditors. Thus, a receiver could choose to sell Asp's assets to pay the bank at a time which suits him and he is not obliged to wait for a rise in the market which might increase the amount of surplus, after the bank is paid, available for other creditors. Receivership does not inevitably lead to liquidation but it is obviously not a very promising sign.

(b) *Administration*

Administration is a relatively recent innovation designed to permit re-structuring of a debt-ridden business — it is comparable with Chapter XI of the American Federal Bankruptcy Code. Administration was introduced to provide a company with a 'breathing space' to enable it to continue as a going concern or at least result in a better realisation of the company's assets than a forced sale on liquidation. Administration may be preferable for the company and the creditors than liquidation — it is likely to be cheaper, it may allow the sale of a going concern rather a 'fire-sale' on liquidation, it allows a company currently trading profitably but burdened by debt from past enterprises to trade on with some form of debt moratorium or re-structuring operating and directors etc owed money by the company may have better prospects of payment than in a liquidation. An administration order, which can be sought by the company, a company's directors or a creditor, is a court order that, for the duration of the order, the company's affairs are to be managed by an administrator who must be a licensed insolvency practitioner. An administrator becomes in effect the board and runs the company on behalf of everyone (unlike the administrative receiver who acts for his client). If the court is petitioned by Asp to grant an administration order, the bank (and any other floating chargeholder) must be informed and can veto the order by appointing an administrative receiver. The power of a floating chargeholder to veto the appointment of an administrator has persuaded some creditors to take such a charge for this purpose alone.

An administrator can be appointed if the company is unable to pay its debts or likely to reach this position but it must not be in liquidation. A court will grant the order only if it is likely to achieve one of four aims — the survival of all or part of the business as a going concern, the approval of a voluntary arrangement under the Insolvency Act, a scheme of arrangement under the Companies Act or a more advantageous realisation of assets on winding up. If an order is made, an administrative receiver can no longer be appointed, the company cannot be put into liquidation and creditors cannot enforce any security against or seize goods from the company. The administrator has three months from appointment to come up with a scheme to achieve the purpose for which the order was made and the creditors then vote on the scheme. If the scheme is approved by a majority in value of creditors, it proceeds, if not it lapses. If the scheme is approved, the administrator continues in office until discharged by the court when his task is complete or it is clear it cannot be completed or a voluntary arrangement is agreed by members and creditors. In this case, Asp's bank may well seek to veto an administration order since it would delay the opportunity of enforcing its security.

(c) *Liquidation (winding up)*

Liquidation or winding up is the process by which the assets of the company are collected and realised, its debts are paid and any surplus is returned to the members — it is the prelude to the company's decease. Liquidation can take one of three forms:

- a members' voluntary liquidation;
- a creditors' voluntary liquidation;
- a compulsory liquidation.

A members' voluntary liquidation is apposite if the members of a solvent company, ie one which can pay its debts, decide that they no longer wish the company to exist, it seems unlikely that this applies to Asp. If the shareholders pass an extraordinary resolution to wind up the company, the directors have five weeks in which to make a statutory declaration of solvency. If a declaration is made (there are rules for determining solvency in this context) the winding up is a members' voluntary liquidation but, if no declaration is made, as seems probable here, it is a creditors' voluntary liquidation. When it is a creditors' voluntary winding up, a meeting of creditors must also be summoned and a list of the company's debts submitted to that meeting. A creditors' voluntary winding up is supervised by a liquidation committee consisting of five members and five creditors — it is the cheapest way to wind up an insolvent company and Jennifer might be well advised to suggest this procedure to the company.

Section 122 of the Insolvency Act 1986 sets out the grounds on which a petition for compulsory winding up may be made (and who can apply) to the court. The commonest ground of application is the inability of the company to pay its debts (which will be presented by a creditor) and the Act specifies how this can be proved. Section 123 says that if a creditor makes a written demand for a sum in excess of £750 and it remains unpaid after 21 days, the company is deemed to be unable to pay its debts (there are other ways of establishing insolvency). Thus, Asp's bank could make a demand for repayment of all or part of the overdraft and, if it was not paid, petition for the company's winding up — compulsory liquidation is both more lengthy and more expensive than a creditors' voluntary winding up and the bank would be wise to avoid compulsory liquidation. It is possible to petition for a compulsory winding up order even if the company is in voluntary liquidation.

Other issues

On the facts given, little can be said about other issues which may be relevant to Asp. The directors should be warned about the possibility of an action for wrongful trading (s 214 Insolvency Act 1986) or fraudulent trading (s 213 IA 86) and Jennifer should note that liability for fraudulent trading extends to any person knowingly party to the carrying on of the company's business with intent to defraud creditors and is not limited to directors, ie she could incur liability. The directors of the company, should it go into insolvent liquidation, might be subject to an action for disqualification. Section 6 of the Company Directors Disqualification Act 1986 provides that a person shall be disqualified (for a minimum of two years) from corporate management where he is or has been a director of a company which has become insolvent *and* his conduct as a director of that, or any other company, makes him unfit to be concerned in company management. The courts are particularly unhappy with directors of insolvent companies who have persistently failed to comply with the accounting requirements of the Companies Act. For example, in *Re Swift 736 Ltd* (1993), the Court of Appeal first accepted that the Secretary of State can appeal against the period of disqualification imposed on a director and then increased the period of disqualification on the principal director of the company. The director in this case had been involved with a series of 'phoenix' companies and had failed to comply with the statutory provisions on accounts. Such failings are 'serious matters' concluded Nicholls VC who went on to stress that the privilege of limited liability carries with it responsibilities. Directors, he said, must be punctilious in observing the safeguards laid down by Parliament for the benefit of others who have dealings with their companies. They must prepare proper books of account and prepare annual accounts; they must file their returns and accounts promptly; and they must fully and frankly disclose information about deficiencies in accordance with the statutory provisions although isolated lapses in filing documents may be excusable.

The efficacy of the floating charge would be of concern to the bank (and liquidator if winding up occurs) but seems not to give rise to any legal difficulties for the company. The directors should be warned that any attempt to protect their own position, eg by creating a charge in their own favour or paying off a creditor whose debt they have guaranteed, could be set aside as a preference. The best advice Jennifer can give, from a legal point of view, is full and frank disclosure to the bank. This may not be the best business advice if the company has a realistic chance of improving its position — which might then obviate any legal difficulties.

Index

A

Ability to bind company 95-96
Accidents
  implications 76, 80-81
Accountants
  claim against company
    for services rendered 19
  reimbursement of fees 22, 23
Accounts, see also
  audited accounts,
    balance sheet,
    profit and loss
    account,
    statutory audit 7, 282-285
  abbreviated accounts 283
  annual returns 291
  criminal offences 284
  failure to comply
    with statutory
    requirements 284
  failure to keep 282
  purpose 283
  statutory provisions 284
Acquisition of non-cash
  assets 203
Action for damages 52
Action to restrain acts
  of Board 101
Actions of company
  unfairly prejudicial
    to interests 171, 173,
      177, 190
Administration 6, 281-303
Administrative rules 6
Agency 85, 87, 95
Agents acting on behalf
  of company liability 68
Agreements
  decisions by
    written agreement 17
  shareholder
    agreements 41, 43, 44, 45, 46
  voting agreements 45, 67
Allotment of shares
  see shares
Annual General
  Meeting (AGM) 293-294
Annual returns 291

A (cont.)

Articles of association 3, 36, 41
  adoption of Table A 16
  alteration 16, 35, 37, 43, 48,
    51, 56, 59, 64-65,
    73, 121, 245
  binding effect 36, 38
  consequential amendment 49, 50
  contents 13, 14
  effect 36
  enforcement 21
  legal effect 35
  nature 35
  status 35
  weighted voting clause 56
Asset-stripping 218
Assets
  augmentation 259, 265
  distribution 261
  increase 270
  sale 53, 55-56
Audited accounts 7
Auditor
  function 286
Auditors' reports 283
Audits 285-287

B

Balance sheet 7
Board of directors 59
Bona fide actions 106-107, 121,
    131, 139, 197
Borrowing see also
  Loan capital,
  Loans 252, 255

C

Capital, see also share
  capital reduction 35
Capital maintenance
  document 193
Change of corporate direction 76
Charitable objects 72
Charges
  fixed versus floating
    charges 256-258
  registration 251

Civil law
  information   137-141
Claim against company
  for services rendered   19
Class rights   38, 127, 195, 219
  comparisons   221
  reduction   221-223
  variation   35, 124, 221-224
Company members
  liability   9
Company secretary
  contract   52
  membership rights   52
  payment   66
  qualifications   287, 288
  requirement to have
    secretary   226
  rights and duties   287, 288
  term of office   48
Compensation   32, 88
Compulsory purchase orders   24, 25
Contracts, see also
  Pre-incorporation contracts,
    Service contracts   79,
                                149-154
  authority to contract   85-86,
                               89-90, 93
  benefits   108, 122, 151
  binding nature   83
  common law   150-152
  disclosure of benefits   151-152
  enforcement   39, 82, 84, 87
                             89, 90, 91
  evasion   82
  legality   83
  made between company
    and third party   108, 122
  shareholders   44
  statutory provisions   152-154
  ultra vires   82, 84, 89
  validity   93
Control   41
  acquisition by purchase
    of shares   194-199
Corporate personality   3, 8-12
Corporate property
  director's role as
    constructive trustee   108-109

Creditors, see also
  Preferred creditors   28
  action to restrain
    acts of Board   101
  action against directors   100
  directors regard for   103
  duty of care owed to   103
  enforcement of
    company rights   104
  enforcement of own
    rights   104
  payment   262-264
  protection   199, 200
  right to litigate   103-105
Criminal offences   136-137, 282
  accounts   284
  directors   4, 5
  effect of prosecution   88
  employees   4, 5
  liability   4, 9
  right to sue directors   104
Crystallisation clause   278-279

D
Damages   52
Dealings with non-members   69-98
Debentures   251
Debts
  rank order of payment   259
Decisions
  by written agreement   17
Declarations
  power to make   27
Derivative actions   218
Direction
  change   77-78
Directors, see also
  Board of
    directors,
  Executive directors,
    Non-executive directors   99-154
  allotment of shares   115, 197
  appointment, payment
    and dismissal   35, 59
  authority of single director   97
  authority to contract   99
  benefit of contract made

between company
  and third party   108, 122, 151
bona fide actions   106-107,
                                 121, 197
breach of duties   58, 61, 69,
                             101-102, 118
care and skill   110-112, 117,
                             142, 145-147
compensation for
loss of office   88
conduct   163
constructive trustee   108-109
contract   79
control of conduct   163
corporate duty versus
  personal interest   121, 122,
                                     123
creditors action against
  directors   100
criminal offences   4, 5
'director for life'   186
disclosure   108
dismissal   61, 65, 88,
                             99, 101, 185
disqualification   142-145, 302
duties   17, 27, 35, 58,
                              61, 99, 100,
                        110-112, 113, 130
effect of appointment
  of liquidator on directors   259
failure to act with due
  care and skill   142, 145-147
fiduciary duties   62, 101-102,
                         105, 110, 115, 217
'general knowledge,
  skill and experience'   27
loans to   132-133
liability   4, 5, 24, 26, 69
locus standi   113
numbers   17, 99, 100
payment   66, 244
power to issue shares   126
powers   6-7, 59, 99,
                             104, 131, 198
purchase of shares
  from existing shareholders   195
refusal to register
  transferee of shares   225

regard for creditors   103
remuneration   99
retirement   185, 244
role   99
sacking on restructuring   53
statutory duties   101-102,
                                 105, 110
subsidiary companies   131
term of office   79
termination of office   94
tortious acts   4, 5
trusteeship   138-139
use of information for
  own benefit   140
wrongful trading   260-261
Directors' reports   283, 285
Disclosure   1, 99, 151-152, 260, 282
duty of   30, 108
'Distributable profits'   204
Dividends   174
failure to pay   254
payout of distributable
  profits   204
requirement of
  company to pay   176
Duties   17, 20, 27, 113
breach   58, 69, 100, 118
care and skill   110-112, 117,
                             142, 147-148
enforcement   28
extent of directors'
  duties   99
Duty of care   103, 110-112,
                         117, 142, 147-148

E
Elective resolutions   17, 294
Employees
  criminal offences   4, 5
  liability   4, 5
  locus standi   35, 54, 114
  tortious acts   4, 5
Equal shareholdings   169
Equitable winding-up   172
Executive directors
  service contracts   28, 29
Exempt transactions   133

Expenses
  reimbursement   19, 20, 22
Extraordinary General
  Meeting (EGM)   293-294

F
'Facade' case   10, 11
False representation   30, 31
Family business   13
Fiduciary duties   62, 101-102,
                                   105, 110, 115, 116,
                                   121, 149, 164, 167,
                                   198, 217
Financial reporting   284
Financing
  long-term projects   207
Fixed charges   256-258
Floating charges   235, 256-258
  redemption   270, 273-274
  validity   266-269
Foreign judgments
  enforcement   11
Forgery   87, 91
Formation   1-34
  expenses incurred   19
  financial benefits   5
  obligations of promoters   19
Foss v Harbottle rule   94-95,
                                   100, 101, 104,
                                   117, 119, 156
Fraud   160
Fraud on a minority   214
Fraudulent or
  wrongful trading   10, 142,
                                   145-147, 260-261
FSA
  remedies   32, 33
  rules   30

G
General fiduciary duties   149
General meeting
  alteration of articles
    of association   59
  powers   59, 60
Group accounts   10

Group of companies
  lifting the veil between
    individual companies   11

H
Hire purchase contract   134-135

I
Incompetent management,
  see also
    Management competence
  rights of shareholders   160-162
Incorporation
  advantages and
    disadvantages   1, 2, 3, 13
  consequences   1-34
  effects   2
  restriction on effects   9
Information   135-141
Insider dealing   136-137
Insolvency   16, 114
  rights of individuals   179, 180-184
  subsidiary   183

J
'Just and equitable'   181, 182

L
Land transactions   97
Legal personality   2, 5, 6
  effects   3, 9, 9
  situations where separate
    personality can be ignored   6, 9
Liability
  agents acting on behalf
    of company   68
  company members   9
  criminal and tortious acts   4, 9
  debts of subsidiary   25
  directors   4, 5, 24, 26, 69
  employees   4, 5
  false representation   31
  limited liability   5
  pre-incorporation contracts   2

shareholders 4, 5, 164
third parties 99
'Lifting the veil' 1, 8, 11, 179
Liquidation 234-235, 298, 301-302
  validity 266-269
Liquidators 231
  effect of appointment 259
  obligations 265
  powers 259
  role 259
Listing particulars 30
  misleading particulars 32
  responsibility for 31
Litigation
  right to litigate 83, 103-105, 113
Loan capital
  comparison with share capital 253-255
  fixed versus floating charges 256-258
  marketable loans 251
  risk versus return 253-254
  secured by fixed charges 252
  specific debt 251
Loans 131-135
  secured loans 18, 267
  unsecured loans 267
Locus standi 93
  directors 113
  employees 35, 54, 114
  shareholder employees 54
  shareholders 3

M
Majority shareholders
  powers 42
management buy-out 230
Management competence,
  see also incompetent
    management 188-191
Meetings, see also
  Annual General Meeting,
  Extraordinary
    General Meeting,
  General Meeting 17, 287, 293-294

conduct 6
failure to hold 189
voting 45
Members 35-68
  non-removal from register 225
  register 228
  rights and duties 35, 39, 40
Membership rights 52
Memorandum of
  association 3, 14, 36, 41
  alteration 37, 43
  binding effect 36, 38
  contents 36
  effect 36
Minimum share capital
  requirement 200
Minority shareholders
  ability to sue on own behalf 157-158
  action to restrain acts of Board 101
  causes of action 100, 156
  enforcement of rights 116, 158
  problems caused by majority shareholders 163
  sale of shares 157
Minority shares
  compulsory purchase 178
Misleading listing particulars
  compensation 32

N
Name
  change 76, 78
Natural persons
  ability to bind company 85
Negative pledge clause
Non-executive directors
  prosecution for criminal acts 88
  service contracts 28, 29

O
Objects
  alteration 48, 73, 76-78
Objects clause

alteration   84
purpose   70-75
'Off the shelf' companies   2, 3, 14
Officers
   appointment, dismissal
      and payment   35
Ordinary resolution   195
   dismissal of directors   101

P
Payments   35, 59, 66, 79, 239,
                        244, 268, 269
Percival v Wright rule   100, 101, 119
Permissible capital
   payment (PCP)   231, 246
Perpetual succession   4, 9
Petitions to court   171, 177, 192
Powers
   acting on behalf of
      the company   94
   determination   69
   directors   6-7, 198
   division   35, 58, 60
   implied powers   89
   non-compliance with
      limits on powers   69
   shareholders   7, 120
   to operate   68
   ultra vires   69
Pre-incorporation contracts   1
   liability   2
Preference shares   18, 209
Preference shareholders   213, 215,
                               219, 221
Preferential debts   270
Preferred creditors   114
Private company   1
Private company limited
   by shares   13
Private limited company   3
Profit and loss account   7, 283
Profits
   'distributable profits'   204
   proceedings to recover   19
Promoters   1, 2
   obligations on formation
      of company   19

reimbursement of
   expenses   20, 21, 22
Property
   sale of   270-273
Prospectuses   30
Public company   1
   registration   295

Q
Qualification shares   93
Quasi-loans   133-134
Quasi-partnership   1, 17

R
Receivership   298-300
Register of substantial
   shareholdings
      content   287, 289-291
      purpose   287, 289-291
Registered office   287, 289
Registration   295
Remedies   32, 33, 52,
                          68, 95, 135
Reports, see also
   Auditors' reports,
   Directors' reports   282-285
Representatives   69
Resolutions, see also
   Ordinary resolution,
   Special resolution   17, 287,
                          295-297
Restructuring   53, 54, 55
Rights and duties   3

S
Secured loans   18, 267, 276-278
Securities   254-255
Service contracts   79
   claim against company
      for services rendered   19
   Company secretary   52
   enforceability   76
   executive directors   28, 29
   validity   76
Share capital   15, 193-249

capital maintenance
    document   193
comparison with loan
    capital   253-255
maintenance   199, 200, 203-206
minimum share capital
    requirement   200
raising capital   201-203
raising capital for new
    projects   207-211
reduction   35, 219,
                           220-221, 233-234
Shareholder employees   53
    locus standi   54
Shareholders, see also
    Majority shareholders,
    Minority shareholders
agreements   41, 43, 44,
                                           45, 46
appointment of directors   59
challenge of allotment
    of shares   115
classes   219
conduct   163
contractual rights   216-217
contracts   44
control of directors'
    conduct   163-168
dividends   174
enforcement of articles
    of association   21
enforcement of company
    rights   104
enforcement of own rights   104
entitlement   213, 215
equality   215, 221
fiduciary duties   164, 167
liability   164
locus standi   3
ordinary   213, 215
participation in running
    of company   255
powers   7, 42, 100, 120
preference   213, 215, 219, 221
relationship
    within company   162
rights and duties   42, 155-193,
                           213, 215, 216-217

rights arising from
    incompetent
    management   160-162
right to litigate   103-105
right to sue directors   62, 104
sale   174
voting for *bona fide* benefits
    of the company   164-166
voting rights   37
Shareholdings
    increase   194
    register of substantial
        shareholdings   287, 289-291
Shares, see also
    Minority shares,
    Preference shares
acquisition   235-237, 297
acquisition of company
    by purchase   194-199
allotment   53, 57-58, 99,
                        114, 115, 119, 124,
                        125-128, 197, 199,
                              203, 213, 238
certificate   228-230
class rights   127
compulsory acquisition   48
consideration for   238
failure to pay dividend   254
financial assistance to
    purchase own shares   239-243,
                                              248
forged share transfer   225,
                           227-228, 230
increase   125
issue   254
issue at discount   199, 202
issue for purpose of
    long term projects   207
ordinary shares   251
partly paid shares   226
payment   239
preference shares   18
private company   170
procedure   226
purchase   232-233
purchase by directors
    of shares from existing
    shareholders   195

purchase of own shares
  by company   7, 204-205,
                     230, 231, 236
  qualification shares   93
  redemption   232-233
  reduction   204, 205
  refusal to register
    transferee of shares   225
  sale   244-249
  sub-division   194-195
  transfer   225
  transferable shares   5
  validity   126
  voting rights   194
Small companies   6
  statutory audits   7
Special resolution   56, 64-65,
                   73, 121, 169
Statutory audits   7
Statutory declaration   236-237, 247
Statutory duties   101-102,
                     105, 110
Statutory rights
  primacy   47
Subsidiary
  bona fide actions   131
  directors' powers   131
  insolvency   183
  liability for debts   25

T
Table A   14, 16, 36, 60,
                     121, 151
Tables A-G   41, 100, 101
Take-over bids   187-188
Third parties
  liability   99
Tortious acts   103
  directors   4, 5
  employees   4, 5
  liability   4, 9
Transferable shares   5
Trusteeship   138-139

U
Ultra vires   41, 69, 71, 72, 73,
           74, 77, 82, 83, 84, 89
Unsecured loans   267

V
Voluntary winding up   175, 216
Voting
  amendment of articles
    of association   51
  bona fide benefits of the
    company   164-166
  control   194
  weighted voting
    clause   56, 194, 196
  voting agreements   45, 67
  Voting rights   37, 45, 194

W
Weighted voting clause   56, 194, 196
Winding-up, see also
  voluntary winding up   170-171,
              172, 180, 235
  claims for payment   266-269
  participatory rights   222
Withholding tax
  non-payment   274-275
Written agreements   17
Written resolutions   17
Wrongful trading   10, 142,
          145-147, 260-261